EARLY CHILDHOOD EDUCATION SERIES
Sharon Ryan, Editor

(continued)

Moral Classrooms, Moral Children

Creating a Constructivist Atmosphere in Early Education

SECOND EDITION

Rheta DeVries
Betty Zan

Teachers College
Columbia University
New York and London

Published by Teachers College Press, 1234 Amsterdam Avenue, New York, NY 10027

Library of Congress Cataloging-in-Publication Data

DeVries, Rheta.
    Moral classrooms, moral children : creating a constructivist atmosphere in
        early education / Rheta DeVries, Betty Zan. -- 2nd ed.
            p. cm. — (Early childhood education series)
    Includes bibliographical references and index.
    ISBN 978-0-8077-5340-8 (pbk. : alk. paper)
        1. Moral education (Early childhood) 2. Constructivism (Education)
    3. Moral development. I. Zan, Betty. II. Title.
    LB1139.35.M67D48   2012
    370.11′4—dc23   2012008613

ISBN 978-0-8077-5340-8 (paperback)

Printed on acid-free paper
Manufactured in the United States of America

19   18   17   16   15   14   13   12   8   7   6   5   4   3   2   1

Contents

127 144

Acknowledgments

This book is the result of collaboration with many teachers over a number of years. For the first edition, we drew mainly from videotapes made in preschool classrooms at the Human Development Laboratory School at the University of Houston and also from videotapes at the Sunset-Pearl Elementary School, the University of Illinois at Chicago Child Care Center, and public school kindergartens. We thank teachers Karen Amos, Terry Anderson, Linda Carlson, Karen Capo, Dora Chen, Stephanie Clark, Maureen Ellis, Peige Fuller, Rebecca Krejci, Cory Levendusky, Marilyn Luttenin, Rebecca Peña-Hines, Coreen Samuel, Angie Quesada, Kathryn Saxton, Mary Wells, and Marti Wilson for allowing us to quote from their work with children. For the second edition, we draw from additional videotapes made during the 6 years we worked at the Freeburg School in Waterloo, Iowa, operated by the Regents' Center for Early Developmental Education at the University of Northern Iowa. We express our gratitude to teachers Gwen Harmon, Sherice Hetrick-Ortman, Beth Van Meeteren, Christina Sales, and Kathryn Thompson for all their efforts in meeting the challenges of developing a constructivist program in a new school and to audiovisual specialists Catherine Richey and Seth Vickers, who diligently monitored and videotaped all four classrooms simultaneously.

To Lorraine Bradley Goolsby we express appreciation for help in developing social and moral dilemma discussion stories that we address in Chapter 9.

The Limited-Grant-in-Aid Program at the University of Houston supported classroom videotape research, and the Harry S. and Isabel C. Cameron Foundation supported program development reflected in the first edition. We also thank the Spencer Foundation for support of the research described in Chapter 1 that serves as the inspiration for this work and the U.S. Department of Education (Grant U215K032257) for funding that supported the videotaping at Freeburg.

We owe special thanks to Deborah Murphy and the late Hermina Sinclair, who reviewed the entire manuscript and offered many helpful suggestions for the first edition. We also thank our editor, Susan Liddicoat, at

Teachers College Press for her faith in the idea for the book and for all her help with the first edition and Marie-Ellen Larcada for her editorship of the second edition.

Finally, we want to express our deep appreciation to all the children and unnamed teachers whose efforts have contributed so much to our understanding and formation of constructivist education.

Moral Classrooms, Moral Children

Creating a Constructivist Atmosphere in Early Education

SECOND EDITION

Introduction

The first principle of constructivist education—that a sociomoral atmosphere must be cultivated in which respect for others is continually practiced—is the basis for this book. By *sociomoral atmosphere* we refer to the entire network of interpersonal relations in a classroom. These pervade every aspect of the child's experience in school. Our conviction is that all interactions between children and their caregivers/educators and among children affect children's social and moral development. This book addresses the question of how to establish and maintain an interpersonal classroom atmosphere that fosters children's intellectual, social, moral, emotional, and personality development.

Readers of the first author's previous books will probably not be surprised to learn that our work on sociomoral atmosphere is grounded in the research and theory of Jean Piaget. Some may be surprised because Piaget's own main focus was genetic epistemology—the origins and development of knowledge. However, Piaget (1948/1973) emphasized that social life among children is a necessary context for the development of intelligence, morality, and personality. Although Piaget did not continue in the direction of his early work on moral judgment (Piaget, 1932/1965), he is consistent in later works in emphasizing the indissociability of intellectual, social, moral, and affective development. In this book, we try to follow the direction indicated by Piaget (1954/1981, 1965/1977) when he hypothesized parallel and intertwined evolution in the child's construction of knowledge of the physical and the social worlds.

The theoretical foundation for our work on sociomoral atmosphere and sociomoral development rests on three parallels in Piaget's theory of sociomoral and cognitive development. The first parallel is that just as knowledge of the object world is constructed by the child, so too must psychosocial knowledge be constructed. That is, sociomoral thought and sociomoral understanding in action undergo qualitative transformations. The second parallel is that just as affect is a motivational element in intellectual development, socioaffective bonds (or their lack) motivate social and moral development. The third parallel is that an equilibration (or self-regulating) process can be described for social and moral development as for cognitive development. For example, this equilibration involves af-firmation of the self and conservation of the other as a desired partner. In particular, we emphasize how decentering to become conscious of differ-ent points of view is necessary for reciprocal adjustments, comprehension of shared systems of meaning, and social coordination. In addition, intra-personal conflict and interpersonal conflict play crucial roles in the devel-opment of self-regulation in both intellectual and sociomoral domains. By *self-regulation*, Piaget referred to an internal system that regulates thought and action. These parallels suggest that the conditions for sociomoral de-velopment are the same conditions as for intellectual development.

This book extends the definition and articulation of constructivist education offered in previous publications. Although these earlier works acknowledge the importance of socioemotional and sociomoral devel-opment, overviews (DeVries & Kohlberg, 1987/1990; Kamii & DeVries, 1975/1977) emphasize the educational goal of cognitive development, as did books on group games (Kamii & DeVries, 1980), physical-knowledge activities (Kamii & DeVries, 1978/1993), and arithmetic (Kamii, 1982, 1985, 1994, 1989/2004, 1994). In this book we argue that implementing constructivist education in its most essential aspect involves more than just physical-knowledge activities, group games, arithmetic debates, whole language literacy activities, and so on. In *Constructivist Early Educa-tion: Overview and Comparison with Other Programs* (DeVries & Kohlberg, 1987/1990), Piaget's view of the necessary role of social life in the develop-ment of intelligence was elaborated.

In his work on adolescent moral education, Kohlberg (Kohlberg et al., 1987; Power, Higgins, & Kohlberg, 1989) advocated social and moral dis-cussion, rule making, capitalizing on conflict, and an emphasis on com-munity and responsibility. He pointed out that children must construct their moral understandings from the raw material of their day-to-day social interactions. Our book on early education takes off from this idea. We provide a constructivist rationale for a cooperative sociomoral atmo-sphere and describe the practical ways in which teachers can cultivate it. Kohlberg's "Just Community" approach to the education of high school students emphasizes democratic principles as well as caring relationships. These are also reflected in our view of the sociomoral atmosphere. How-ever, our own conception of the constructivist sociomoral atmosphere as it applies to younger children encompasses more than democratic principles of justice and care. Piaget's work also leads us to emphasize the coopera-tive nature of the constructivist teacher-child relationship and the influence of the entire interpersonal school atmosphere on the child's development.

Further, our perspective on the sociomoral atmosphere is influenced by the ideas of Jackson (1968/1990) and Kohlberg (Power, Higgins, &

Kohlberg, 1989) on the "hidden curriculum" of moral education in schools. The hidden curriculum consists of the norms and values embedded in the social structure of schools, especially those related to discipline.

One unifying theme of this book is that of development as the aim of constructivist education. Therefore, the most desirable school atmosphere is one that optimally promotes the child's development—social, moral, and affective, as well as intellectual. Unfortunately, the sociomoral atmosphere of many schools and child care institutions so emphasizes the acquisition of knowledge that sociomoral and affective development are negatively influenced. This leads to a second unifying theme of this book, the conception of the constructivist teacher-child relationship as one of mutual respect in which the teacher minimizes the exercise of unnecessary authority in relation to children. In previous publications cited above we emphasize the theoretical importance of a cooperative teacher-child relationship. Here we flesh out this general guideline with specific principles of teaching and examples drawn from videotapes of classrooms.

The aim of our book is decidedly practical. However, practicalities are rooted in theoretical rationales based on child development research. We are aware that many educators have been disappointed with the lack of practical help offered by much research and theory in child development. Yet we are committed to contributing to the development of a science of educational practice that has theoretical coherence and scientific validity. Without such a steadying framework, educators' convictions swing with the pendulum. Open to the appeals of one bandwagon or fad after another, the field stumbles along and makes little progress.

We are encouraged to continue in our efforts to travel a two-way street between theory and practice by the responses of teachers with whom we have worked. The theory is useful to them. Convictions about what they do are anchored in knowing why they teach as they do. When Peige Fuller was director of an infant and toddler program, she expressed this attitude in the following way:

> Theory has a negative connotation in education. Teachers seem to say, "Give us a bag of tricks." I say, "Give us a foundation for being able to figure it out ourselves." You're not giving teachers a prepackaged thing. You're trusting them and encouraging them to grow and learn as teachers and as people. Not to give that to teachers is a grave disrespect. Just giving teachers a bag of tricks is like giving teachers a worksheet. That's exactly an analogy. Not to give teachers theory is just to give them worksheets. If you don't understand the theory, even all the good ideas that come from constructivism—all the good activities—amount to a sophisticated bag of tricks. Every

good method, if it isn't backed up by knowledge of why you're doing it, is going to reach limitations. If teachers don't understand the why of teaching in a particular situation, the next situation will be different, and they won't be able to go into their understanding of children and their understanding of what it means to facilitate children's learning, in order to know what to do next. (Personal communication, June 1992)

In this book, we try to provide the theory and rationales that will enable teachers to "go into their understanding" and make professional educational decisions. We believe that teachers should be not technicians but theoretically sophisticated professionals.

In Chapter 1, we address the question, What do we mean by "moral classrooms"? Drawing from research on teacher-child interactions in three kindergarten classrooms in mostly Black, urban public schools for children from low-income families (DeVries, Haney, & Zan, 1991; DeVries, Reese-Learned, & Morgan, 1991), we describe three very different sociomoral atmospheres that illustrate conflicting educational paradigms.

In Chapter 2, we answer the question, What do we mean by "moral children"? When we speak of "moral children," we do not mean children who are merely obedient or who simply know moral rules of others, act in prosocial ways, conform to social conventions of politeness, have certain character traits, or are religious. Instead, we refer to moral children as people grappling with interpersonal issues that are a natural part of their lives. We discuss Piaget's research on how children think about moral rules and right and wrong. Selman's work on interpersonal understanding, a theme throughout the book, is introduced. In addition, Piaget's conception of mental relationships is introduced.

In Chapter 3 we turn to the question, How does the sociomoral atmosphere influence the child's development? Here we present perhaps the most important aspect of Piaget's theory with regard to the sociomoral atmosphere: the distinction between two types of adult-child relationships that result in very different effects on the child's development. We discuss Bowlby's complementary theory of attachment and research on the attachment relationship between teacher and child. We also talk about the role of social interaction in the construction of the self and discuss the benefits of peer interaction in a constructivist classroom, as well as the teacher's role in promoting peer interaction.

Chapter 4 focuses on establishing a constructivist sociomoral atmosphere. Constructivist education is defined in terms of three characteristics: interest, experimentation, and cooperation. To get started, we suggest organizing the classroom to meet children's needs, then organizing it for peer interaction and child responsibility. Examples include how a 1st-grade teacher socializes children for self-regulation during the 1st week of school.

A unique feature of constructivist education is conflict resolution, the topic of Chapter 5, in which we discuss the role of conflict in development and the constructivist teacher's general attitude toward children's conflicts. Principles of teaching are offered with many examples of classroom interactions, showing how resolution of conflict is cooperation through negotiation, even in the context of angry feelings.

Four chapters are devoted to group time and its activities. In Chapter 6 we discuss how group time can promote children's development and contribute to the cooperative sociomoral atmosphere of the classroom, describe different types of group time, point out how the teacher's role in leading group time is different from activity time, list some common problems, and discuss the controversial issue of show-and-tell, ending with several detailed examples of group times. In Chapter 7 on rule-making, we talk about how constructivist teachers foster children's self-regulation by allowing them to make rules by which the class lives, how children's rules are distinguished from the teacher's norms, and how the constructivist teacher can establish necessary norms and still respect children's autonomy. Chapter 8, on decision making and voting, deals with their contribution to the sociomoral atmosphere, principles of conducting discussions in which children make certain decisions, and teaching the democratic use of voting, ending with a tale of voting gone awry. Chapter 9 on social and moral discussions presents Piaget's and Kohlberg's moral judgment theory, defines moral dilemmas, describes how these discussions contribute to children's social and moral development, points to sources of good dilemmas for discussion, and offers principles of teaching with examples.

In Chapter 10 we consider cooperative alternatives to discipline. The constructivist emphasis on children's self-regulation does not mean that teachers are permissive. Constructivist teachers develop cooperative ways of "working with" rather than "doing to" children in order to manage a classroom and cope with inevitable breakdowns in cooperation. We offer principles of teaching to guide teachers in developing a cooperative sociomoral atmosphere through dealing with children's misbehaviors.

Activity time is the subject of Chapter 11, in which we discuss its important role in promoting children's development by appealing to interests, purposes, reasoning, and cooperation. We consider how Piaget's distinctions between kinds of knowledge can help teachers in planning and implementing activity time. We discuss why we prefer to talk about logico-mathematical relationships rather than logico-mathematical knowledge. It is important to understand that Piaget's use of the term *mental relationships* refers to both content and organization of content. We hope this discussion will assist teachers in thinking about children's thinking in the classroom. Finally, we suggest principles of teaching, with examples from constructivist classrooms.

Finally, in Chapter 12 we discuss the sociomoral atmosphere of the school for children and teachers. An Appendix provides constructivist rationales for general categories of activities.

One caveat concerns our use of the term *constructivist*. This word refers to a psychological, not an educational, theory. Therefore, when we say *constructivist education* and *constructivist teacher*, we are using a convenient shorthand to refer to an educational approach.

The children described and quoted in this book are diverse in many ways, representing many ethnicities, social classes, parent education levels, and family incomes. The teachers we describe are also ethnically diverse. Since the first edition of this book, we were able to build the Freeburg School in a low-income neighborhood of Waterloo, Iowa, under the auspices of the University of Northern Iowa. The many examples we add in this edition come mainly from our 6 years of experience in operating this school for children 3 through 8 years of age. The book reflects the authors' many years of work with teachers who are striving to implement education of young children that is informed specifically by Piaget's research and theory.

Sadly, we report that the schools described in this book no longer exist as constructivist schools (with the exception of the University of Illinois at Chicago Child Care Centers), victims of budget cutting and budget difficulties in trying to establish high-quality programs with competitive teachers' salaries. The Freeburg School now serves as a Head Start center. The prevalence of balancing day care and early education budgets with low teachers' salaries (and often low qualifications) is a result of society's failure to adequately support children's early education.

Yet we know that teachers in those schools who struggled with developing their convictions about how to use Piaget's theory have extended the influence of constructivist education. Many of them are in public school systems, teaching, or in administration, and some are engaged in teacher education. Teachers were influenced by visiting and studying those demonstrations of constructivist education and carry the benefits with them. We hope to extend further those benefits with this book.

1

What Do We Mean by "Moral Classrooms"?

When we speak of *moral classrooms*, we are talking about classrooms in which a particular kind of sociomoral atmosphere supports and promotes all aspects of children's learning and development—moral, social, affective, and intellectual. The sociomoral atmosphere is the entire network of interpersonal relations that make up a child's experience of a classroom. To begin our exploration of the meaning of "moral classrooms," we ask the reader to ponder the following vignettes describing children's experiences in three kindergarten classrooms. What do these different kinds of experiences mean for children's intellectual, emotional, and moral construction of relationships with others?

VIGNETTES FROM THREE CLASSROOMS

Vignettes involving mathematics illustrate different types of sociomoral atmospheres in three kindergarten classrooms in low-income neighborhoods of a large urban public school district. These vignettes are not meant to convey complete pictures of the mathematics programs of the classrooms but to illustrate the nature of the teacher-child interactions. Our accounts are drawn from transcripts of videotapes focused on the teacher in each classroom for 2 entire days near the end of the school year. Each brief account comes from an approximately 30-minute experience. Consider what it is like to be a child in the classrooms described below.

Classroom 1

Twenty-two kindergarten children sit at desks arranged in rows. The teacher stands in front of the class, frowning and speaking in a stern tone.

Listen, my patience is not going to last very long with you today. Sit down (yelling and pointing her finger at a child)! Three, 6, get ready. (As the

7

teacher claps once for each number, children and teacher chant in unison.)
Three, 6, 9, 12, 15, 18, 21, 24, 27, 30. Fives to 100. Get ready. Five, 10 . . .
100. Tens to 100. . . . It's a close call between row 2 and row 4. Excellent
job. Good counting by 3s and 5s. We're going to do some problems here.
Those of you who did not finish this part of your work today, you're out
of luck right now (erases arithmetic homework assignment). Eyes up here.
Our first problem is 6 + 3 (writes on board). We don't know what 6 plus 3
equals, but we do know what 6 plus 1 equals. Remember, when we plus
one, we say the next number. (Children chant, "6 + 1 = 7.") I'm seeing
which row can answer me. Get ready. 6 + 1 = 7 (children chant in unison
as the teacher hits the numbers on the board with a yardstick to direct the
chant). (Same procedure for 6 + 2 = 8 and 6 + 3 = 9.) Eyes on the board,
Tobias. I wonder why row 3 [Tobias's row] is losing. A lot of people aren't
paying attention. Let me see everyone answering. Get your hands folded
and your eyes up here. Now it's time for the teacher game. Listen carefully.
I bet I can beat you at this game. I'm going to say some facts. If you get the
fact right, you get a point. If I get the fact before you get it, or if I hear a lot
of wrong answers, I get the point. If you're misbehaving, I'm going to give
myself a point. I'm going to add a new rule to it. Okay, 5 + 2 = (signals for
children to respond with downward motion of hand). (Some children say 6
and some say 7.) I thought I heard a wrong answer. I'm going to give myself
a point. Rameka, want to give me a behavior point? (The teacher scowls at
Rameka.)

We see this teacher as a *Drill Sergeant* and characterize the sociomoral atmosphere of this classroom as a *Boot Camp*.

Classroom 2

Twenty kindergarten children and their teacher sit in a circle on a rug.
The teacher speaks in a concerned tone.

Juanita's mom was going to bring us a snack today, but her mom didn't
get here in time, so she'll bring us something tomorrow. The only food
in the room is some boxes of raisins. Our problem is that we don't have
enough to give each person a whole box. (Children all talk at once and call
out ideas.) "Give them just one in each box." Should we count and see?
(Juanita goes to the teacher, picks up a box of raisins, and opens it.) Juanita
has an idea. What should we do, Juanita? "Do it like this." (Juanita shows
how to open a box and place raisins on plates.) That's an idea. If everybody
had a plate, how many plates would we need (smiles expectantly)? "17!"
We need 17. Lonisha points at Carol, who is videotaping; Norris, who

is waking up from nap; and two sleeping children. Oh, we didn't count enough. "That's 21." Elliot just noticed there's another person here. We counted 17. If we count Carol, that's 18. Did we count . . . ? "Her and her." Seventeen, 18, 19. "And her." If we count Laurie, that's 20. "And Norris." We counted Norris. "And the other girl is 20." "Twenty, 21." (Children disagree on the total number.) How many kids are usually in our room? "Twenty-one." And who's missing today? (Lonisha says Jake is missing.) So 21 minus 1, Jake, is how many? (Lonisha and Elliot say 20.) If you count Carol and myself, it will be 20 plus 2. So how much will that be? "Twenty-two!" So we need 22 sets of raisins. "How about we give two people the boxes and take them out on the plate?" That's an idea! What if each person had a partner and shared? That's a good idea, Dontavious. (Several children say, "Yeah.") Okay, everyone wash your hands and find a partner. (Children pair up, two hugging each other in anticipation.) I'm coming around with the plates. When you get this, how are you going to decide with your partner how much you get? "Count 1, 1, 2, 2" (demonstrates by putting a raisin on one plate, then the other). Okay, that's an idea. Make sure you do it in a fair way so you get the same amount. Dontavious, this was a good idea. (Children break into pairs, divide raisins from a single box, and chat while they eat.)

We see this teacher as a *Mentor* and characterize this classroom sociomoral atmosphere as a *Community.*

Classroom 3

Twenty kindergarten children sit on a rug in rows, looking up at their teacher, who stands in front of them at a chalkboard, speaking in a calm, serious tone.

Let's zip this up (makes zipping motion across mouth) because we're going to be listening and looking. Those people who want to learn, sit up and listen. If you want to play, you'll have to do it another time. Okay, Braden, have a seat. (Child asks to get some water.) No, I'm sorry, we're ready for you to sit down. Yesterday, we worked in our workbooks on a big word, *subtraction* (writes word on board). We had a lot of turtles swimming together (draws 3 turtles). We had a big set of turtles (draws circle around the turtles). Remember, we took the little one out, and you put him in a box (partially erases one turtle so that its broken outline remains, then draws a turtle outside the circle). Okay, how many did we have in the circle when we started? (All children say 3.) And then how many went away? (Some children say 2 and some say 1.) We took 1 away, and then how many did we have left? (Almost all children say 3.) Two. We had only 2 left. We call that subtraction. We really had two sets inside a great big set. We kept this set, and we took this one away. (The teacher writes several other subtraction problems. Children give many wrong answers, sometimes adding instead of subtracting and sometimes calling the minus sign "equals.") Okay, we're going to go to our tables and turn to page 120. Do I have everybody's eyes up here? I hear some people talking. Shhh, I don't want your mouth up here. (Children go to their tables and work on arithmetic problems from workbooks.)

We see this teacher as a *Manager* and characterize this classroom socio-moral atmosphere as a *Factory*.

A STUDY OF THE SOCIOMORAL ATMOSPHERES IN THREE KINDERGARTEN CLASSROOMS

The three vignettes above were drawn from a study (DeVries, Haney, & Zan, 1991) of sociomoral atmospheres in three kindergarten classrooms following different curriculum approaches: *Direct instruction* (vignette 1 of the Boot Camp), *constructivist* (vignette 2 of the Community), and *eclectic* (vignette 3 of the Factory). These curriculum approaches were selected for study because they reflect different conceptions of learning and teaching—different educational paradigms. A paradigm is a theory or set of beliefs providing the accepted (perhaps unquestioned) background for work by scientists. Educators, too, can often be identified with a paradigm or theory that guides their work.

The importance of paradigms in educational research was discussed in a classic article (Tuthill & Ashton, 1983) in which the authors state that almost all classrooms are "conglomerates of contradictory elements" and that teachers "eclectically apply teaching strategies derived from conflicting paradigms, using a little behaviorism here and a little humanism there, for example" (p. 10). They argue that in order to know whether an educational approach results in better outcomes for children, we must study children from classrooms where teachers implement clear paradigms. Tuthill and Ashton challenge us to consciously develop and study "pure prototypes" that avoid the usual eclecticism, in order to learn the practical effects of educational paradigms.

Taking this challenge seriously, the first author designed a study of kindergartens to compare the sociomoral outcomes of children from classrooms reflecting two opposite paradigms, behaviorist and constructivist, and a third, eclectic, approach. The Direct-Instruction classroom followed a DISTAR (Direct Instruction System of Teaching Arithmetic and Reading) curriculum that reflected behaviorist theory and practice. The Constructivist classroom followed recommendations by Constance Kamii and Rheta DeVries (1978/1993, 1980) that reflected Piaget's constructivist theory and practices derived from that body of work. The teacher in the Eclectic classroom termed her theoretical orientation "eclectic" and explained that meant she took the "best from all approaches" (personal communication in interview, 1987).

To study whether the three classrooms did, in fact, differ in sociomoral atmosphere, each teacher was videotaped for 2 entire days in her classroom (9–10 hours total for each teacher). Results of analyzing videos and transcripts revealed clear differences in the typical ways the three teachers related to and taught children. We describe each classroom in more detail, drawing from coding of over 20,000 specific teacher interactions with children. (Although it was impossible to analyze children's interactions in the classrooms, peer interactions were recorded in the second part of the study, and these are reported later in this chapter.)

The Boot Camp

In classroom 1, the pervasive sociomoral atmosphere is strong pressure for obedience. Children follow the Drill Sergeant teacher's directions, not only for arithmetic but also for exactly how to sit and where to put their hands. Coding of a 33-minute video segment, including the vignette above, shows that children are kept under strict teacher control through 87 test questions, 157 demands, 21 threats (such as "This will just go into our art time today," "You'd better not be faking today [about need to go to bathroom]," "You can stand in the corner the rest of the afternoon"), 36 criticisms (such as "That's the kind of behavior that gets you into trouble," "I see some people that aren't sitting the right way. Sit with your back up against the chair," "You're acting silly"), 2 instances of yelling and emotional intimidation, and 3 arbitrary punishments (such as telling a child to finish a paper in the school counselor's office [where children are often spanked, as spanking was not prohibited at the time] and sending a note home). Continual regulation by the teacher leaves the children little or no opportunity for self-regulation. Their regulation comes from outside themselves, from the teacher, who tells them what to do and what to think. Children experience praise for rote answers and threats or punishments for deviations in behavior.

The children's experience of arithmetic is that learning arithmetic means reciting "facts" or using a "trick" procedure to get the right answer (for example, "When you plus 1, you say the next number"). The mindlessness of the recitation is manifested by frequent wrong answers despite hours of drilling over the course of the past year. Mathematical truths for these children come from the teacher, not from their own reasoning, and thus must be memorized as if arithmetic were arbitrary rather than logical.

The vignette from classroom 1 is typical of the children's experience of their teacher during 2 whole days of videotaping in this teacher-centered direct instruction program (considered to be an exemplary classroom by the principal). Small-group lessons in reading are conducted in the same fashion as the arithmetic lesson. Children not participating in a small group lesson sit at their desks doing worksheets or assignments written on the chalkboard. Throughout the day, children are exhorted to work, be quiet, and refrain from interactions with classmates. On the whole, children are very compliant, though eyes may drift or glaze, and some children "misbehave" by surreptitiously communicating with a classmate through silent looks and whispering.

Besides conducting the large- and small-group lessons in reading, arithmetic, and language, the teacher reads stories to the class and leads "discussions" that are filled with test questions. These activities are also conducted in the same stern manner as lessons. For example, discussion of things found on a poultry farm is the occasion to "see which row knows the most." Children leave the classroom to go to the library, the computer room, physical education, and lunch, supervised by other teachers. Occasional opportunities for a period of outdoor recess depend on whether children are "good." The teacher imposes and strictly enforces rules.

Toileting is at set times, and the bathrooms in the school are locked 30 minutes before children leave. Children who ask to go to the bathroom are viewed as suspect. For example, when Lebron asks, "Can I go to the bathroom? I have to go," the teacher accuses, "No, 'cause you're lying." Lebron insists, "No, I'm not," but the teacher replies, "You're telling me a story, Lebron." Later, she allows him to go, but sends another child along, saying, "You're going to go with Lebron to the restroom right now, and (to Lebron) I want a report on you. Young man, you'd better not be faking today. (To other child) Come back and tell me, and (to Lebron) you have 1 minute in the restroom." To another child, the teacher says, "Do you have to go, or do you just want to get out of your seat? Tomorrow I think I'm going to have to come in the restroom and make sure we're all going when we're supposed to."

Children spend most of the classroom time seated at desks or in chairs, and opportunities for physical movement are limited. The teacher uses recess time as a reward for good behavior and frequently threatens children with its loss. After lunch, children rest for 15 minutes by putting their heads on their desks. When some children have difficulty waking up, the teacher pulls them out of their seats and makes them stand up.

Few open conflicts among children occur in this classroom. For example, when a child seems to be on the verge of aggressing, the teacher says, "Mind your own business and no one else's. Ignore him, and that will help you be good." When one child complains, "Lena kicked me in my nose," the teacher advises, "Then sit at the end, and nobody will be able to." One conflict does occur during a story when children are sitting on the floor. Cassie protests, "He pinched me," and the teacher asks why. Terrell replies, "She wouldn't give me something I want." The teacher scolds Terrell: "Come here. What have we talked about with you? This is the fourth time in 2 weeks. You got in trouble for this last week, didn't you? When someone does something to you, what do you do? You do what? [Terrell says, 'Tell the teacher.'] You tell the teacher. You don't do anything yourself. You apologize to her right now. [Child mumbles something.] You say it again, *nicer*."

In order to find out more about whether the regulation of children's behavior is internal or whether it comes from external teacher control, we asked the teacher to leave the room while children did assigned seatwork. Our videotape shows that most children in Boot Camp do not go on with their work. Instead, some just engage in talking while others run around the room and chase each other, grab others' belongings, and behave aggressively toward others. Some look out the window to see if the teacher is coming and then commit some kind of rule violation. (Note that the videographer was in the room while the teacher was absent.) This experiment suggests that behavioral regulation in the classroom comes from the teacher's control and not from children's autonomous self-regulation.

Data on the overall sociomoral atmosphere of this direct instruction classroom show that it is characterized by oppression, anger, anxiety, and social isolation or withdrawal. Children's energies, rather than being fully engaged in learning activities, seem pent up and frustrated. Children in this class go to the teacher with more physical complaints than children in either of the other classrooms. This may be due to classroom stress or to the fact that the only time this teacher expresses personal concern for children is when they say they do not feel well. In a nutshell, we can say that children in this authoritarian classroom have to suppress their personalities, feelings, and interests in order to meet the teacher's demands and avoid punishment.

What are the effects of such a controlling sociomoral atmosphere on children? It appears to us that children feel they are powerless. Only if they submit completely to the will of the teacher can they "control" what happens to them. However, the teacher's will (that is, the exact behavior she deems unacceptable) is not always predictable, and the most eager-to-please child also elicits criticism and punishment. Further, the expectation that young children can control their behavior to meet such rigid standards makes children's failures inevitable.

Are these children paying too high a price for academic performance? Is it possible that the results of this heavily academic Boot Camp will be manifested later in rebellion against a system unsympathetic to children's needs and interests? Or will they become calculating by pretending to go along but violating school/societal rules when not under surveillance? Or will they give up their *will* to the control of others? What happens to the development of children's social and moral competence in this atmosphere? Will they develop this competence outside the school? What happens to active reasoning and initiative?

The Community

In classroom 2, the sociomoral atmosphere is one of respect. The teacher respects children by consulting them about how to solve the snack problem and by following their suggestions. Children's ideas are valued, and the Mentor teacher affirms them and encourages their pride in having good ideas. (Such appreciation is very different from praise that is automatically given no matter how well a child does.) She takes a "we" attitude, frequently identifying with the children as a group member. She facilitates children's interactions among themselves. Fairness is upheld as the goal of interaction with others. The attitude of the group is positive and reflects a feeling of community.

Analysis of a video segment of this classroom during a 30-minute period that includes the vignette reveals that the Mentor used 151 persuasive strategies (such as making suggestions, elaborating on children's ideas, reminding children of reasons for rules, offering choices, encouraging the generation of ideas, and upholding the value of fairness), asked 4 test questions, made 23 demands and 1 criticism, and never threatened or punished children. Such persuasive strategies are respectful because they take into account the child's perspective and appeal to cooperative tendencies. In contrast, the Drill Sergeant used only 11 persuasive strategies and the Manager only 7 in their 30-minute segments.

Children's experience of arithmetic in the vignette is that it is used for the purpose of solving the problem of limited snack. They actively think about the calculations involved in determining how many people need snack. Although answers are not always correct, no one is criticized, because criticism can stop thinking. The teacher guides children in pursuing two different procedures for figuring out the correct number of people who need snack. She challenges them to figure out a fair method of division, with the goal of equal portions for all. A child suggests a logical way to be sure both partners have the same amount of raisins, that is, to count systematically "1" (for the self), "1" (for the partner), "2" (another for the self), "2" (another for the partner), and so on. The arithmetic in this activity is embedded in children's purposes and is integrated with a social aim (to negotiate with a peer to resolve a problem) and a moral aim (to achieve equality in the distribution of raisins so as to be fair to both partners). The teacher also has in mind a moral goal that children may yet achieve—that is, cooperation motivated by a desire to maintain a good relationship with another person.

The vignette from the Community classroom is typical of children's experience of their teacher during 2 days of videotaping. They sing together (and children suggest what to sing), plan and recall a trip to the zoo, act out stories, and discuss common concerns (such as what to do for a classmate who has chicken "pops" and how to solve the problem of the messy pretend center).

In the rather noisy Community classroom, the curriculum is integrated. Children interact with each other, choosing from among activities such as making boats from a variety of materials and experimenting to see if they float, pretending in a center furnished as a restaurant, writing names and telephone numbers of classmates in order to call them during the summer, dictating a story for the teacher to write, inventing ways to use black strips of construction paper, playing math games, and building with unit blocks.

In addition to engaging in indoor classroom activities, children go outdoors every day (often extending classroom activities such as flying kites or catching air with adult- and child-made parachutes). Besides having ample opportunity for physical activity, children nap for at least an hour each day. Although the communal toilet facility is down the hall, bathroom needs are met on an individual basis. Children simply let the teacher know when they want to go. The only rule is that children go one at a time.

Conflicts do arise among children in this classroom, and the teacher takes time to help children work through their conflicts. Conflicts are taken seriously as opportunities to help children think about others' points of view and figure out how to negotiate with others. The teacher says to children, "If you don't tell people, they don't understand," "What could you say to him?" "Can you talk to her yourself, or do you need my help?" Sometimes, the teacher gives children words to say (for example, "Say, 'Brendon, that hurts my feelings.' Say, 'Tell me in words'"). In a passionate argument among three boys over how many marbles each child could use in a marble rollway, the teacher solicits the children's ideas, asks each child if he likes each idea, and supports them through a long procedure of negotiation to decide how many and then who should distribute the marbles and how to ensure equality.

The teacher is a companion and guide who organizes a program of activities designed to stimulate children's reasoning and provides them with a supportive environment in which to explore and experiment, to make inevitable errors in reasoning, and to invent new ways of reasoning.

Children vote to make many group decisions, and rules are made together by children and the teacher. When problems arise, children often suggest making new rules. For example, when some children handle the guinea pig roughly, the children create a set of rules to regulate handling the guinea pig. In an interview on life in the classroom, children from the Community clearly express a feeling of ownership of classroom rules. When asked, "Who makes the rules in your class?" they say the children make the rules.

When we ask the teacher to leave the room, children in the Community simply go on with their activities. They work with a balance game, model clay, play cards, and draw and write. Because they pursue their own purposes, they have no desire to become rebellious or sneaky.

The emotional tone of this constructivist classroom is friendly and cooperative, reflecting a feeling of community. Children appear to feel comfortable about speaking their minds to the teacher and to each other. Conversations between teacher and children focus on the many shared experiences and negotiations that concern participants in the Community. Humor is expressed. Expressions of affection are abundant in the Community as children often spontaneously hug the teacher, and she returns their affection. Although intense conflicts sometimes arise, children can also be observed expressing affection toward each other. Children actively engage with one another, and it is clear that this educational approach is decidedly social. The teacher fosters children's interactions and friendships with one another. In a nutshell, we can say that children are free to pursue their interests within the boundaries of respect for others, including safety; figure out problems related to physical phenomena; form friendships; learn how to resolve conflicts with others and how to collaborate; and communicate effectively with others.

What are the effects of such an accepting, respectful, and stimulating sociomoral atmosphere on children? It seems to us that children have the opportunity to feel effective in acting on their world. They exercise their will and initiative by experimenting with objects and people and observing the results of their actions. They learn to moderate their exercise of will in the context of clashes with the wills of others. With teacher assistance in conflicts, children's interpersonal understanding evolves from impulsive, self-centered actions to negotiations that respect the rights and feelings of others.

Do children from the Community become respectful of one another? Do they come to restrain their impulses as a result of experience in mediated conflicts? Do they become more socially and morally competent? Will children be prepared academically for later schooling?

The Factory

In classroom 3, the sociomoral atmosphere is pressure for obedient production of academic work. However, it is neither as negative as that in the Boot Camp nor as positive as in the Community. Children seem more willingly obedient, more docile, than those in the Boot Camp. In the vignette, they listen quietly to the teacher and watch as she and a few classmates write answers to subtraction problems on the chalkboard. The teacher speaks to children calmly, but at times appears to be emotionally disengaged. Analysis of a 30-minute video segment of this classroom shows that the teacher asked 91 test questions and made 51 other demands.

The children in this class, like those in the Boot Camp class, are kept under strict teacher control throughout and have little opportunity for autonomous self-control. As in the Boot Camp, children are praised for right answers, but in the videotaped segment the Manager teacher offers only 12 criticisms, and the tone of this classroom is generally more positive.

Like the Drill Sergeant, this teacher believes strongly in the value of the right answer and corrects all errors. She clearly tries to appeal to children's interests with the turtles in the math lesson. However, children may be confused by the fact that when one turtle is "taken away" and redrawn outside the circle, a broken outline of the "subtracted" turtle remains. Later, when children sit at their tables, the teacher "walks" them through every step of the worksheet, instructing them to put 3 turtles (loose cutouts) at the top of their page, take 2 away, write "$3 - 2 = 1$," and glue 1 turtle in the "pond." Again, children may be confused by the fact that although they "take away" the turtles from the pond, they still have them. The second and final problem is $4 - 2 = 2$. After telling children what to do and what the answers are, the teacher retires to her desk to check children's work as they come to show it to her. When approved, a child's page is imprinted with the stamp of a nickel.

Children's experience of arithmetic in this Factory classroom is one of uncertainty. Faced with puzzling stories and formalisms they do not understand, children seem very unsure and rely on the teacher to tell them what to do at every step. The experience of many children seems to be of isolated steps that are not understood as a coherent whole. Failure to understand leads some children to disengagement.

Once during the 2 days of videotaping the teacher loses control. A child standing in line at the teacher's desk is being crowded and says, "Stop pushing!" Rather than responding to the child's problem, the teacher impulsively pushes the complaining child out of line and says, "You sit down till you can stop all that noise in the line." Other than this incident, she did not threaten or punish children in our 2 days of videotaping. However, children reported in interviews that she punished children by having them put their heads on their desks and shutting them in the bathroom, and that she threatened them with spanking in front of the class.

The Factory vignette is typical of instruction in this eclectic classroom. We call this classroom "eclectic" because that is the teacher's own term, and because this program shares some characteristics of both direct instruction and constructivist programs. After Factory children complete their assigned academic work, they can pretend in a housekeeping center, paint at an easel, slide down a small slide, feed gerbils and fish, water plants, do a prescribed "art" activity that involves following the teacher's model, or play dominoes. Before the formal beginning in the morning, they can build for a short time with Legos™ or put together puzzles. Children leave the classroom for physical education, library, music, lunch, and outdoor play, supervised by other teachers. Book reading by the teacher that we recorded focuses on informing children about dinosaurs.

Emphasis in this Factory classroom is on production. In addition to filling out worksheets, children paste white paper "bones" on black paper just like the teacher showed them, to represent a dinosaur skeleton. They follow the teacher's model of how to make dinosaur footprints and how to draw a scene with blue water, green plants, purple mountain (she explains, "People use purple because that's a good color for showing distance"), and yellow sun. They use the dinosaur stamp to put a dinosaur in the picture and copy the word *brontosaurus*. The teacher shows how to draw a vicuna (explaining that it is something like a camel), color it light brown, and write the letter *v*, lowercase and uppercase. During rest time, children are called individually to a table and tested on whether they can count to 10; say the days of the week and months of the year; recite their birthday, telephone number, and address; say the name of their school; write their names; identify a circle, square, triangle, and rectangle; order numerals to 20 and read the ones the teacher points to; and name their city, state, and country. As they pass groups of these tests, children are rewarded with red, blue, and gold medals posted by their pictures on the bulletin board.

When the teacher plays dominoes with children, she takes the role of a player in the game (as a constructivist teacher does). However, because she takes charge and directs the game to avoid mistakes, children's possibilities for exercising autonomy and cooperating with one another are lost. (For examples of constructivist teachers using group games in the classroom, see Kamii & DeVries, 1980.)

In a visit to the pretend center, the teacher engages in pretense but in a rather dominating and negative way. For example, when a child offers her a drink, she rejects the pretend idea with her reply: "That's okay, but I'd rather have coffee. Haven't you got some coffee in this place? Dump that out and give me some coffee, please. Oh, it's hot. Who made this so hot? I'll just have to sip it. Pretty good, though. Sure is messy in your house. Who keeps house around here? I think when your house is cleaned, I'll come back."

Despite the teacher's impersonal and sometimes negative comments to children, she does appeal to children's interests in feeding gerbils and fish and looking at a live snail and a dead dragonfly. She shares friendly conversations with children, as one child tells her, "My daddy bought me some perfume," and another, "I know where a bird nest is."

This classroom is not so rigidly controlled that conflicts do not occur. Generally, the teacher responds to conflicts between children by forcing an apology, sermonizing, and exhorting children to be more careful in the case of physical harm. She tends to "gloss over" situations without taking children's feelings seriously. She ignores Shapria, who complains, "Gregory called me an ugly coon." The teacher frequently "blames the victim." For example, when LaToya complains, "Portia hit me on the head," she replies, "Why was she doing that? Are you 'meddling' her? I want you to stay clear of LaToya, okay? When I get through here, I'm going to see how nicely you all have settled." In another instance, LaToya complains, "He step on my hand." The teacher replies, "What are you going to say? Say, 'Excuse me.' Next time, LaToya, let's put our hands in our lap. Be careful to look if you're going to put them on the floor to stand up."

In the most serious conflict, when Beatrice bit Angelica several times, and Angelica bit Beatrice once, the teacher minimizes the experience and does not try to find out what led to the biting. (It is unclear to us from viewing the videotape what precipitated the biting.) She jokes, "Were you hungry, Beatrice?" and continues, "I think little babies bite sometimes, but we're big people, and we're able to say if we don't like something. Are you going to bite anymore, Beatrice? I'll be so glad if you don't bite. Are you through biting? Now I want you and Angelica to be friends. Say to Angelica, 'I'm not going to bite anymore.' (Child does not respond.) You don't feel like saying that? When you feel like talking about it, you'll have to talk to each other about it." No follow-up occurs in the classroom, and the teacher simply tells Beatrice's mother about the incident at the end of the day.

When we ask the Manager teacher to leave the Factory classroom, production slows but does not stop altogether as children generally continue to work on assigned arithmetic papers. However, many children laugh and talk loudly. The entire group gasps, "Ohhh!" and one child comes to the cameraperson to tattle: "He said a bad word." Many times, children threaten, "I'm gonna tell," on classmates for seemingly minor infractions. After placing their completed first assignment on the teacher's desk, several children run, dance, and tease each other. Overall, the emotional tone in this eclectic classroom is calm. Children are expected to be quiet during instruction and relatively quiet during activities. Because the teacher maintains almost continual control, children's interactions with one another are, for the most part, stifled. Except for the opportunity to play with each other in the pretend center, children have little opportunity to express their feelings or pursue interests. It is the teacher's interests and personality that predominate.

What are the effects of this teacher's interpersonal style on children? Many children seem very unsure about what the teacher wants them to do. This leads to heavy dependence on the teacher's direction. Most children seem to lack confidence. Although this atmosphere is less negative than that of the Boot Camp, children in the Factory are almost as tightly regulated by teacher control, except during short periods of activity time.

Is the eclectic combination of instruction and free activity the best of both worlds? Do children in this classroom learn content as well as develop moral personalities and social competence? Does the teacher's calm but firm style enable children to be autonomously self-controlled? Or does the teacher's overbearing dominance have a stifling effect on children's cognitive, social, and personality development?

COMPONENTS OF THE SOCIOMORAL ATMOSPHERE

We state earlier that the sociomoral atmosphere is the entire network of interpersonal relations that make up a child's experience of the classroom. Constructivist teachers think of this network in terms of its two primary parts: the teacher-child relation and children's peer relations.

The teacher establishes the sociomoral atmosphere of a classroom through personal relationships with children. A teacher may be more or less warm/cold, close/distant, and respectful/disrespectful. Based on our data, we would characterize the Drill Sergeant as consistently cold, distant, and disrespectful, with the exception of occasional warmth over symptoms of illness. The Manager was rarely warm, usually distant, and sometimes respectful and sometimes disrespectful with children. The Mentor was warm, close, and respectful in her relationships with children.

The sociomoral atmosphere may also be viewed in terms of differences in child activity and positive affect. The most child activity and the most positive affect occur in the Community, with the Factory next, and the Boot Camp a distant last.

The sociomoral atmospheres of our three classrooms may also be viewed in terms of differences in the teachers' exercise of power. The Drill Sergeant exerts the most power over children, with the Manager not far behind. The Mentor exerts the least amount of power *over* children because she aims to cultivate power *in* children—power to act and think about the moral issues of daily life with deep convictions and feelings of respect for self and others. In this cultivation process, the Mentor is highly influential as she encourages a reciprocal process of give-and-take in discussions about how they want their class to be, reasons for and against making certain decisions, and how to solve problems and resolve conflicts.

Peer interaction, too, plays a very important role in determining the quality of the sociomoral atmosphere in a classroom. When teachers forbid children to interact with one another, as in the Boot Camp, the teacher-child relation constitutes almost the *total* sociomoral atmosphere, except for what interaction children can sneak behind her back. In Boot Camp, children have the experience of shared domination by the teacher, who encourages an adversarial relationship among children. On the other hand, when children have the possibility to engage with one another, as in the Factory and Community, peer relations also contribute to the sociomoral atmosphere. Children's interactions may be harmonious, ranging from silliness to friendly play to sharing secrets and other self-disclosures. Children's interactions may also be tense, ranging from verbal and physical aggression to one-way controlling actions to two-way negotiations aimed at satisfying both parties. The constructivist goal is for children to become more and more able to take other perspectives and to cooperate.

Peer interaction in and of itself does not guarantee a sociomoral atmosphere that will promote children's development. The teacher influences the quality of children's interactions in a variety of ways, including the provision of activities that engender children's needs and desires to interact, and active support of children's friendships, cooperation, and negotiation. We will discuss throughout this book how a constructivist teacher promotes children's sociomoral development by encouraging peer interaction.

SOCIOMORAL OUTCOMES OF CHILDREN
FROM THREE DIFFERENT SOCIOMORAL ATMOSPHERES

To explore children's *sociomoral development* in the three very different *sociomoral atmospheres*, children from these classrooms were studied in pairs in two situations. In one, children played a teacher-made board game in which players roll a die to determine how far to move a marker around a path from Start to the end. The children were taught the game by a research assistant, who played the game with them until it was clear they understood the rules. When the children came with the research assistant a second time (a few days later), they were told, "This time you're going to play the game by yourselves. I have some work to do over here. You just let me know when you're ready to go back to the classroom." In the other situation, pairs of children were given five stickers to divide between them. Based on children's expressed preferences, stickers included only one desired by both children and four disliked by both. The goal in these situations was to see how well children are able to engage and negotiate with each other when no adult intervenes to control or influence them. Bias in analyzing children's behaviors was avoided in a number of ways. Coders worked from videotapes and did not know the program from which pairs of children came because each pair was videotaped against the same white background to avoid any clues to the identity of the children's classroom or school. Interested readers may read other technical details in the *Early Childhood Research Quarterly* (DeVries, Reese-Learned, & Morgan, 1991).

Analysis of transcripts and videotapes (according to a detailed coding manual) of children's behaviors in these two situations shows differences in interactions of children from different classrooms. All differences reported are statistically significant. Children from all three groups try to achieve their own desires by controlling the other (for example, through commanding and telling the other what to do). In comparison with children from the other classrooms, children from the Community are more actively engaged with one another, as shown by the greater number of interactions in this group. They had more friendly *shared experiences* with each other. Examples include telling secrets, helping one another, and laughing together when one lands on the ghost space and has to go back to the haunted house space. These behaviors are in contrast with grabbing the die away from the partner, playing in an automatic fashion without speaking to each other, or insulting the other (for example, "You can't count, boy."), as observed in pairs from the Direct Instruction classroom. Children from the Community, in comparison with the other groups, not only negotiated more but negotiated more successfully. The analysis of all the conflicts among children as they played the game showed that Community children resolved 70% of their conflicts, in comparison with 40% and 33% for the children from the Boot Camp and Factory, respectively. Data showed that Boot Camp children tended to try to resolve conflicts by overwhelming the other physically or emotionally. Children from the Community used significantly more strategies reflecting consideration for the other's point of view and efforts to achieve mutually satisfactory interactions. Further, in harmonious interactions, children from the Community were also more reciprocal (for example, recalling past shared experiences) than children from the Boot Camp and Factory (who engaged in much more impulsive silliness).

The results of this study suggest that educators must seriously consider the possibility that heavily academic, authoritarian programs may hinder children's development of interpersonal understanding and sociomoral competence. Results also suggest that providing traditional child-centered activities alongside traditional academics does not compensate for the sociomoral disadvantages of a heavy academic emphasis in a controlling atmosphere.

But what about school achievement? Although standardized achievement tests do not adequately assess the achievement of cognitive goals of the constructivist Community, we obtained scores on these tests from the school district and compared the three groups. Children from the Boot Camp had significantly higher scores than both other groups at the end of 1st grade, but by 3rd grade no such differences were found. On some 3rd-grade tests, the children from the Factory scored at significantly lower levels than both Boot Camp and Community children.

It therefore appears that Boot Camp children pay a price in terms of low social and moral competence for their early academic achievement. The price is especially questionable, since its advantage is lost by 3rd grade.

We cannot say that all direct instruction classes are as negatively authoritarian as Boot Camp. However, the structure of the curriculum requires its implementation in an authoritarian manner. In our view, authoritarian experiences in DISTAR classrooms communicate unfortunate "lessons" about what it means to go to school and what it means to learn. In this paradigm, schooling means being physically and mentally passive in submission to the all-knowing teacher. Learning means memorizing many things that do not make sense—an uninteresting endeavor in which it is difficult to invest one's best energies. What impact does this kind of classroom atmosphere have on children's possibilities for constructing moral knowledge and convictions? We will address this question in Chapter 2.

Although the Boot Camp classroom is an extreme case of authoritarian experience for children, the experience of children in the eclectic classroom is also predominantly authoritarian. Unfortunately, many adults do not view children as having a right to respect from adults. They view the adult-child relation as one in which children are supposed to respect adults, and the adults are supposed to wield the power of their authority in order to socialize and teach children. We agree that children should respect adults. The problem is in the definition of *respect*. Many adults interpret the notion of children respecting adults as meaning that children should obey adults without question. Here we agree only up to a point. Children should obey adults; but obedience is not the same as respect. Respect is an attitude toward another person with whom one has a relationship. It cannot be commanded but must be cultivated.

Disrespectful attitudes toward children permeate our educational system, public and private, and reflect an authoritarian orientation to children in our society. Perhaps this is why disrespectful attitudes among children have also increased. The hidden "lesson" in authoritarian teaching is: Be submissive to those who are more powerful. Piaget (1932/1965) pointed out three unfortunate effects of too much adult control: rebellion, mindless conformity, and calculation (this last evident when children do what adults say only under surveillance). Are these the characteristics we want to foster in our children? From the authoritarian perspective, the answer is yes: Keep children obedient to authority. From the perspective of democracy and equity, the answer is no: Children should be given opportunities to think autonomously. How can we expect to educate children for democracy with totalitarian methods?

THE SOCIOMORAL ATMOSPHERE AS HIDDEN CURRICULUM

Some people feel that the school should not be concerned with social and moral education but should focus on teaching academics or promoting intellectual development. The problem with this view is that schools *do* influence social and moral development, whether they intend to or not. Teachers continually communicate social and moral messages as they moralize to children about rules and behavior and as they provide sanctions for children's behavior. So the school or child care institution is not and cannot be value free or value neutral. For better or for worse, teachers are engaged in social and moral education. Most often, the sociomoral atmosphere is a hidden curriculum. It is hidden from teachers who are not conscious of the sociomoral atmosphere they provide. It is less hidden from children who are acutely aware of the social pressure of the classroom. When teachers tell children what they are supposed to do and what they are not supposed to do, what children hear is what is good and bad, right and wrong.

Unfortunately, in most schools, the sociomoral atmosphere is mainly controlling and requires children to be submissive and conforming, at the expense of initiative, autonomy, and reflective thinking. Even well-meaning teachers feel that it is their responsibility to be the authority in the classroom, to provide children with behavioral rules and expectations, and to discipline children through the use of rewards and punishments. While most teachers are not as negative as the Drill Sergeant, and many try to combine an authoritarian attitude with affection and child-centered activities, children know when they have no power.

Some people say that you have to exercise authority over children because they will have to live with it in the larger society. This idea is dangerous for democracy because it contradicts the basic idea of freedom within a system of justice. Mindless conformity to authority is not social-ization into a free society. It is more like socialization into a prison atmo-sphere. Consider some characteristics shared by most prisons as well as most schools. Liberty is suppressed. There is no possibility of demanding rights from authorities. Inmates and children are excluded from power in decision making. Rewards are manipulated as exchange for compliance with authorities. Punishments are decided bureaucratically, sometimes for minor infractions of petty rules. Let us not force our children to be imprisoned in school. Instead, let us empower children to take their place in a democratic society where government is derived from the will of the governed.

SO WHAT IS THE CONSTRUCTIVIST SOCIOMORAL ATMOSPHERE?

Having demonstrated that the constructivist Community sociomoral at-mosphere is associated with more advanced sociomoral behavior and development in children, we explore this atmosphere in more detail in the remainder of this book. We talk about the ways in which constructiv-ist teachers respect children as having a right to their feelings, ideas, and opinions. We talk about how constructivist teachers use their authority selectively and wisely. We talk about how constructivist teachers refrain from using their power unnecessarily in order to give children the oppor-tunity to develop self-confidence; respect for self and others; and active, inquiring, creative minds. We try to show how the sociomoral atmosphere permeates every activity, every part of the day, and every type of class-room interaction.

2

What Do We Mean by "Moral Children"?

When we speak of moral children, we are talking about children grappling with issues concerning others in their own lives. Although the content of moral issues in the lives of children differs from that of adults, the basic issues are the same. Children worry about how people (first of all, themselves) are treated long before they can understand the Golden Rule. They worry about aggression, fair use (for example, of dress-up clothes), equal participation (for example, in a new activity or cleanup), and fair distribution (for example, of snack). These are issues of rights and responsibilities just as are adult concerns with crime and violence, equal educational and employment opportunities, and the need to protect the environment. We are also talking about a process by which children wrestle with questions of what they believe to be good and bad, right and wrong. They form their own opinions and listen to the opinions of others. They construct their morality out of daily life experiences.

To begin our explanation of what we mean by "moral children," we state what we do *not* mean by "moral children." Then we discuss how children think about moral rules and how they think about others. Finally, we give examples of children in constructivist classrooms struggling with moral and social issues.

WHAT WE DO *NOT* MEAN BY "MORAL CHILDREN"

First, when we speak of moral children, we do *not* mean children who simply follow moral rules out of obedience to authority. Obedience is often motivated by fear of punishment or desire for rewards rather than by self-constructed principles. (We discuss this at greater length in Chapter 3.) Our country's extensive prison systems attest to the fact that fear of punishment is an inadequate motivator of moral behavior.

Not all obedience is undesirable. Obedience that emerges out of affection and attachment is different from obedience motivated by fear. Such obedience results from the adult's appeal to the child's feelings toward the adult. Because affection engenders a more willing attitude on the part of the young child, obedience arising from a secure attachment relationship with a trusted adult provides a foundation for later moral development. However, if this type of obedience is continued when the child can begin to understand reasons for rules and demands, it can have unfortunate effects in the long run. That is, the child who continues to obey just to please the adult may not construct his or her own reasons for following moral rules.

Similarly, we also do not mean that moral children simply *know* what others consider moral. Moral principles are not arbitrary rules such as the custom to stand during the playing of the National Anthem. Instead, they are rooted in the universal ideal summarized by the Golden Rule, "Treat others as you want others to treat you." This ideal underlies other moral principles such as refraining from harming others, respecting the rights of others, acting out of consideration for the feelings of others, and taking responsibility for one's own actions. Such principles cannot be taught directly; they must be constructed out of the entirety of social experience. To construct a moral value such as not harming others requires a gradual process of understanding its meaning. In the course of social interactions we become gradually conscious of how our actions affect others, and, in the best of circumstances, we come to care about how others think and feel. Moral people come to understand the spirit of the Golden Rule and feel a personal moral necessity for treating others as they themselves would wish to be treated.

Second, when we speak of moral children, we do not mean children who are simply taught to engage in certain prosocial behaviors such as sharing, helping, and comforting, although we hope children will share, help, and comfort others. The problem with defining morality in terms of a list of desired behaviors is that this definition fails to consider the motivation for engaging in such behaviors. Teaching children *simply* to behave in certain ways ignores the cultivation of feelings of caring about others and feelings of necessity for behaving in moral ways. If a child helps another child in order to get the teacher's approval, is this moral? We would say no.

We recognize that children often imitate moral behaviors without having moral intentions in mind. Such imitation can occur before children are able to think about another's point of view and may be a precursor to decentering (taking the other's perspective) and moral feelings. We are not saying that such behavior should be discouraged, of course. On the contrary. For example, a child imitating the teacher by patting a crying classmate may find out that the distressed classmate stops crying. The constructivist teacher may say, "I think you made her feel better when you did that." From this experience, the child may decenter somewhat to recognize the other child's feelings. This is the constructivist goal. We are concerned with the child's development of moral feelings and intentions, not just behaviors. Therefore, constructivist education does not stop short with a limited goal of getting children simply to exhibit moral behaviors.

Third, when we speak of moral children, we do not mean children who simply follow conventional rules of politeness such as saying "please," "thank you," and "I'm sorry." Parents and teachers often feel a responsibility to force children to say these words even when children do not feel respect, gratitude, or contrition. Certainly it is necessary to teach children to say "please," "thank you," and "I'm sorry" because these are important conventions in our society. Teaching strategies may range from gentle reminders to use polite language (for example, when a child demands something from a teacher, the teacher might say, "I would feel better about giving that to you if you asked me kindly") to more direct teaching. For example, when a 1st-grade teacher confronted a situation in which one child had borrowed something from another child's cubby without permission and the child protested to the teacher, the teacher helped the child ask politely if she could borrow the item, and the owner graciously agreed. In this situation, one child experienced the difference between borrowing without permission and asking permission, and the other experienced the difference between her feeling when a possession was taken without permission and her feeling when permission was requested. Each changed her feelings about the other. Although goals include teaching and supporting children's use of polite conventions, the more important constructivist goal is to help children develop moral feelings that are reflected in polite approaches to others. Therefore, constructivist teachers do not force children to use polite language. Instead, when occasions arise, they themselves express sincere politeness, gratitude, and contrition to children. Thus, children have the opportunity to experience how it feels to have another care about his or her feelings. In other words, we believe it is crucial that even these conventions be learned in a context of affection and respect.

Fourth, when we speak of moral children, we are not referring to children who exhibit certain character traits such as "honesty," "integrity," and "generosity." Kohlberg and Mayer (1972; DeVries & Kohlberg, 1987/1990) call this the "bag of virtues" approach to defining morality. They point out numerous problems with this approach. One problem is that of deciding which virtues go in the bag. Who decides what is virtuous? Another problem is that of defining virtues. Who decides what a virtue means? Meaning of what is good and right can vary even within a subculture. As Kohlberg points out, one person's "integrity" may be another person's "stubbornness." Or, to an adult, a child's fantasy may appear as an intentional lie.

Finally, when we speak of morality in children, we are not speaking of religion. Although religion is concerned with morality, morality transcends particular religions. It is possible to be moral without being religious, just as it is possible to be "religious" without being moral. Religions vary across and within cultures, but certain moral principles—such as the Golden Rule—remain the same across all religions.

HOW CHILDREN THINK ABOUT MORAL RULES

An enormous body of research makes the persuasive case that young children think about moral and social issues and relations in ways that differ from the ways in which older children and adults think. Research on child morality was stimulated by Piaget's seminal work, *The Moral Judgment of the Child* (1932/1965). Lawrence Kohlberg (1984; Kohlberg et al., 1987; Colby & Kohlberg, 1987) further defined stages of moral judgment, and Robert Selman (1980; Selman & Schultz, 1990) elaborated Piaget's theory of perspective-taking in levels of interpersonal understanding.

According to Piaget (1932/1965), young children base their judgments about right and wrong, good and bad, on what is observable or "real" to them. Thus, Piaget calls young children "moral realists." The first characteristic of moral realism is that young children view moral rules (and other rules as well) as arbitrary impositions by adults. Moral rules seem arbitrary and senseless to children who cannot understand their reasons. This intellectual limitation means the young child is unable to consider nonobservable factors such as others' intentions and feelings. Reasoning about others' intentions and feelings occurs only when children's general intellectual progress enables them to decenter—that is, take another's perspective. Therefore, when the adult says not to lie or steal, the moral realist experiences this command as an arbitrary adult rule. Following such adult commands can thus be done only out of obedience to authority. Piaget calls this attitude of mindless obedience *heteronomy*, in contrast to an attitude of reflective understanding or *autonomy*. (These attitudes are discussed further in Chapter 3.)

The second characteristic of moral realism is that the letter of the law rather than its spirit should be followed. Because the young child cannot think beyond what is observable, the spirit of many rules is unknowable. The child can only try to follow rules literally. Following a rule not to hit others, for example, may not mean to the moral realist that he or she should also not push someone down or bite someone.

The third characteristic of moral realism is that acts are judged in terms of observable material consequences rather than in terms of intention and motivation. For example, the young child whose block structure is destroyed by a playmate's accidental stumble will be just as angry as if the action had been intentional. Concern with material consequences leads children to think that it is right to give "an eye for an eye." The classic example is the child who when hit by another is convinced that the right thing to do is to hit back. (This is exacerbated when parents instruct their children to do so.) It also leads children to believe that retribution (making a wrongdoer suffer) is right and proper.

HOW CHILDREN THINK ABOUT OTHERS

Young children's difficulties in understanding the reasons for treating others in moral ways are due in part to a limited ability to take the perspectives of others and to think about others' feelings and intentions. It is especially difficult for young children to think about another's point of view in situations when their own self-interest is at stake. For example, consider a situation in which two preschoolers are fighting over possession of a toy, each one crying and screaming, "I had it first!" Children in such a situation are so overwhelmed by their emotion and certainty in the moment that it is difficult for a teacher to get either to listen to the other.

Selman (1980) elaborated Piaget's (1932/1965) work on perspective-taking in the domain of interpersonal understanding. He examined the progressive development of children's ability to take the perspective of the other and coordinate it with one's own. We describe in detail Selman's work on perspective-taking and interpersonal understanding because of its practical value to constructivist teachers.

Interpersonal Understanding

Selman and his colleagues developed a model for assessing children's interpersonal understanding by observing their social interactions. This approach offers to teachers the advantage of being able to assess a child's interpersonal understanding during a social interaction. It is particularly useful in assessing young children who lack sophisticated verbal skills. This model is based on Selman's (1980) levels of perspective-taking (see center column of Figure 2.1). At Level 0 (approximately ages 3–6 years), the young child has an egocentric perspective and does not recognize that others' inner, subjective experiences (feelings, intentions, and ideas) may be different from his or her own. The child simply does not realize that the

Figure 2.1. Selman's Levels of Enacted Interpersonal Understanding

	Negotiation Strategies	Core Developmental Levels in Social Perspective Coordination	Shared Experiences
↑ ↑	Negotiation through collaborative strategies oriented toward integrating needs of self and other	Mutual Third-Person Level (3)	Shared experience through collaborative emphatic reflective processes
	Negotiation through cooperative strategies in a persuasive or deferential orientation	Reciprocal Reflective Level (2)	Shared experience through joint reflection on similar perceptions or experiences
↑	Negotiation through one-way commands/orders or through automatic obedience strategies	Unilateral One-Way Level (1)	Shared experience through expressive enthusiasm without concern for reciprocity
↑	Negotiation through unreflective physical strategies (impulsive fight or flight)	Egocentric Impulsive Level (0)	Shared experience through unreflective (contagious) imitation

(The left margin is labeled vertically: Development)

other has a point of view. Others are viewed as a kind of object. At Level 1 (approximately ages 5–9 years), the child decenters enough to know that each person has a unique subjective experience, but the child at this level cannot consider more than one perspective at a time—usually his or her own. At Level 2 (around 7–12 years), the child decenters further to consider feelings and thoughts of both self and other—an awareness of reciprocal perspectives. At Level 3 (generally beginning in adolescence), the child decenters still further to simultaneously coordinate these reciprocal perspectives into a mutual perspective. (We do not discuss Level 4 here because it usually emerges only in late adolescence or adulthood and so does not pertain to young children.)

Although Selman's levels of perspective-taking focus primarily on how children *think* about others, his levels of interpersonal understanding describe what children actually *do* in social interactions, along with how they think and feel. Selman distinguishes two types of interactions with others. The first is negotiation, when some degree of tension exists between people in an interaction. The second is shared experience, when the interaction is friendly or relaxed. In the course of these two basic types of daily interactions, children construct interpersonal understanding, an integral aspect of morality. After reviewing Selman's levels of perspective-taking, we discuss levels of interpersonal understanding expressed in negotiations and shared experiences.

Negotiations

Negotiations are interactions that occur when an interpersonal dynamic is in disequilibrium—that is, characterized by some tension. The disequilibrium may be mild, as when one person casually asks another for something, or it may be strong, as when one person forcefully demands that another do something. The separateness of the actors' goals and purposes is therefore emphasized. The left column of Figure 2.1 summarizes the developmental levels of negotiation strategies described below.

Level 0 strategies are egocentric and impulsive, are often physical, and reflect a lack of awareness of the other's perspective. Included are exertions of force, such as hitting, grabbing, or yelling, and reactions to force such as fleeing, hiding, or other types of withdrawal. When a toddler wants a toy that another child has, he or she may simply say, "Mine," and grab the toy out of the other child's hands. This is classic Level 0 behavior in which the perspective of the other is not considered because it is not even known. The other is viewed as an object or nonpsychological being.

Level 1 strategies are unilateral and reflect a beginning awareness of another's perspective. These include "will-less" submission or obedience as well as one-way demands, threats, or bribes. To continue the above example, a preschooler who wants a toy that another child has may simply use a Level 1 command, such as "Give me that." The other person's perspective is considered to the extent that the child recognizes that in order to get the toy, the other person has to give it up. Thus at Level 1, the other is seen as someone to command or control (or be controlled by).

Level 2 strategies are self-reflective and reciprocal and involve the coordination of perspectives. These include strategies such as choosing to defer to the wishes of the other, suggesting or accepting a barter, and persuading or being open to persuasion. The child who wants something that another has may try to convince the other to give it up: "If you let me use that block, I'll push you on the swing at recess." Thus at Level 2, the other is seen as someone to persuade (or be persuaded by).

At Level 3, negotiations become mutual and collaborative, with more complex perspective coordinations. Strategies include trying to find mutually satisfactory solutions to problems and compromising to preserve the relationship over the long term. Although we do not generally see Level 3 strategies among young children, we can imagine that at Level 3, an older child who wants something another person has may engage that person in a dialogue about each other's relative needs. Thus at Level 3, the other is seen as someone to understand (and be understood by).

Shared Experiences

Shared experiences are characterized by an interpersonal dynamic that is in equilibrium—in other words, without tension. Since there is no disequilibrium to be resolved, shared experiences are usually relaxed and friendly and foster connection and intimacy between individuals. The right column of Figure 2.1 summarizes the developmental levels of shared experiences described below.

Shared experiences have in common with negotiation strategies the developmental levels of perspective-taking, moving from egocentric and impulsive, to unilateral, to reciprocal, to mutual. At Level 0, shared experiences are characterized by unreflective, contagious imitation. An example might be two children engaging in a burping contest or giggling together uncontrollably. Level 1 shared experiences are characterized by expressive enthusiasm without concern for reciprocity. An example might be children's parallel pretend play, where one child asserts, "I'm the mommy," and the other child asserts, "I'm Superman." Level 2 shared experiences reflect conscious commonality such as cooperative pretense or two children reflecting on the good time they will have together on a field trip. Level 3 involves collaborative, empathic reflective processes such as an intimate discussion in which two children engage in self-disclosure, and each affirms the other.

Examples of Interpersonal Understanding

In Chapter 1, we describe our research showing that children in the Community classroom were more advanced in sociomoral development than children in Boot Camp and Factory classrooms (DeVries, Reese-Learned, & Morgan, 1991). In our study of those children, sociomoral development was defined in terms of Selman's levels of interpersonal understanding. The results showed that Community children engaged in more Level 2 interactions with classmates in a board game and in a situation where two children had to decide how to divide some stickers, including one that both wanted. Many of their interactions were even coded at Level 2 during conflict. This undoubtedly explains why they were so much more successful in resolving their conflicts than Boot Camp or Factory children. Consider the following examples of child interaction in the board game.

Kevion and Cody are two boys from the Boot Camp. The overall dynamic of their play is irritable. Cody is irritated because Kevion makes a consistent counting error (counting the space he is on as "1" rather than going forward one space). Kevion is irritated because Cody keeps on criticizing and interfering with his play. Cody is condescending, critical, and insulting, saying, "That ain't no 5, boy" (*Level 1 negating*), "You can't count" (*Level 0 insulting*), and "Look, lemme count this for you" (*Level 1 demanding*); grabs the die (*Level 0 grabbing*); and demands, "Boy, can't you count?" (*Level 0 insulting*). Cody manifests an antagonistic competitive attitude, gleefully gloating, "Boy, I'm whippin' you up" (*Level 1 competing*). Numerous times, they argue over the counting, but conflicts do not come to a resolution satisfactory to both. Cody usually prevails by force, and Kevion becomes increasingly frustrated and surly. This interaction is characterized by Levels 0– and 1–enacted interpersonal understanding. No Level 2 understanding is manifested, and no shared experience occurs.

Travis and Jake are two boys from the Community classroom who have the same difference in point of view on counting as Kevion and Cody in the example above. Travis makes the logical error consistently. Jake is transitional, sometimes making the error but often correcting himself. It is clear that he is aware of the error and is trying to overcome his tendency to make it. To prevent the error, Jake uses the strategy of saying, "Mmm," for the starting space, then moves one space and says, "One." It is as though he feels he must acknowledge the starting space somehow with a corresponding verbalization, just as he counts each of the other spaces with a verbalized number. Jake frequently notices Travis's logical error. We were amazed that, instead of criticizing and insulting Travis, Jake tries to teach him his own strategy. When Travis makes the error, Jake takes Travis's hand with his marker (*Level 0 grabbing*) and moves it correctly, saying, "Mmm, 1, 2, 3" (*Level 1 showing*). When Travis continues to make the error, Jake says, "Look at my mouth" (*Level 1 demanding*), emphasizing, "Mmmmm, 1, 2, 3" (*Level 2 showing and explaining*). Even though grabbing Travis's hand or body impulsively is Level 0 negotiation, it initiates the helping effort that even includes some Level 2 showing and explaining in attempts to coordinate the two perspectives. Travis resists at first but then accepts Jake's obvious effort to be helpful. He learns Jake's strategy and says, "Mmm," on the starting space. This equilibrium is obviously satisfying to both boys as they exchange triumphant smiles (*Level 2 shared experience*). Conflicts are resolved in this pair's engagement with one another. Shared experiences occur in the form of friendly talk about the game and teasingly setting the die on a number without rolling it, then giggling at the inevitable protest and rolling it correctly.

The interaction between another pair of boys from the Community classroom, Adam and Daeton, is characterized by even more shared experiences that embed their conflicts in a predominantly friendly dynamic. Considerable Level 2 shared experiences occur in the form of whispering secrets and playful teasing. At one point, Daeton puts the die behind his back and says, "I haven't got it" (*Level 2 teasing*) as he shows empty hands, then playfully offers and withdraws the die. Negotiation includes Daeton's inquiring into Adam's motivation when he states, "Wanta play it again?" (*Level 2 checking out with the other*). In one of the most engaging moments, Daeton complains after rolling a series of low numbers, "I always get 1" (*Level 1 complaining*). Adam responds to his friend's frustration, offering, "Okay, you want me to give you 6?" (*Level 2 helping*). He then rolls lower numbers several times. When he finally rolls 5, he asks, "You like 5?" (*Level 2 inquiring into feelings*). Daeton refuses, "Nope, I want 6" (*Level 1 demanding*). Adam then sets the die down, saying, "Here's 6" (*Level 2 helping*), and Daeton happily moves his marker 6 spaces. In the most serious conflict, Daeton and Adam disagree about the rule that when one player lands on the space occupied by the other, the marker there first goes back to Start. With both markers on the same space, each says the other has to go back. Having no way of checking the rules to know who is right, Adam suggests, "So me and you're gonna stay there, okay?" (*Level 2 compromising*). Neither goes back to Start, and the game continues. These boys have profited from their experience with negotiation in the classroom. When they both want to be first in the game, they settle the argument peacefully by reciting a choosing rhyme similar to "Eenie, Meenie, Miney, Moe" that they used in their classroom. Such negotiation never occurred among the children from Boot Camp or Factory classrooms. Adam and Daeton clearly enjoy one another's company and are able to work through difficulties by using Level 2 negotiation strategies. In contrast, one Boot Camp pair played the game without ever saying a word to each other.

Our examples illustrate the ways in which Community children are better able to self-regulate their interactions when in disequilibrium than are Boot Camp children. Similar but less extreme differences were observed between children from Community and Factory classrooms.

MORAL CHILDREN IN THE CLASSROOM

As morality is basically concerned with interpersonal understanding, we find that Selman's levels provide a practical tool for assessing children's sociomoral development. Level 0 understanding is typically observed in the social behavior of 1- to 3-year-olds and is to be expected in this age range.

Its extreme form can be seen, for example, in tantrums, biting, and crying when a child does not get his or her own way in a situation. Most of the interpersonal understanding of children ages 3–6 years (and perhaps beyond) is Level 1. In fact, Level 1 is appropriate in many life situations, not only for children, but for adults as well. For example, "Pass the salt, please," is a Level 1 negotiation. Nevertheless, with cooperative experiences, young children are often capable of Level 2 interpersonal understanding. Its appearance marks the leading edge of young children's moral and social development and is an occasion for celebrating children's moral progress.

The following example of precocious moral engagement takes place in the Explorers class in the Human Development Laboratory School at the University of Houston. The teacher, Marti Wilson, observed this almost unbelievable incident in the classroom and recorded it in her weekly observations.

Sara (35 months) and Reggie (35 months) were engaged in cooperative pretend play. Each one had a hat, purse, and doll and were going to the "store" for apples and eggs. As they walked across the classroom, another child, Tyree (31 months), decided that he wanted the purse Reggie was carrying. Tyree pulled on the purse so hard that he caused Reggie to fall backward. When Reggie fell, Tyree grabbed the purse and ran. Reggie cried. Sara went after Tyree and brought him back to Reggie. Looking at Tyree, she said, "He's having a turn. It's Reggie's purse. He's sad you took the purse. See, he's crying." Then she turned to Reggie and said, "He doesn't understand your crying. Tell him, 'I'm having a turn.'" So Reggie said to Tyree, softly, "It's my purse. It's my turn." Tyree gave the purse back to Reggie. Sara then told Tyree, "Thanks for listening. Do you want to go to the store, too?" Tyree nodded. "I'll help you find a purse," Sara offered. She found a purse for Tyree, and the three children continued their pretend play.

Sara's truly remarkable negotiations illustrate our goal for young children to become involved in the moral life of their classrooms. Undoubtedly, Sara's competence also reflects her home experience as the daughter of a constructivist teacher. Some of her actions may have been imitations, but their complexity, coherence, and precise adaptation to the other children suggest that her behavior is more than just imitation. In terms of Selman's levels of interpersonal understanding, Tyree's initial behavior is Level 0. Sara seems to enact Level 3 as she states Reggie's point of view and feelings to Tyree. She ends with Level 2 inquiry into Tyree's desires and offer to help him. We should point out that Sara was not in a situation in which her self-interest was at stake. It may be easier to mediate another's conflicts at advanced levels than to deal with endangered self-interest in such ways.

We can only surmise what the children learned in this drama. Sara may have learned that she is an effective mediator, and Reggie that he can stand up for his rights. Perhaps Tyree learned that when he snatches something from someone else, he makes them sad, and this is not tolerated in the community.

We want to emphasize that even at young ages, children can care about others and grapple with moral issues by requiring others to respect property, giving injunctions against hurting others, and helping victims of aggression. Our goal for children is that they become involved in the moral issues of their classrooms. We want them to recognize unfairness when they see it, to prefer fairness to unfairness, and to feel compelled to speak out against injustice.

Let us consider another example of children involved in a moral issue in their 1st- and 2nd-grade classroom in a constructivist school in Houston called the Sunset-Pearl Elementary School. This involves Vera, a 6-year-old whose limited peer experience manifested itself earlier in the school year in lots of Level 0 hitting and grabbing. In this incident, we see that she has progressed to Level 1 negotiations, though restraint of Level 0 urges is observable. The situation in Vera's classroom is that children are engaged in making simple machines. The conflict involves the use of a plastic section necessary as the support for the revolving part of Vera's merry-go-round. Emily has one of the scarce parts Vera wants. Throughout a 40-minute period, Vera repeatedly returns to Emily, using increasingly strong Level 1 demands: "Give it to me, please"; passionate assertions: "Emily, I *need* it!"; and mock barter (offers Emily a piece Emily does not want). Several times Vera puts her hand on Emily's machine but does not follow through with a Level 0 grab. She appeals to the teacher, Linda Carlson, with a Level 1 complaint: "She won't give me one." Later, Vera complains again: "She still won't give it to me. I asked her three times"; "Linda, I need that thing desperately. I can't get that machine to work without this part. Emily won't give it to me. She just says, 'Maybe next time you'll get it'" (sarcastic mimicking tone). Throughout, it seems that Vera simply believes she should have what she wants and is unable to decenter from her own perspective. The teacher asks, "Vera, do you understand why she's upset with you?" Vera honestly does not know and asks curiously, "Why?" Linda tries to help Vera decenter by saying, "You see, she feels she needs that for her project." Vera replies, "Well, she's just not considerate. She's got tons more than I do."

We want to point out that these classroom examples illustrate that a person's level of enacted interpersonal understanding depends more on experience than on age. We saw at least Level 2 in a child of about 3 years. We saw a child of 6 years perseverating in Level 1 strategies because she could not take another's point of view when it conflicted with her own self-interest.

The teacher familiar with the levels of interpersonal understanding can quickly learn how to recognize negotiation strategies and shared experiences when a child is being impulsive and physical, when a child is being unilateral, when a child is being reciprocal, and when a child is being collaborative.

The teacher familiar with the Selman model can also recognize educational needs based on children's predominant mode of interacting. The task of children at Level 0 is to learn to be unilateral (Level 1). Thus the teacher mediating a conflict between two Level 0 children might suggest that each child tell the other in words what he or she wants the other to do, the logic being that a demand (Level 1) is better (higher level) than a grab (Level 0). Likewise, a teacher might suggest to a child who demands a toy from another child that the other child also wants to play (pointing out the perspective of the other) and that it might be more effective to suggest taking turns or playing together. Chapter 5 addresses the issue of how constructivist teachers can interact with children in conflict situations to promote their development and social competence.

MENTAL RELATIONSHIPS

Another way to think about moral children is to think about the mental relationships they make in the course of social interaction. According to Piaget (1975/1985), a mental relationship is a connection in the mind between something and something else. It was in his theory of cognitive development (after his work on moral judgment) that Piaget proposed the idea of mental relationships. Drawing from examples cited above, we can list some of the mental relationships moral children might construct in the course of life in a cooperative classroom:

Mental relationships between/among

- Grabbing a toy and the other's protest
- Limited number of spaces in a new activity and everyone's desire for a turn
- Amount of snack and number of children to be served
- Asking permission to borrow something and borrowing without permission
- Comforting a crying classmate and the classmate's appearing to feel better
- Disagreement and negotiating

When a child hits another, the teacher who calls attention to the other's tears, facial expression, and cries is attempting to get the first child to make an empathetic connection between his feelings when he himself has cried and the feelings of the child facing him in tears, as well as a causal connection between his action of hitting and the crying child. Thus a mental relationship has both cognitive and affective aspects.

The moral child is an intellectually active child. In the course of interactions with others, the moral child finds out how another reacts when he or she acts impulsively or unilaterally, finds pleasure in shared experiences, comes to know the joy of mutual friendship and caring, learns the advantages of working on problems together with others, and comes increasingly to take other people's points of view. In short, the moral child engages with others in ways that lead to greater consideration of points of view. Moral engagement involves intellectual as well as emotional engagement. As we discuss further in Chapter 3, the sociomoral atmosphere affects a child's moral development.

3

How the Sociomoral Atmosphere Influences a Child's Moral Development

Moral feelings have their origin in interpersonal relationships, according to Piaget (1954/1981). Interpersonal relations are the dynamic context in which children construct their ideas and feelings about themselves, the world of people, and the world of objects. Depending on the nature of the overall sociomoral atmosphere of a child's life, he or she learns in what ways the social world is safe or unsafe, loving or hostile, coercive or cooperative, satisfying or unsatisfying. In the context of interpersonal activities the child learns whether or not he or she is lovable, trusted, admired, respected, and so on. Within the social context, the child also learns in what ways the world of objects is open or closed to exploration and experimentation, discovery and invention.

The sociomoral atmosphere colors every aspect of a child's development. Relationships with adults determine the nature of the sociomoral atmosphere in which a young child lives, through daily interactions that communicate approval and disapproval, acceptance and rejection, respect and disrespect. For the child, the sociomoral atmosphere is made up, in large part, of the countless adult actions toward and reactions to the child that form the adult-child relationship. Peer relations also contribute to the sociomoral atmosphere at home or at school, and peers' reactions to a child, especially when the adult is not present, play a large role in children's conceptions of self and others. However, adults often establish the framework of limits and possibilities for peer relations.

Teachers who want to establish a constructivist sociomoral atmosphere in their classrooms must begin by reflecting on the nature of their relationships with children. In this chapter we discuss first how social interaction in general influences children's construction of the self. We then focus on how the teacher-child relationship influences the child's development and talk about the role of peer relationships in the sociomoral atmosphere of school. Finally, we discuss the constructivist teacher's role in peer interaction.

SOCIAL INTERACTION AND CONSTRUCTION OF THE SELF

The young child has not yet constructed a unified personality with a certain consistency and coherence in thoughts, feelings, and values. The reader may recall Piaget's classic experiments on intellectual development. In one of these, he showed that although children below age 7 say that two balls of clay have the same amount, most believe one has more when it is rolled into a hot dog or pancake shape. Piaget pointed out that such children do not *conserve* the original equality relationship between the balls. He extended this notion of conservation to feelings, interests, and values (Piaget, 1954/1981). That is, young children's feelings, interests, and values are labile and tend not to be consistent from one situation to another. The young child only gradually constructs a more stable system of feelings, interests, and values that acquires some permanence.

A central task for the child is to construct a self separate from others. This means coming to view the self as one among others. Consciousness of the self as a social object, according to Mead (1934) and Piaget (1932/1965, 1954/1981), comes about through social interactions—through experiencing the reactions of others to what the child does and says. Without going into all the technical details, we can simply say that it requires viewing the self from the point of view of others (decentering from one's own perspective).

Consider our own adult experiences when we become aware that someone perceives us in a certain way (for example, as generous, intimidating, diplomatic, threatening, inconsequential). These revelations often surprise us and contradict our own self-concepts. Experiences of realizing how others see us lead to a new consciousness of ourselves as social objects and thus to new elaborations of our self-concepts. Becoming conscious of the attitudes of others toward the self requires decentering—viewing the self from their point of view. Such decentering is necessary for reflection on social relations with all the complexities of thought and feeling involved in construction of the social world and one's place in it. For example, when Andy expresses anger toward Brian, Brian (a 3-year-old) may be jolted into self-consciousness through realizing that he or his behavior can be the object of anger. The idea that "I am a person with whom someone else can be angry (or pleased or loving, etc.)" marks an advance in the child's conception of self. If the child actively takes on the attitude of the other toward the self, it is reasonable to conclude that the others' attitudes (positive or negative) determine in part the nature of the self-system that the child constructs—a complex network of feelings and values concerning the self.

The construction of a self proceeds at the same time as and parallel to the construction of others as having thoughts, feelings, and values, just as the self does. When a child becomes aware that another's inner feelings exist, it is then possible for the child to begin to think about (coordinate) differences in points of view and, for example, resolve a conflict over use of a toy.

Piaget (1954/1981) talked about the construction of stable schemes of social reaction—a growing consistency in reactions to others. Thus the personality becomes organized into increasingly stable characteristics.

Competence plays an important role in construction of the self. For example, a child may find that he or she is good at building with blocks, running fast, or making people laugh, but not good at riding a bicycle or playing tic-tac-toe. These feelings of competency, of course, occur in a social context that values the competency or not. The ability to make people laugh may be positively valued by peers but not by some adults, especially in a traditional classroom.

Early feelings of liking and disliking (for self and others) are, for Piaget (1932/1965), the starting point for moral feelings. In the course of opportunities to make choices, the child begins to construct a hierarchy of what he or she does and does not value—people, objects, or situations. That is, the child prefers chocolate ice cream over other flavors, likes to play with one child rather than another, or likes active science time over less active reading instruction. The child who prefers science may find pleasure in writing about a photograph of his or her investigation during science time. These preferences gradually become organized and reorganized into permanent values. According to Piaget, affectivity, morality, and intelligence are developed and transformed in interconnected ways.

The current dominance of literacy and mathematics in early childhood classrooms (stemming from the federal No Child Left Behind Act) has led many teachers to say they have no time for the effort required to work on interpersonal relationships among children. Considering the importance of social interactions for all aspects of children's development, we cannot afford *not* to take time for planning, offering socially active curriculum, and intervening when necessary (especially in conflicts) to assist children in constructing more and more advanced ways of relating to others (see Raver, 2002 for the excellent review *Emotions Matter: Making the Case for the Role of Young Children's Emotional Development for Early School Readiness*). As we shall see, the social is also interconnected with the intellectual.

CONSTRUCTIVIST THEORY

The most important aspect of the sociomoral atmosphere is the teacher-child relationship. We find the most useful guide to thinking about adult-child relationships in Piaget's constructivist research and theory. Piaget's research on children's moral judgment (1932/1965) led him to describe two types of morality in children corresponding to two types of adult-child relationships, one that promotes children's development and one that retards it. The first type of morality is a morality of obedience. Piaget called this "heteronomous" morality. The word *heteronomous* comes from roots meaning "regulated by others and following rules made by others." Heteronomous morality is conformity to external rules that are simply accepted and followed without question. The individual who is heteronomously moral follows moral rules given by others out of obedience to an authority with coercive power. An extreme example of heteronomy is the Nazi soldier who justified his role in the execution of Jews and gypsies by stating that he was just following orders.

Heteronomous teachers give children little or no choice about what happens to them and what they do in the classroom. Thus children become heteronomous by following orders without question. Moreover, heteronomous teachers who are negative or punitive especially strengthen children's natural tendencies to heteronomy. That is, children know adults are superior to them and may fear the potential and real power of adults over them. According to Piaget (1932/1965), a mixture of fear of and respect for adults makes children vulnerable to heteronomous treatment by adults. For example, discipline through threat of punishment is found in the system of putting a child's name on the board for misbehavior, with certain consequences arbitrarily chosen for misbehaviors.

The second type of morality is "autonomous." The word *autonomous* comes from roots meaning "self-regulating." By autonomy, Piaget did not mean simple "independence" in doing things for oneself without help. Rather, the individual who is autonomously moral follows moral rules of the self. Such rules are self-constructed, self-regulating principles—a part of the self. These rules have a feeling of personal necessity for the individual. The individual who is autonomously moral follows internal convictions about the necessity to treat others with respect. For example, a police officer who reports another officer for unnecessary brutality demonstrates autonomous morality. Similarly, teachers who refuse to allow standardized tests to determine their entire curriculum are autonomous. Their integrity and personal convictions about what is the best education for children leads them to resist pressures, for example, to teach mathematics through rote drill and practice. Instead they appeal to children's interests in group games such as Add Up to Twelve Bingo and in mathematical problems that arise in the classroom such as how to divide 12 boxes of raisins for snack among 21 people.

Surely no educator or parent would support a goal of heteronomous morality in children. We probably all agree that we want children to believe with personal conviction in such basic moral values as respect for others. Without belief that rises from personal conviction, children will not be likely to follow society's moral rules. Nevertheless, many educators manage children in authoritarian ways that promote children's heteronomous reliance on external authority rather than cultivating children's construction of internal convictions about what is right and wrong.

The Coercive or Controlling Relationship

A heteronomous relationship is coercive or controlling. In this type of adult-child relationship the adult prescribes what the child must do by giving ready-made rules and instructions for behavior. In this relation, respect is a one-way affair. That is, the child is expected to respect the adult, but the adult does not feel an obligation to respect the child. The adult controls the child's behavior. The child's reason for behaving is to please the adult or to avoid punishment. Heteronomy can range on a continuum from hostile and punitive to sugarcoated control.

In adult-child interactions heteronomy is often appropriate and sometimes unavoidable. That is, for reasons of health and safety, as well as practical and psychological pressures on the adult, parents and teachers must regulate or control children in many ways. However, consider the situation from the child's perspective in ordinary life with adults. At home, children are forced to submit to a whole set of rules whose reasons are incomprehensible to them. The obligation to eat disliked foods, to interrupt play at bedtime, or not to touch certain delicate or important objects, for example, can only be felt by children as coming from outside themselves because the necessity to carry out these obligations cannot be felt from within. At school, too, children do not understand the reasons for most of the rules to which they must submit.

Imagine how it would feel for you as an adult to be continually obliged to do things that do not make sense to you. Such a work or family situation, for example, may lead to a feeling of coercion by another's arbitrary demands. Some might react with defeat and passive acceptance of the other's right to be in control, especially if that person is sometimes affectionate or kind and if a feeling of attachment has been established. Some might react with anger, suppressed or expressed, while others might react with the secret rebellion of intelligent calculation, obeying only when under surveillance. Certainly, none of these reactions is good for mental health or future development.

Well-meaning teachers often feel that it is their responsibility to manage every detail of children's behavior. The Drill Sergeant (in Chapter 1) dictated a right way to sit as well as every correct answer in lessons. The Manager dictated the details of children's actions in academic lessons and art. In contrast, the Mentor organized her classroom so that she could leave many details of children's behavior to their own self-regulation.

Some external control of children in classrooms, of course, is unavoidable. However, when children are governed continually by the values, beliefs, and ideas of others, they may practice a submission that can lead to mindless conformity in both moral and intellectual life. The child who lives a life dominated by obedience to the rules of others may develop a morality of blind obedience. Such an individual may be easily led by any authority. Or, because of failure to develop a personal feeling about the necessity of moral rules, the obedient child may eventually rebel, openly or privately. So long as adults keep children occupied with doing what adults want, children will not be motivated to examine, question, or analyze what the adult tells them to think, feel, or do. Such mindless submission leads to superficial learning and conforming (or nonconforming) behavior that fails to bring understanding.

In Piaget's view, following the rules of others through a morality of obedience will never lead to the kind of reflection necessary for commitment to internal or autonomous principles of moral judgment. Piaget warned that coercion socializes only the surface of behavior and actually reinforces the child's tendency to rely on regulation by others. By insisting that the child only follow rules, values, and guidelines given ready-made by others, the adult contributes to the development of an individual with a conformist mind, personality, and morality—an individual capable only of following the will of others. Tragically, obedience-based schools simply perpetuate qualities needed for submission.

Piaget (1954/1981) drew on psychodynamic theory in discussing the child's construction of self-esteem, which begins when the toddler asserts his or her will against adult will. Some people say it is necessary to "break a child's will." However, such defeat of a child's will can lead to inferiority feelings, lack of confidence, and general self-doubt. (We discuss the issue of power struggles in Chapter 10.) Doubt about the self is a continuing issue for young children who are in the process of constructing their personalities. When a child experiences adults as predominantly controlling, the self that is constructed may be weak and indecisive. The child accustomed to control by others may need or seek control by others who will make the child's decisions and prop up the weak self. In contrast, constructivist teachers encourage the construction of personality and will by providing many opportunities for children to follow their own ideas and interests as far as possible, even when these are problematic for the teacher. In Peige Fuller's classroom one year, some of her 4-year-olds wanted to learn about breaking glass. She saw it as her responsibility as a teacher to find a way to make this happen safely, described in Chapter 4. Most teachers would probably have dismissed this question, but in constructivist classrooms, children's ideas are sought out and taken seriously.

Piaget (1954/1981) talked about will as conservation of values, noting that an individual without will is unstable, believing in certain values at certain moments and forgetting them at other moments. Continual external control can lead to a personality defined by control—giving in to it or struggling against it. Such a relation does not provide the possibility for constructing positive self-esteem or cooperative moral feelings. The patterns of social reaction constructed by the child regulated by too much external control may be defensive. Social reactions can also become habitually hostile or dependent.

So is obedience bad? Not necessarily. In certain situations, adults must insist on obedience (for example, when a 2-year-old is poised to run into the street). However, strong pressure for obedience for the sake of obedience can lead to unfortunate results. Adults often insist on obedience to an arbitrary demand when an opportunity for self-regulation could be offered. For example, when two children both want to play with the same toy, some teachers impose a sequence of time-sharing in which one child (chosen by the teacher) is allowed to use the toy for a certain length of time (decided by the teacher), and then the other child gets to use the toy for the same amount of time. How much more effective it is, in terms of children's self-regulation, to encourage children to come up with and follow their own ideas about how to solve their problem (see Chapter 5).

Emotionally, children who are continually pressured to obey for the sake of obedience may react to adult control in several ways. One reaction is a submissive attitude to dominance, feelings of inferiority and acceptance of others' superiority, lack of confidence, and low motivation to think about reasons for rules. Intellectually, the heavily controlled child may react with a passive orientation to the ideas of others, an unquestioning and uncritical attitude, and low motivation to think, instead parroting rote-memory answers. Such a reaction may not be viewed by adults as problematic. The "good child" (the conformist child) may even be viewed positively. Not so well known is the emotional cost to such a child. When children are preoccupied with just giving back correct information, their curiosity is repressed. The result may be intellectual dullness, superficial knowledge, and frequent misunderstanding. Children of the conformist type may not learn to think for themselves, with the danger that they may follow anyone viewed as an authority. Limited opportunity for personal constructive activity can lead to a constricted personality with inadequate social, emotional, intellectual, and moral competence.

External control of children has its limits. Children may conform in behavior, but feelings and beliefs cannot be so easily controlled. As children grow larger physically, the possibility of behavioral control decreases. The only real possibility for influencing children's behavior when they are on their own is to foster their gradual construction of morality, knowledge, intelligence, and personality.

The Cooperative Relationship

Piaget contrasts the coercive or controlling adult-child relationship with a second type that is characterized by mutual respect and cooperation. The adult returns children's respect by giving them the possibility to regulate their behavior voluntarily. This type of relation Piaget called "autonomous" and "cooperative." He argued that it is only by refraining from exercising *unnecessary* external control that the adult opens the way for children to develop minds capable of thinking independently and creatively and to develop moral feelings and convictions that eventually take into account the best interests of all parties.

The method by which the mutually respectful relationship operates is that of cooperation. Cooperating is a process of striving to attain a common goal while coordinating one's own feelings and perspective with a consciousness of another's feelings and perspective. For children, the motive for cooperation begins in feelings of mutual affection and trust that become elaborated into feelings of sympathy and consciousness of the intentions of self and others.

Cooperation is a social interaction with a shared goal by individuals who regard themselves as equals and treat each other as such. Obviously, children and adults are not equals. However, when the adult is able to respect the child as a person with a right to exercise his or her will, one can speak about a certain psychological equality in the relationship. Piaget, of course, was not advocating that children have complete freedom because such freedom is inconsistent with moral relations with others.

We also want to assure the reader that cooperating with children does not mean that the teacher dispenses entirely with authority. It is not always possible to cooperate with children. However, when external control of children is necessary, it is important *how* it is done. The adult can be disrespectful by saying, "Do it because I say so," or respectful, by explaining in a way the child can understand why something is required.

Constructivist teachers we know monitor their use of unnecessary authority by asking themselves, "Is this coercion necessary?"

We are *not* saying that disobedience is acceptable. Here, it is useful
to think about *three types of obedience*. In the first type, the child does not
understand the reason behind an adult directive, and obeys blindly out
of fear. In the second type, the child understands the reason behind the
directive, and obeys with understanding. In the third type, the child does
not understand the reason behind the directive, but obeys out of trust and
affection for the adult giving the directive. The first type reflects heteronomy, the second type autonomy. The third type, while not yet reflecting full autonomy, protects the child's developing autonomy by making it
possible for the child to obey willingly.

Does obedience occur in constructivist classrooms? Yes, it does. Constructivist teachers try to elicit the second type of obedience defined
above. For example, they think about how to explain necessary rules such
as the daily schedule and proper behavior related to toileting and using
the water fountain. However, young children are naturally heteronomous
and can sometimes *feel* controlled even when a teacher uses cooperative
methods. Trying to avoid this, the constructivist teacher appeals to children's cooperation and trust rather than to their obedience and fear.

Does constructivist education encourage children to expect immediate gratification of desires? No. An atmosphere of cooperation requires
balancing one's desires with those of others. The constructivist teacher
considers the child's point of view and encourages the child to consider
others' points of view. Respect for both self and others is emphasized.

*A general constructivist principle of teaching is that external control of chil-
dren be minimized to the extent possible and practical.* Note the word *minimized.*
We do not state that external control of children should be eliminated.
Some critics of constructivist education misunderstand this point and say
that children in constructivist classrooms do anything they like and that
classrooms are chaotic. We would call this permissive, not constructivist.
The constructivist teachers with whom we have worked have clear expectations for children, set reasonable limits, and support children in abiding
by those limits. As children become more capable of regulating their own
behavior, constructivist teachers give children more opportunities to do
so. What is most desirable is a mixture of cooperation and control that
increasingly favors children's regulation of their own behavior.

Encouragement of self-regulation leads to many fortunate effects on
children's development. Emotionally, children feel acceptance and respect
for their concerns and ideas. Children often respond to cooperation with
a reciprocal attitude of cooperation, feelings of equality and confidence,
and active thoughtfulness about reasons for rules. Intellectually, the child

may react with an open and active orientation to new ideas; an attitude of questioning and critical evaluation; and motivation to think about causes, implications, and explanations. With skilled adult guidance and extensive peer interaction, children move toward moral reasoning that considers all points of view. An educational experience full of opportunities for exploration and experimentation with the physical world leads to intellectual sharpness and understanding. Extensive opportunity for personal constructive activity leads to a highly differentiated personality with social, emotional, intellectual, and moral competence.

ATTACHMENT THEORY

Attachment theory (Bowlby, 1969/1982; Ainsworth et al., 1978) and research on its educational effects (Howes & Ritchie, 2002; Watson, 2003) are also useful in conceptualizing the kind of adult-child relationship that is most effective in promoting children's development and learning. John Bowlby (1973, 1980, 1982) drew from evolutionary theory to describe the role of the child's attachment relationship with his or her primary caregiver (usually the mother) in the child's development. According to attachment theory, a biologically based desire for proximity with the primary caregiver leads to the formation of an attachment relation between attachment figure and child. This relationship provides the child emotional support and protection. The child with a secure attachment bond to a primary caregiver uses the caregiver as a secure base from which to explore the world.

The attachment relationship also colors a child's sense of self and relationships with others through the formation of what is known in attachment theory as *internal working models* (Bretherton & Munholland, 1999). Bowlby drew on Piaget in his development of this idea of internal working models. Similarities between Piaget and Bowlby can be seen when Bowlby writes:

> Starting, we may suppose, towards the end of his first year, and probably especially actively during his second and third when he acquires the powerful and extraordinary gift of language, a child is busy constructing working models of how the physical world may be expected to behave, how his mother and other significant persons may be expected to behave, how he himself may be expected to behave, and how each interacts with all the others. (1969/1982, p. 354)

These working models serve as the lens through which children view the world. Bretherton and Munholland explain how the child's internal working model colors the child's view of self:

A working model of self as valued and competent, according to this view, is constructed in the context of a working model of parents as emotionally available, but also as supportive of exploratory activity. Conversely, a working model of self as devalued and incompetent is the counterpart of a working model of parents as rejecting or ignoring of attachment behavior and/or interfering with exploration (1999, p. 91).

Bretherton (2005) further explains that children whose internal working models include unresponsive attachment figures would "come to see the world as unreliable and unpredictable, leading them to either retreat from it or to fight it" (p. 16).

Internal working models are not static, but rather are dynamic, responding to the child's changing life situations and developing competencies. For example, while the infant relies on physical proximity to the attachment figure in order to feel safe and secure, the older child's ability to represent the absent attachment figure mentally allows him or her to feel secure even when the attachment figure is not present.

A vast body of research over several decades has demonstrated the power of the attachment relationship (either secure or insecure) to influence children's development, both short term and long term (see Grossmann, Grossmann, & Waters, 2005, for detailed summaries of longitudinal studies of attachment, and Thompson, 1999, or Watson, 2003, for reviews). Briefly, these studies show that children with secure attachment relationships, as compared to children with insecure attachment relationships, tend to be more cooperative with both adults and peers, more confident, more resilient, less aggressive, more socially competent, and better able to cope with stress.

Although most of the studies conducted on attachment examine the attachment relation between parent and child, some researchers are looking at the teacher-child relationship as a secondary attachment relationship (for example, Howes, 1999; Howes & Ritchie, 2002; van IJzendoorn, Sagi, & Lambermon, 1992; Watson, 2003). In many ways, the teacher-child relationship resembles the parent-child relationship. The teacher attends to the child's physical needs (providing food, drink, rest, first aid, etc.), social needs (offering assistance in entering play groups, negotiating conflicts, etc.), and emotional needs (comforting a child who is hurt, sharing a child's pride in accomplishment, etc.). According to Howes (1999; Howes & Ritchie, 2002), young children frequently form attachment relations with their teachers and caregivers and use these attachment relationships in similar ways in early childhood settings, as a secure base for exploring their environments.

The teacher-child attachment relationship can be characterized as either secure or insecure, just as the parent-child relationship can be. In some ways, results of research on secure and insecure teacher-child attachment relationships parallel results found with parent-child relationships. That is, when children are securely attached to their teacher, they are cooperative, confident, and able to seek and accept help from their teacher (in academic work, interpersonal relations, etc.). However, when children are insecurely attached to their teacher, they are likely not to trust their teacher, have conflictual relationships with the teacher, and frequently exhibit behavior problems in the classroom.

Teachers encounter unique problems when working with children who are insecurely attached to their primary caregivers. Such children bring to their classrooms internal working models of adults as coercive, untrustworthy, and incapable of meeting their needs, and models of themselves as unworthy of the teacher's care (Watson, 2003). These children present significant challenges. They may be highly suspicious, negative, defiant, aggressive or withdrawn. Resistant to offers of affection, they may be hypervigilant, mistrustful, and hostile. They may also have difficulty managing strong emotions, such as becoming overwhelmed by seemingly small disappointments. Watson (2003) describes them this way:

> These children will enter the classroom with low social and emotional skills, low self-esteem, little or no trust that teachers can be relied upon to care for them, and a belief that their survival depends on their ability to manipulate and control others. They are likely to be anxious and passive or angry and aggressive as they struggle to make their way in the world of school. Initially, they will view our efforts to teach, guide, and direct them as efforts to control or coerce them (pp. 282–283).

When children who are insecurely attached at home enter classrooms where the sociomoral atmosphere is coercive and controlling, their internal working models of adults as coercive are reinforced. The only hope of reaching children with attachment problems is to first gain their trust. We therefore find that this body of research is consistent with Piaget's conception of the cooperative adult-child relationship as most conducive to children's optimal development.

The reader may rightly protest that no child's experience is totally coercive or totally cooperative. We agree. We describe here how a predominance of coercion or cooperation influences children's development. However, each child presents a unique history of coercive and cooperative experiences. Our stance is optimistic. We are convinced that no child has experienced so much external control that a cooperative teacher cannot ameliorate, at least to some extent, the effects of heteronomy. Each classroom, too, will provide a mixture of controlling and cooperative experiences. Again, our stance is optimistic. We believe that moral classrooms will promote moral development in children—as well as emotional, social, and intellectual development.

PEER RELATIONSHIPS

Peer interaction is sometimes vaguely justified as beneficial for socialization, as necessary for children to learn to share and live in a world with others. Unfortunately, many classrooms are not organized to provide children with the experiences favorable for social competence and moral development.

In classrooms where interactions among children are forbidden, peer relationships play little role in the overall sociomoral atmosphere. Of course, sympathies and antipathies may develop based on children's interactions outside the classroom. However, life in traditional classrooms is not designed to promote peer relationships. Children's tendencies to aid each other are usually classified as cheating and may be punished. In the Boot Camp described in Chapter 1, the Drill Sergeant often pitted children against each other (by row or gender) in competition for praise and avoidance of criticism. The resulting sociomoral atmosphere was stifling, and it is difficult to imagine that anyone wanted to be there together.

In classrooms where interactions among children are encouraged, peer relationships play an important role in the sociomoral atmosphere. Although some peer interaction was permitted in the Factory classroom described in Chapter 1, it played a minor role in children's classroom experience. The Manager emphasized the primary importance of academics, insisting on individual work rather than cooperation. Conflicts were squelched, and peer interactions muted. The resulting sociomoral atmosphere was a kind of "nicey-niceness" in which no one was very invested in the experience of being together. In contrast, the Mentor not only organized her classroom to optimize its interactive character, but also actively engaged children with each other. Life in the Community was the main "subject matter," and the Mentor took advantage of spontaneous incidents to maximize children's opportunities for confronting social, emotional, intellectual, and moral problems. The resulting sociomoral atmosphere was one of vitality and energy invested in the experience of being together.

According to Piaget's theory, peer interactions are crucial to the child's construction of social and moral feelings, values, and social and intellectual competence. As indicated in our discussion of the teacher-child relationship, we do not agree with those who interpret Piaget as saying that it is *only* in relations with peers that autonomous morality and intelligence develops. We build on Piaget's ideas and describe throughout this book how the constructivist teacher can engage with children in co-operative ways.

Peer relations are especially conducive to social, moral, and intellectual development for two reasons. The first is that peer relations are characterized by more equality than can ever be achieved in adult-child relations, no matter how hard the adult tries to minimize heteronomy. Peer relations can lead to recognition of real reciprocity implicit in relations of equality. This reciprocity can provide the psychological foundation for decentering and perspective-taking. As autonomy can occur only in a relationship of equality, children are sometimes able more easily to think and act autonomously with other children than with most adults. However, as Piaget pointed out, inequalities also exist among children, and autonomy can be violated in child-child interactions.

The second reason peer relations provide a good context for development is that seeing other children as like themselves results in a special feeling of interest that motivates peer contacts. These contacts are social, moral, and intellectual endeavors. In the course of peer interaction, children have opportunities to become conscious of others and differentiate self and others, construct schemes of social reaction, and cooperate in thought and action.

THE CONSTRUCTIVIST TEACHER'S ROLE
IN PROMOTING PEER INTERACTION

Cooperative peer interaction in a constructivist classroom requires considerable teacher support. The constructivist teacher's important role in children's peer interactions involves planning and setting up the classroom so that it can occur, facilitating peer interaction, and making cooperative peer interactions a part of the culture of the classroom.

Planning for Peer Interaction

Constructivist teachers consciously plan opportunities for children to engage with one another. They may design activities to be done in pairs, such as making snack for the class or cleaning the rabbit's cage. On a typical day in Beth Van Meeteren's 1st- and 2nd-grade classroom at the Freeburg School, two children might make bread in the morning, using a bread machine, so that the bread will be done during the afternoon activity period. The bakers survey everyone in the classroom (children and adults), write down what they would like on their slice of fresh-baked bread (usually butter or peanut butter), and then prepare each slice to order for an afternoon snack. Making something to feed classmates can arouse feelings of responsibility and caring. Being fed by classmates can arouse feelings of gratitude and a sense of being cared for. All this contributes to a shared sense of community in which people care for each other and meet each other's needs.

Constructivist teachers also devote attention to how the selection and arrangement of furniture and materials can support peer interaction. For example, they may create cozy places for two or more children to read or work together uninterrupted; provide sufficient room and materials (such as blocks, puzzles, etc.) in certain learning centers for several children to work together; provide two chairs at the computer, so that children can collaborate if they wish; or choose equipment that two children can use together (for example, a tape or CD player, one book for following a recorded story, and two sets of earphones). When activities appeal to their interests, children gravitate individually to the same activity, and the stage is set for interaction.

Facilitating Peer Interaction

The value of peer interaction depends on the ability of the teacher to intervene when children have difficulties and to help them maintain a sociomoral atmosphere that is cooperative. Young children do not necessarily come to early childhood settings proficient in peer relationships. Problems with peer interaction are inevitable with young children who are just learning how to take the perspectives of others, control their own impulses, and interact respectfully with one another. Conflict can be a constructive context, but it can also be destructive. Because children are limited in their abilities to restrain impulses and because of limited perspective-taking, children left entirely to their own devices can fail in their efforts to overcome interpersonal difficulties. Without the guidance of a skilled teacher who promotes cooperation, children can end up with a sociomoral atmosphere in which might makes right and in which many unresolved conflicts create a climate of insecurity, anger, and anxiety. When problems occur, constructivist teachers take an active role in facilitating peaceful resolutions. Chapter 5 is devoted to this very important topic of conflict resolution. Let us simply state here that constructivist teachers consider this an extremely important aspect of their responsibilities as teachers, and do not shy away from this very difficult and time-consuming work.

Some children in early childhood classrooms experience considerable difficulties engaging successfully in peer interactions, for a variety of reasons, including disabilities and lack of good adult role models at home. Constructivist teachers devote considerable attention to monitoring children's developing abilities and determining the most appropriate assistance. Sometimes this assistance takes the form of more-or-less direct teaching. For example, if a teacher observes that a child's only strategies for getting what he or she wants are physical (hitting, grabbing, etc.), the teacher may intervene to give the child words to say to another (for example, "Can you ask him if you can use the truck when he is finished with it? Say, 'Can I use that truck when you're done with it?'"). If a teacher notices that a child does not seem to know how to enter a group, he or she may coach the child on ways to do so successfully, such as watching from the sidelines first to see what the children are doing. The teacher may give the child information about how to "read" how others are feeling (for example, taking a child to the side privately and saying, "Did you see her back up when you asked her that? I don't think she liked it when you put your face so close to hers. You might try standing a little further away when you ask her a question"), as well as feedback about how a child's actions may affect others (for example, "Did you see her smile when you handed her the baby chick? I think she appreciated you doing that").

The constructivist teacher influences the peer culture of the classroom by establishing expectations concerning how others are to be treated and how disagreements are to be resolved. For example, at the Freeburg School, an expectation is that if someone has a conflict with you and asks to talk to you about it, you have to talk to them. Sometimes this occurs at the Peace Bench, but a Peace Bench or other designated place in the classroom for resolving conflicts is not crucial to the process. What is most important is simply the expectation that this is how we solve our problems here.

Constructivist teachers also provide a model of respectful interactions with others, both adults and children. They are careful always to treat others with dignity. They use proper manners (saying please, thank you, and excuse me, and apologizing when they accidentally bump against someone). They look for opportunities to demonstrate how adults can disagree respectfully (for example, in a vote about what to name the class pet). Another way constructivist teachers do this is to engage sometimes as a peer. For example, in a board game, the teacher can take the role of a player alongside children. As a player, the teacher must agree on the rules, abide by them, and accept their consequences, just as children must. As a player, the teacher can ask direction from children and allow them to assume the instructional role. As a loser, the teacher can model how to cope with defeat. As a winner, the teacher can model how to refrain from gloating.

We know that no teacher can be perfectly cooperative all the time. However, we hope the ideas presented in this book will help teachers as they assess their relationships with children and develop cooperative ways of teaching and "being with" children.

4

Establishing a Constructivist Sociomoral Atmosphere

A moral classroom begins with the teacher's attitude of respect for children, for their interests, feelings, values, and ideas. It is sustained by the teacher's efforts to establish a classroom atmosphere in which children's unique developmental needs are accommodated. In this chapter, we offer a succinct definition of constructivist education, discuss each of its three elements, suggest some ideas for getting started, and provide an extended description of how a 1st-grade teacher socializes children for self-regulation during the first 2 weeks of school.

DEFINITION OF CONSTRUCTIVIST EDUCATION

Respect for children leads to the definition of constructivist education as active. Specifically, constructivist education

1. Engages the child's interest
2. Inspires active experimentation with all its necessary groping and error
3. Fosters cooperation between adults and children and among children themselves

We discuss below how interest, experimentation, and cooperation are important for the sociomoral atmosphere and give examples of teachers implementing these ideas.

Engaging Interest

By *interest* we refer to the child's positive emotional engagement in classroom activities. Such interest is crucial to the constructivist sociomoral atmosphere because it reflects respect for the child's point of view.

Why Interest Is Important

Piaget (1954/1981, 1969/1970) referred to interest as the "fuel" of the constructive process. Adults' interests are generally consciously defined and ordered in priorities. Adults are thus often capable of constructive effort even when their interest is at a low level and they feel the pressure of some kind of coercion. Even for adults, however, the absence of interest can prevent effective effort. When our interest is thoroughly engaged, our efforts are most productive. This condition is even more necessary for young children whose interests are still relatively undifferentiated. According to Piaget, interest is central to the actions by which the child constructs knowledge, intelligence, and morality. Without interest, the child would never make the constructive effort to make sense out of experience. Without interest in what is new to him or her, the child would never modify reasoning or values. Interest is a kind of internal regulator that frees up or stops the investment of energy in an object, person, or event. Thus, methods aimed at promoting the constructive process must arouse the child's spontaneous interest, which is inherent in constructive activity.

It surprises many people to learn that constructivist education for cognitive development focuses equally on affectivity. This Piagetian principle was elaborated well before Piaget by John Dewey (1913/1975), who argued that the aim of education is increase in ability to put forth effort. Dewey cautioned, however, that some kinds of effort are *un*educative. These are efforts in tasks that involve nothing but sheer strain and external motivation for keeping at them. Such tasks he described as not only uneducative, but *mis*educative. They are miseducative because they deaden and stupefy, leading to a confused and dulled state of mind that always results when action is carried out without a sense of personal purpose. They are also miseducative because they lead to dependence on the external pressure of the taskmaster. When the child's interest and motivation lie in avoiding punishment or getting reward from the teacher, it is focused outside the task itself. Dewey said we should look not for motives external to activities, but for motives *in* activities. When teachers have to look for artificial ways to motivate children, something is seriously wrong.

Interest in activity is at the heart of constructivist education. Both Dewey and Piaget recommended that we start from the active powers of children. In what ways can young children be mentally active? A partial answer to this question is that young children are motivated to be mentally active in the context of physical activity. For Piaget, intelligence originates in infancy in action that is simultaneously mental and physical. Mental development is in large part a matter of gradually freeing mental activity from physical activity. For many years in childhood, however, physical activity continues to be closely associated with and necessary for mental activity. Another part of the answer to the question of how young children can be mentally active is that they must be emotionally engaged. Children have intellectual needs for activities that stimulate their interests and provide *content that inspires them to figure out something*. This inspiration is simultaneously intellectual and emotional.

Examples of Appealing to Children's Interests

In constructivist classrooms, large blocks of time (at least 1 hour in length) are scheduled for activity time, during which many different activities go on simultaneously. These activities include those long associated with the child-development tradition in early education that appeal to children's interests (for example, painting and other art activities, blocks and other construction activities, and pretend play). Additional activities usually include physical-knowledge and other science activities (DeVries & Kohlberg, 1987/1990; DeVries, Zan, Hildebrandt, Edmiaston, & Sales, 2002; Kamii & DeVries, 1978/1993); group games (DeVries & Kohlberg, 1987/1990; DeVries et al., 2002; Kamii & DeVries, 1980).

The Project Approach (Helm & Beneke, 2003; Helm & Katz, 2001) has put the emphasis on children's interests in recent years as a basis for study in which "the children, in discussion and consultation with their teacher, take initiative, make decisions, and take major responsibility for what is accomplished" (Helm & Katz, 2001, p. 12). Documentation of how children construct knowledge is a strength of this approach. It complements our own because it honors children's wrong ideas and shows progress of individual children from those ideas to better ones. Projects have always been part of constructivist education, but the writers of *The Project Approach* have given us new conceptualizations and new practical directions.

Children do not, of course, create an entire curriculum, and teachers frequently propose activities by putting out materials in centers that might pique children's curiosity and lead to experimentation and disequilibrium. Children can, however, provide ideas that will guide decisions about curriculum content. At the Human Development Laboratory School at the University of Houston, Peige Fuller asked her Investigator class (3½- to 4½-year-olds) at group time what they wanted to know about. The list generated by the children then provided the content for the rest of the semester. Here is a partial list of topics: spacemen, breaking glass, moms and dads, going to college, apples, washing your hands, dinosaurs, and flower girls. In an interview (June 1992), Peige explained her thinking:

The challenges were to respect children's desires and somehow to make constructivist activities from the topics. The teacher has in mind, too, what she wants to include in the curriculum, what she wants children to know about in the world. Being a facilitator means that you're looking at the topics they want to know about and trying to figure out how to bring activities that will jump from their idea and create opportunities for disequilibrium—interpersonal and cognitive. Constructivist teachers understand that that is where the real learning happens.

I learned as a teacher by involving children in their learning from the beginning. It takes teachers who respect children's ideas and who know how to raise them to a new plane. It's a matter of thinking about what things to pull in—investigations, places to go, arguments and struggles we could have. That's where the excitement of early education is—the excitement of being with your kids to figure out your curriculum. You make the commitment to be the best facilitator of their learning that you can be. Then you find out what they want to know about. And then you have these really hard planning meetings where you figure out what all there is in the world that you can bring into the topics.

Taking children's interests seriously led Peige to many unexpected experiences. We recount a few of these in order to illustrate the rewards of following children's interests.

Breaking glass. Peige said, "We were very concerned about this topic when we first heard it. In retrospect, it was the easiest to do." The study of breaking glass was expanded into a unit on safety. Of course, children were not allowed to break glass. Peige explained to them that it would be unsafe and that she could not let children be hurt. Instead, children watched as a teacher did this in a safe way (in a box covered with a towel). Peige explained that children just wanted to see what happened when glass broke. She speculated that they learned why adults "freak out" and say to be careful when children handle glass.

Flower girls. This was perhaps the most challenging topic to elaborate into something that led to not only new knowledge but also reasoning and understanding. As the assistant director was planning her wedding, she was invited to group time, where she talked about loving relationships, getting married, and starting a family. Children had a chance to think about what it means to form a family, and, of course, they asked if she was going to get babies. She replied, "Yes, someday" and added that children make families even more special. In other group times, the group talked about the many different kinds of families represented in the classroom. Children learned about family names and began to write initials of last names after first names. The dress-up center was appropriately organized. Peige comments:

> For me, the flower girl part was not the major focus, but for the two or three who thought this was important, it was a chance to explore that fantasy. Maybe it was a reality in their lives, a special time they wanted to relive, when they felt sort of grownup and fancy.

During the exploration of this theme, an argument arose about whether boys could be flower girls. Peige comments, "We didn't see why someone couldn't have a flower boy if they wanted to, so all the little boys got to wear lace and flowers and all the sparkly stuff, too."

Washing hands. This curriculum suggestion came from a boy who was mystified about why his parents and teachers told him to wash his hands so often. We are reminded of the story told by the first author's mother, Lorraine Goolsby, about the child who, when asked to wash his hands before cooking, said, "I don't need to. I already had a bath this morning." Peige reflected that although children talked about germs, they had to take their existence on faith. She engaged the help of a mother, a microbiologist, who provided Petri dishes. Peige thought of the occasions when adults tell children to cover their mouths as well as to wash their hands. After children played in sand, Peige took fingernail clippings from them for one dish. After children washed their hands, she took more nail clippings for another dish. At group time one dish was passed around for everyone to cough on without covering their mouths. With another, children covered their mouths and coughed. To get the effect of an uncovered sneeze, one child suggested using a cotton swab to take mucous from her nose. One dish was merely exposed to air. All dishes were labeled and discussed so that children would be clear about what they were doing. The mother took the dishes to a warm and moist place in her lab. When she brought them back 2 days later, dramatic results were visible to the naked eye. One container had become so toxic that it had to be sealed and returned to the lab for disposal! Children remembered what they had done and discussed the findings at group time. During activity time they examined the dishes closely. This project made germs observable and more real to children.

Inspiring Experimentation

By *experimentation*, we refer to the child's actions on physical objects, together with observations of the reactions of the objects to these actions as well as new actions informed by previous observations. Our definition should not be equated with the formal scientific definition of *experiment* that includes formal research questions and hypotheses; independent, dependent, and control variables; systematic data collection; and statistical analyses.

Why Experimentation Is Important

Up to the age of about 7 years, child thought is dominated by the physical, material, observable aspects of experience. The child's main interest in objects is what happens when he or she acts on them. In the course of examining objects and trying to see what they can do, children inevitably confront surprises—contradictions to their expectations. These are the moments constructivist teachers hope for because it is then that children have the possibility to construct something new—to make new mental relationships.

Constructivist teachers are guided by Piaget's theory that describes development in terms of a process of experiencing and resolving moments of uncertainty or *disequilibrium*, as noted in Chapter 2. According to this theory, learning does not occur without disequilibrium. In the course of trying to figure out how to do something, children experience disequilibrium when something unexpected occurs. According to Piaget, in the course of experimenting and making new mental relationships, a child constructs not only physical knowledge but also intellectual power—intelligence itself.

The reactions of adults to children's experimentation are crucial to the sociomoral atmosphere. If experimentation is viewed as misbehavior, it may be punished. It is easy to squelch a child's experimental attitude. The challenge for the constructivist teacher is how to foster it.

Examples of Classroom Experimentation

In a constructivist classroom, the teacher actively promotes experimental attitudes among children. In a sink-and-float activity in the kindergarten of the Human Development Laboratory School, for example, Coreen Samuel encourages children's curiosity by providing objects that might arouse feelings of contradiction between children's expectations and observations of objects. She asks questions and makes comments such as "What is going to happen? Is it going to float?" She calls children's attention to individual experiments: "Let's see what happens when _____ tries _____." Children are heard saying, "Let's see what this does," "Let me show you something," "Let's test these," "Try these." They announce their discoveries with pleasure and, frequently, surprise, indicating conscious reflection on a problem. The teacher capitalizes particularly on surprise, as this indicates disequilibrium through a contradiction between children's expectations and their observations. For example, Sally seems surprised that a medium-sized wooden truck (with metal axles and rubber tires) partially submerges while a larger wooden school bus floats. Coreen (T) suggests further experimentation and comparison, and nudges Sally to think about differences between the two trucks and the ways they each act in water.

S: Watch this. Look, Coreen, it [medium wooden truck] sank.
T: I wonder, how about a big one?
S: (Puts large wooden school bus in the water; she looks at Coreen with a surprised expression.)
T: Oh, my gosh, look at that! I never saw a school bus float before.
S: And this one sank (holds up truck).
T: How could this one have sunk? And this [truck] is even smaller.
S: Because it's small.
T: It's smaller, and this one is bigger. Is this [school bus] heavier? Let's feel it. Which one do you think is heavier?
S: This [bus].
T: How come this one is floating?
S: (Drops tiny wooden car in water; it floats) How do little bitty things float if they're little?
T: You thought that only big things float?
S: Yeah, but the little car floats.
T: Pretty strange.
S: (Gets cardboard paper towel roll) It's gonna float. Look at it. It's floating like a snake!
T: How about that! Look at this toothpick. What do you think is going to happen?
S: (Drops toothpick in water and sees that it floats)

In this activity, Sally does not resolve the feeling of contradiction between her expectation that only big things float and her observation that small things also float. However, her puzzlement is the foundation for further experimentation, reflection, and eventual resolution of her disequilibrium.

This example illustrates that children's expectations can surprise us. Thus the teacher, too, continues to construct knowledge about how children reason and how they modify their reasoning.

Coreen supports children's ideas, even when wrong, but attempts to help children become aware of contradictory evidence. For example, when Timothy hypothesizes that a piece of Styrofoam floats because it has a hole in it, Coreen repeats, "Timothy says if it has a hole in here, it doesn't sink." Then Coreen tries to challenge children's reasoning by observing, "This [plastic strawberry basket] sinks, but it has holes in it." Later, when other children infer that wooden things seem to float, she calls attention to the partially submerged truck with metal axles and rubber wheels, saying, "What's different about this one?" A child says, " 'Cause it's carved." He refers to the fact that the truck is made from a single piece of wood. When one group of children concludes that metal sinks and wood floats, Coreen introduces a wooden ruler with a metal edge and asks for predictions. She continually challenges children to refine their conceptualizations.

We would like to point out that Coreen does not avoid including objects having properties of both sinkers and floaters in sink-and-float experiences. Although some observations lead to clear conclusions according to classifications by material, others do not. Coreen does not try to protect children from the ambiguities of the real world.

In a shadows activity, Coreen observes that Brad, a kindergarten boy in the Human Development Laboratory School, has figured out that moving back from the screen results in a bigger and bigger shadow of his wooden elephant. Wondering whether Brad has taken the light source into account, she asks, "How big can you make it? Make it as big as you can." Brad responds by moving back and back until he is behind the slide projector serving as light source. "What happened to the elephant shadow? I don't see it any more." Brad is startled by the unexpected result and waves the elephant in the dark. Seeing no shadow, he moves forward, but out of the path of the light. Waving the elephant from side to side, Brad accidentally catches the light and glimpses the shadow. This leads him to move into the full path of the light. "There it is!" Coreen again asks, "So how big can you make it?" Brad again backs up, still unconscious of the light source, and loses the shadow again. "Darn!" He waves the elephant around, places it on top of and beside the projector, and finally re-creates the shadow by going back to stand in the place where he saw it last. Over the course of the year, Coreen continues to create situations that challenge Brad to experiment further with shadows. (See DeVries, 1986; DeVries & Kohlberg, 1987/1990.)

Fostering Cooperation

By *cooperation*, we refer to thinking or behaving in relation to another's desires, feelings, ideas, and other psychological states. When people talk about cooperation between adults and children, they often mean children's compliance with adult demands. This is not what we mean. Our view of cooperation is drawn from Piaget (1932/1965), who refers to cooperation as *reciprocity* (a "give and take") in relationships among people and as *reciprocity* in thinking about these relationships. When we talk about cooperation in the classroom, we refer to the teacher's attitude and demonstration of respect for children. Of course children are expected to respect adults, but the reverse is not usually discussed. Cooperation is important for the sociomoral atmosphere because it reflects respect for the equality of class members—equality in rights and responsibilities. The general principle of teaching is that the teacher minimizes the exercise of adult authority as much as practical and possible (see Chapter 3 for the rationale).

Why Cooperation Is Important

As noted in Chapter 2, Piaget talked about the cognitive and moral importance of decentering from awareness of a single perspective. Cooperation is not possible unless children decenter to think about the perspective of the other. Cooperation, with its implicit reciprocity, is critical to the sociomoral atmosphere. Cooperation requires coordination of points of view, progressive adjustments in understanding the other, accepting another's initiatives, reciprocating proposals with counterproposals, and so on. The necessity for coordination becomes clear when children act in contradictory ways or openly disagree. The desire to play together arises from children's friendly relations—their socioaffective bonds. The habit of playing/working together makes possible more complex forms of cooperation. The motivation to cooperate and resolve problems when interactions break down is stronger between friends than non-friends. Therefore constructivist teachers promote children's interactions and friendships.

The desire to share one's thoughts with another leads to efforts to understand and make oneself understood. The feeling of understanding another and being understood can create the conditions for development of friendship. Frequently in children's play, what they are most interested in is not so much the content but the social interaction. Experiences in cooperation provide the foundation and context for developing interpersonal understanding and thinking about issues of fairness and justice.

In the absence of external organization, children who play together must construct agreements on what to do, in light of one another's desires. In pretend play, the meaning of symbols must be shared; in play with a doll, if one child holds out a block and says, "Give the baby some water," the other has to accept the block as meaning a container with water if the play is to succeed. In group games, children confront the need to agree on rules; if one child makes a certain move, but the other says, "No, you can't do that," they must co-operate (that is, "operate together") to negotiate if the game is to succeed. These kinds of interactions illustrate how *decentering* looks in the classroom. These situations are moral in that the equilibrium of trust and friendly feelings is at stake. If one child refuses to accept and acknowledge the other's overture, a breakdown in the relation occurs. Cooperation is therefore important for intellectual as well as social and moral development.

Examples of Classroom Cooperation

A classroom organized to promote interest and experimentation also invites cooperation. Children who want to use the blocks may decide to work together on a structure. In pretend play, children can develop complex shared symbols as they coordinate their roles and ideas. Cooking the class snack can be organized so two cooks need to agree on what to cook and how to divide the responsibilities.

As noted above, group games require cooperation. Consider, for example, the case of two 5-year-old friends who play checkers together frequently over the course of a year. The progressive adjustment of points of view is clear as they simultaneously construct rules along with interpersonal understanding. In the beginning, they do not know all the classic rules and unconsciously modify the game. For example, Kerrick decides that the checkers can move diagonally any number of spaces, as long as the path is clear, like the bishop in chess. Jordan thinks he can jump over two spaces in order to capture an opposing checker. Kerrick decides they can move backward. As the teacher had provided rules written especially for the game, she is able to refer to these when children are at an impasse. Rather than just telling children a rule, the teacher says, "Let's see what the rules say." She thus moves authority from herself to the written rules. Over time, the boys learned to play by the written rules as one of several ways to play they had invented. However, they became able to coordinate with one another by clarifying which rules to play by before beginning a game. Their ability to cooperate progressed dramatically, and we believe that one particularly serious conflict they could not resolve (described in Chapter 5) may have played an important role in their recognition of the need to cooperate more closely. A more detailed description of the Checkers play of Kerrick and Jordan may be found in Zan (1996, 2002).

An example of how the constructivist teacher minimizes authority is that the teacher often takes part in a group game as a player alongside children (Kamii & DeVries, 1980; DeVries et al., 2002). In this role, the teacher has to abide by the rules and accept their consequences, just as children do. This role allows the teacher to think aloud as a player and thereby help children become more conscious of rules and strategies (for example, in a game of Checkers: "If I move that one here, it would be safe, but if I move it here, you'd jump me, so I think I'll move it here so it will be safe"). Children thus are challenged to think ahead and reason about possible moves on the part of the opponent. All good group games involve social and moral benefits, but possibilities for the construction of knowledge must be analyzed for individual games to determine the educational benefit. For example, spatial reasoning is fostered in games such as Tic-Tac-Toe and Checkers, math in Add-Up-to-10 Bingo, Rat-A-Tat-Cat, and UNO, physical knowledge in Drop the Clothespin, Shuffleboard, and Pick-Up Sticks. Constructivist teachers cultivate over time children's thinking and ability to play cooperatively.

The long-term goal of cooperation among children includes construction of emotional balance and coping abilities. Emotional balance is a continual effort on the part of young children whose emotions can change drastically even from one moment to the next—from laughing with a peer as they both tug on a toy to an angry *no* when the other does not release it. As noted in Chapters 2 and 3, young children have not yet constructed stable personality characteristics and coping competencies, a process that occurs gradually over many years. This is related to intellectual limitations in thinking about the perspectives of others and the complexities of social interactions and relationships.

Constructivist teachers foster the development of self-knowledge by helping children reflect on their feelings and reaction tendencies. When children become upset, the teacher can ask what happened to make them upset. Sympathetically, the teacher can acknowledge children's feelings, letting them know that how they feel is recognized. In the case of an issue with another child, the teacher can use conflict resolution techniques, discussed in the following chapter. If the child comes to school upset with a parent, the teacher can listen and perhaps help the child figure out how to talk to the parent about the problem. If the child continues to be upset or is upset about something that cannot be changed, the constructivist teacher can help the child let go of and master the difficult feelings, making suggestions such as "Sometimes you can make yourself feel better" or "Sometimes when I am upset, it helps if I play with play dough. Would

you like to try that?" Consider the following interaction between Peige
Fuller (T) and 4-year-old Colin, who has been in her class just a few days.

C: (Cries)
T: So, are these tears because something is upsetting you? What makes
    you sad?
C: I want my mommy.
T: Right. Did something in our classroom happen that made you very
    sad?
C: (Nods)
T: What happened?
C: I just want my mommy.
T: You just want your mommy? I see that you got your paper towel.
    Would you like to eat some snack?
C: (Shakes head)
T: No, okay. You know what you could do that would be a big help to
    us would be for you to have a seat here and help us to clean up some
    Legos. That would be a very big help. (She holds Colin in her lap while
    they pick Legos from the floor and put them in a container.)

Peige later offers Colin several other ways he might cope with separation from his mother and tries to help him consider his possible control over his feelings of loss. Finally, she leaves him to figure out what
to do. After a while, he tentatively begins observing and then engaging
in classroom activities. This may represent some progress in Colin's construction of emotional balance and coping ability, but children usually
have to struggle again and again with separation over a period of time.
In schools where we have had children as young as 14 months to 3 years
routinely separating from parents with no upset, we have sometimes been
surprised at the occasional separation trauma (sometimes with screaming and tantrums) of much older children who have not been in a school
setting before. This reminds us that the need for help in constructing new
coping abilities can occur at any age, in one form or another.

We generally recommend that teachers not initiate group discussions
of problems between two children. However, when many children are
concerned about an individual's behavior, group discussion may be fruitful. For example, in the Human Development Laboratory School kindergarten, children come in one day from early morning outside time with
a concern about Harry's behavior on the playground. Nancy enters the
classroom, saying, "We need to discuss the problem of Harry." The teacher, Coreen Samuel, asks if it is for the whole group or if it is something to
do at activity time. Nancy is too angry to wait, and other children join in

her complaint. Nancy explains, "Harry was hurting and tearing up my picture, and he threw me down on the hard platform slide." Harry denies this, saying he doesn't remember pushing Nancy down. Nancy accuses him, "Yes, you did! You're just lying so you can get out of the problem." Other children support Nancy's story, and Andrea (age 5 years) argues eloquently and passionately about the implications beyond this particular incident. She says:

> I think what we should do about it is let Harry know how we feel. These problems are really important because if we don't help these problems, they're not going to get any better and kids won't be taught very well and when they grow up, they're prob'ly not gonna know—if we go on letting people hurt, people will learn to hurt. If we don't stop this, then people will learn to hurt when they grow up. And I don't think that's a very good idea to leave these problems in front of us and not go ahead and help these problems.

The teacher follows up, "Nancy, Andrea said she saw the same thing with her eyes. She had a suggestion. Maybe you need to tell Harry how you feel about that. Do you want to talk to Harry, since it's yours and his problem?" Nancy says to Harry, "Harry, I don't like that when you push me down and try to tear my paper up." Other children also express concern about getting hurt on the playground. Coreen remarks, "It seems like the playground is not a fun place to be anymore." She asks, "What can those children do when they're having this kind of lack of control?" Andrea again acts as the moral spokesperson:

> We should tell them how we feel. Everybody in the world has feelings. It's like I said, they'll grow up and hurt other people, and I'm not sure we can help it when they're all grown up. That's just the way they've learned and there's no other way they've learned.

Coreen emphasizes decentering, "What we try and tell children to do is to think of other people's feelings. Even the teachers do it. If you're really upset, then we think about what you might be feeling, and we try to help you." Jay offers, "It's not fun when you're fighting all the time." Andrea once again speaks:

> You know, we're the big class, and we're trying to teach the little kids by our actions. I'm not sure if we're really showing them how a big kid should act—and then they're going to do the same thing when they're in our kindergarten class.

Coreen says, "Let's see what Harry has to say. Maybe he can help control himself. What can you do to make the playground a better place? It's no fun anymore." Harry replies, "I can not hit." Coreen asks how he is going to work toward not doing that. Then Harry shows that he heard Andrea's plea, yet assimilated it to an internal morality that is motivated by fear of punishment (see Chapter 2):

> Well, I think what the same thing Andrea said. Like if you hurt someone and then when you grow up, then you'll learn that hitting is what you should do, and if you hit, then you'll get into trouble.

In this example, we see a feeling of moral concern and responsibility that even goes beyond the immediate problem situation to long-term effects on the kindergarten children themselves as well as the younger children whom they influence.

IDEAS FOR GETTING STARTED

For teachers new to these ideas, planning how to establish a constructivist sociomoral atmosphere can be daunting. We discuss several ideas for getting started—organizing the classroom to meet children's needs and helping children feel welcome in the classroom. We close with a description of how one constructivist 1st-grade teacher socialized her children for self-regulation in the first 2 weeks of school.

Organizing to Meet Children's Needs

Organizing to meet children's needs includes consideration of children's physiological and emotional needs as well as their needs for peer interaction.

Physiological Needs

In Chapter 1, we describe different attitudes toward children's physical needs for eating, toileting, and resting. It seems obvious that adults should meet children's physical needs. However, we have observed rather callous disregard for these needs on the part of some teachers and schools. Perhaps part of the reason this occurs is that school rules and facilities sometimes make it difficult and inconvenient for teachers to respond to young children's physical needs. Nevertheless, failure to meet children's physical needs creates stressful situations for children that interfere with learning. When children are preoccupied with their physical needs, they cannot devote mental energy to what the teacher has planned (for example, listening to a book being read, generating a list of favorite foods, or thinking of rhyming words to plug into the song "Down by the Bay"). The sociomoral atmosphere of the constructivist classroom must be characterized by physical comfort.

Emotional Needs

A constructivist sociomoral atmosphere is one that is sensitive to children's emotional needs. In many schools where children's physical needs are met, emotional needs may be overlooked. We discuss in Chapter 3 the unfortunate effects of heteronomy on children's emotional development. The Drill Sergeant described in Chapter 1 may be considered an emotionally abusive teacher. The Manager may be considered an emotionally absent teacher. The Mentor is not only emotionally present and available to children, she continually takes children's feelings into account and tries to help them construct a more stable system of feelings and ways of coping with difficult feelings. Research shows that children whose teachers score high on emotional sensitivity and responsiveness demonstrate greater social competence than children whose teachers score lower on those characteristics (Hamre & Pianta, 2005; Pianta, La Paro, Payne, Cox, & Bradley, 2002; Pianta & Stuhlman, 2004).

Respecting children requires communicating acceptance and affection. It requires providing an environment that encourages and supports children's expressions of feelings, interests, and values. This means accepting the child's right to feel anger and sadness as well as positive feelings.

Need for Peer Interaction

The child's need to be active includes a need to be socially interactive. The constructivist teacher promotes peer interaction by intentionally organizing the program so interpersonal engagement can and will occur.

Activity time (discussed in Chapter 11) offers extensive opportunities for peer interaction. Some activities, such as pretend play and group games, especially motivate children to engage with one another and figure out how to cooperate. In physical-knowledge activities, children experiment, observe others' experiments, and exchange ideas. Similarly, art, block building, and writing can be contexts for peer collaboration. In all these activities, children are free to choose not only their activities but also their playmates. They are also free to work alone if they so choose.

Although it is important for teachers to offer materials and possibilities in various centers during activity time, we caution against overorganizing peer interaction. For example, teachers sometimes try to promote community by assigning children to activities and to play/work with other children, on a rotating basis. When children are old enough to recognize why the teacher is imposing this method of organization, perhaps it can promote better acquaintance and friendship among children, but only if the teacher has already cultivated in the group an attitude of wanting to be a *community* and a willingness to risk the unknowns of getting to know someone new. However, assigning play/work partners to younger children is a different matter. Unable even to appreciate the logic of how everyone can be paired with everyone else, much less why this might be desirable, young children can only experience such assignments as depriving them of working/playing with friends. Having to play/work with a nonchosen peer can lessen investment and mental activity. Thus this method of organizing younger children is not respectful of their feelings and interests. Similarly, rotating groups of children every 15 minutes or so interrupts what children are doing and makes them resentful. We have seen young children sit with arms folded and a glowering look when forced to suddenly stop what they are doing and engage in a different activity. A feeling of community cannot be purchased at the price of individuals' friendships and mental activity. Such control will operate against the establishment of children's feelings of ownership of the classroom, their feelings of belonging, and their possibilities to think. For these reasons, we believe that teachers should maximize children's opportunities to choose their play/work partners and their activities.

Sensitive teachers create situations in which getting acquainted with and interacting with others is unavoidable. For example, a new physical-knowledge activity (where several can work simultaneously) may be so popular that a sign-up sheet is necessary, and taking a turn when a place opens up groups children in new ways. Similarly, placing two chairs at the computer and using a sign-up list to regulate turns leads inevitably to different pairings. Other ways to promote interaction include group time games such as Simon Says or Musical Chairs (without putting anyone out, as described in Kamii & DeVries, 1980).

In early childhood, children are still constructing their feelings, ideas, and values concerning friendship. Even very young children can develop attachments to other children that have all the characteristics of friendship. Two-year-olds can be observed to have stable preferences for play partners, to watchfully anticipate their arrival, to miss them and feel sad when they are absent, and to express special compassion for them.

We caution against trying to break up special attachments among children. Sometimes teachers are concerned about cliques that form. We understand and agree that there are concerns about children feeling left out when excluded from a group's play. However, children's attachments are important to them and mark progress in social development. Stability in preferences reflects conservation of values that is necessary for moral development. When children come to be interested in the psychological states of others and in developing friendships, they construct a repertoire of different types of negotiation strategies and shared experiences. As children become more balanced and better able to emotionally cope, the sociomoral atmosphere of the classroom changes accordingly. Therefore, we suggest that teachers encourage children's special friendships.

If a problem of exclusion and hurt feelings arises, this can be addressed in a variety of ways. It can be a topic for discussion at group time as a general hypothetical issue without naming personalities involved. It can be the topic of a puppet play in which one puppet is hurt because of exclusion by other puppets, and the children can be supported to think of ways to include the hurt puppet. If a child is very upset, the teacher can explore the problem in a private discussion at first. Sometimes it is helpful to suggest that the parents of the excluded child invite a classmate to their home or to share a special occasion. We have seen overnight friendships bloom after such a shared experience. Sometimes it is helpful to coach the excluded child on how to enter into others' play. Sometimes it helps for the excluded child to bring a special game or activity to share with classmates. It is not necessary to mandate that children must play with certain others in order to deal with problems of exclusion.

To organize for peer interaction is also to set the stage for inevitable conflicts. Viewing conflict and its resolution as part of the curriculum, constructivist teachers take advantage of incidents of conflict, as discussed in Chapter 5. In a conflict situation, children have the opportunity to recognize the other's differing perspective. Those who care about each other are motivated to figure out how to resolve the problem.

Helping Children Feel Welcome

Some of the ways to help children feel welcome are to make a personal connection with each child and family, introduce children to each other, and communicate to children that the classroom belongs to them. The following practical ideas are based on our observations of classrooms at the beginning of a school year.

Make a Personal Connection with Each Child and Family

Some teachers are able to contact families before the school year begins. Writing a card or letter to each child is an old tradition in many schools. Home visits also have a long history in early education. Since being required by Head Start and advocated by national and state organizations, this practice has regained an important place in practice. At the Freeburg School, teachers made home visits before school began and took digital photographs—one of the child and family, to post in the classroom, and one of the child and teacher, to keep at home. Families were individually invited and scheduled to visit classrooms before classes began. At these times, children were introduced to the centers, materials, and possibilities. These and other such methods aim to establish positive relationships among a child, family members, and the teacher(s) and to make the child and family feel comfortable and cared for in the classroom and school.

Introduce Children to Each Other

Introductions can be done in various ways and depend on the extent to which children already know each other. When older children do not know each other or someone new is in the class, a round-robin of self-introductions at an opening group time may suffice. The teacher can plan ahead for a mentor child to show a new person around at activity time. Teachers at Freeburg used movable name cards on a board visible to everyone in the group. At the beginning of the morning, all the cards were in a column labeled "Not in School." Either as they arrived or during group time, individuals moved their name cards to the "In School" column. Through attention to these cards, children learned to read one another's names. Singing a "name song" often made it possible to sustain children's interest until everyone had moved his or her card.

In her book about developmental discipline, *Learning to Trust*, author Marilyn Watson (2003) describes how teacher Laura Ecken uses group time activities to help children learn about each other and become aware of similarities and differences. One activity involves having the children stand on one of two sides of the room. The teacher calls out a series of "What would you rather do?" questions, and the children go to one side of the room or the other, depending on the answer. For example, "Would you rather sing or dance?" "At a birthday party, would you rather eat cake or ice cream?" Children have the opportunity to see that sometimes they disagree with their friends and that they may have things in common with others that they did not know about. Mara Sapon-Shevin's book, *Because We Can Change the World: A Practical Guide to Building Cooperative, Inclusive Classroom Communities* (1998) contains many other ideas for helping children get to know each other and building classroom community.

Communicate to Children That the Classroom Belongs to Them

When children feel ownership of the classroom, the stage is set for cultivating feelings of belonging and responsibility. Constructivist classrooms are organized so children can take responsibility for many aspects of the classroom such as rules, decisions, room arrangement, and decorations. Adults often underestimate the amount of responsibility children are willing and eager to accept.

Transferring ownership of some aspects of the classroom to the children may require a shift in thinking for some teachers. A very useful resource for K–6 teachers is a small paperback called *Ways We Want Our Class to Be* (Developmental Studies Center, 1996) that complements our own approach. The primary vehicle recommended in this book is the class meeting, a forum for children to talk about being in school. Over several meetings, children are invited to talk about what they want to do in school during the year, what makes them feel good about school and about themselves, and what they see and experience that makes them feel bad. The teacher makes positive and negative lists, and these provide the basis for later presentation of vocabulary such as *fair/unfair*, *kind/unkind*, and *responsible/irresponsible*; categorization of the lists; and explanations such as that the positive list shows ways of taking care of each other, the classroom, and so on. "Check-in" meetings several times a year allow children to assess whether the class is the way they want it to be and discuss how to improve. Another way to foster children's feelings of ownership of the classroom is to begin a class meeting on the 1st day by calling attention to the bare walls of the classroom and asking children what they would like to make for the walls. The teacher can say, "This is your classroom, and I need your help in figuring out how to make the walls more interesting." Discussion can lead to planning ways to decorate, but it can also give the teacher important information about children's interests. Decorations can be linked to study topics, and children with similar interests may begin to group themselves for work.

SOCIALIZING CHILDREN FOR SELF-REGULATION IN A 1st-GRADE CLASSROOM

Constructivist teachers invent many ways of establishing a cooperative sociomoral atmosphere at the beginning of the year. We studied how Terry Anderson, a 1st-grade teacher in Kirkwood, Missouri, went about socializing children during the first 2 weeks of school into an atmosphere characterized by caring, mutual respect, and self-regulation. As most of Terry's

20 children had not had previous experience in a constructivist classroom, they needed instruction and coaching concerning what they could do at various times of the day. We discuss what Terry did in terms of introducing children to classroom procedures such as the lunch count, bathroom sign-up, work time and choice time, fair turns for journal sharing at group time, and "have-tos." We point to how she used a spontaneous conflict to show children how conflict resolution can resolve problems and how she used self-disclosure and empathy to make the classroom a safe place for openness about feelings. In addition, how Terry used humor to create feelings of community is especially important.

Inspired by Piaget's notion of reducing heteronomy, Terry's priority in the beginning was to establish procedures that gave children responsibility and freed her from regulating them. As she was required by the office to do a lunch count, and children had to go to a centrally located bathroom, these were the procedures she addressed first.

Lunch Count

On the 1st day, Terry set up centers and encouraged children to choose what they wanted to do just as they had in kindergarten. When this was going smoothly, Terry began to call small groups of children to instruct them in how to do the lunch count. She gave each child a small magnet with his or her name glued on the top and called attention to the cards on magnets that she had arranged on the side of a metal file cabinet, labeled *Bringing*, *Choice Number 1*, and *Choice Number 2*. Terry (T) explained:

T: It says, "'Bringing,' and this says 'Choice number 1', and 'Choice number 2'" (reading categories glued in a line across the bottom of the chart to define columns of names). That is, if you are buying lunch, you get two choices, and you choose which one you want. But you don't know what it is today, so I have to tell you what it is. If you look over on the board—Steve is looking at the choices. Tell us, Steve, what are the choices? This says, "Number 1." See that, "Lunch choices, #1."
C: Chicken nuggets.
T: Chicken nuggets, and number 2 is—
C: Burritos?
T: Burrito.

Terry then showed the children how to place their magnets above their choice. After all were instructed, Terry filled out the paper for the office and asked a child to take it there. In the course of explaining the lunch count system, Terry talked with the children about why the office needed a lunch count and what might happen if people forgot to make their choices. On succeeding days, Terry sometimes had to remind a child about the lunch count (she could see which magnets had not been placed), but doing one's lunch count simply became an individual child responsibility, and Terry's time was then freed from this chore.

Bathroom

Inevitably, children began to ask to go to the bathroom. At afternoon group time on the 1st day, Terry introduced the sign-up sheet.

T: Some of you have been coming to me and asking to go to the bathroom. In this class, you don't have to ask as long as you sign out. There is a sign-out sheet over by the light switch, and it looks like this (writing "Boys, Girls" on a small dry-erase board).

Children: Boys, girls.

T: Yes, and it's got a line in the middle like that. So if you're Margot, would you sign up here (pointing to "girls" column)? And do you know why I need you to sign your name?

C: So you know where we are.

C: So you know that we didn't, like, sneak away.

T: Yes, so I know where you are because I am responsible for you, and I need to know where you are.

C: Well, if you can't find us, you will just go over to look at it.

T: Exactly. So if I look around and say, "I need to read with Maggie," and Maggie is not in the room, I would worry. But this way, I will go over and say, "Oh, Maggie is in the bathroom." Now the thing she needs to do when she gets back is cross out her name so the next person can go. Usually just one girl can go at a time and one boy. Okay, so if you see that Ellen's name is like this, and you need to go to the bathroom, it looks like Ellen is not back yet. How can you tell that she is not back yet?

C: Her name.

T: Right. She doesn't have her name crossed out so she must still be gone. So wait until Ellen comes back and crosses her name out, and then you can go.

Children did need reminders on day 2, especially about crossing their names off when they returned from the bathroom. Terry found herself giving a lot of individual instruction. Wanting children to take ownership of the system, Terry asked David, "Would you remember to remind people at our next group time that we need to cross our names out?" She followed up with a revisiting of bathroom procedures at group time. As children became accustomed to the system, they could regulate themselves.

Sharing Journals at Group Time

Terry created a procedure designed to give children opportunities to read their journals at group time but to limit the number of children to the time available. She decided that it was feasible for five children to have a turn each day and asked children who were interested to put their names on the chalkboard. Again, the responsibility was given to children.

Work Time and Choice Time

Terry thought about work time as an experience of "bounded choice." That is, children had choices but within boundaries. At group time on day 3, Terry showed a list of all the possible activities for work time. These included computer (with its sign-up list), three games (Tic Tac Toe, Guess Who, and Connect Four), spinning tops, new book in the listening center (where children could listen to an audiotape of a book and read along), and the handwriting center "have-to." In addition, children could always make or read a book. In fact, children often chose many of their work time activities at choice time as well. Terry also invited children during work time to read a book with her, and children often came to show her the books they made. These were opportunities for encouraging children's authentic writing and for showing conventional spellings, too. Terry made art available only at a choice time period at the end of the day when messy projects could take up a lot of space.

"Have-Tos"

Terry identified some activities as "have-tos" that allowed no choice. During the 1st week, she introduced children to a worksheet handwriting curriculum required by the school district. This did not fit well with Terry's own writing program. Because the teacher had no choice, neither did the children. Terry explained this to her class but tried to minimize the coercion she could not avoid by allowing children to decide when during the week they would do this work. Terry hoped that this element of choice would help children accept this responsibility with some degree of autonomy and give experience in time management. Still, getting some children to do this work required reminding. Another example of a "have-to" is that everyone on day 6 had to draw pictures to illustrate the pages in their class book that was inspired by the book *Mary Wore a Red Dress* (Peek

& Giblin, 1985). Later, Terry consulted children about what makes a good "have-to," and children took more and more initiative in suggesting work to be designated as "have-tos."

Conflict Resolution

During the 1st week of school, Terry dealt with conflicts as they arose. On the 3rd day, she introduced the Peace Chairs during group time and asked two children to act out a conflict. (A similar situation is described in detail in Chapter 5.) She talked about trying first to solve a problem where it arises but going to the Peace Chairs when it is not easily solved, turn taking when talking, the ways in which one might talk in order to express feelings, and how she sometimes goes over to help children work on a problem. Children laugh when Terry humorously acts out grabbing a book from Anthony, and they talk about what she could have done differently.

These mundane classroom necessities are significant for our description of how to establish a cooperative sociomoral classroom atmosphere. Terry took time to solicit children's ideas about why these procedures were necessary. Knowing the reasons gives children the power to follow the procedures autonomously rather than just because the teacher says so. Moreover, Terry's respectful approach and tone of voice communicated to children that she viewed them as responsible persons having the ability to cooperate with the procedures. Forgetting was forgiven as children became accustomed to these ways of doing things. It should be noted that the teacher created these and other procedures and taught them directly (see the discussion of rules and norms in Chapter 7).

Openness About Feelings

During the first group time on the 1st day after activity time, Terry (T) begins her effort to make the classroom a safe place in which to be open about feelings. She begins:

T: How many of you when you came in this morning were feeling kind of scared in your tummies? Yeah, well, guess what? A lot of your friends, if you look around, a lot of your friends were feeling kind of scared, too. . . . I need to tell you something about what I did this last weekend. I have a son. I will show you his picture. Okay, this is my son (shows photograph of a dog).

Children: (Laugh) No, it isn't. It's a dog!

T: (With exaggerated surprise) Oh, this is not my son. Is this my son (shows son's photograph)?

Children: Yes! What's his name? He is pretty big.

T: This last weekend, we loaded up his drums—because he plays the drums—in the car, and all of his clothes and books, and all of his CDs that he likes, and jackets and coats and everything. We took him to Minnesota, which is another state. It takes 10 hours to get there, and we took him to college. He is at college now, and I had to leave him there. I had to leave him there, and I am his mom, and guess how I felt?

Children: Sad.

T: Really sad and scared because I was thinking. What do you think I might be thinking?

Children: He will get hurt. . . . He might not get a education . . . He might get in trouble. . . . He might get a heart attack.

T: That is what I was thinking. I was so worried about him. But you know what? When we called him last night, I said (in an exaggerated, worried tone of voice), "Ryan, how are you?" He said, "I'm fine, Mom."

Children: (Laugh at Terry's impersonations.)

T: I bet if your moms called you on the phone today, they would probably say (with exaggerated, worried tone of voice), "Candy, how are you?" And you would say (calm tone of voice), "I'm fine."

Children: (Laugh) . . .

T: You know what? Your mom is probably worried just as much as maybe you might be, but so far, I guess we are all okay.

Terry effectively uses self-disclosure to communicate to the entire group that being open about feelings is allowed, appropriate, and encouraged. She gives children opportunity to reflect on their own feelings and to leave feelings of discomfort behind. Moreover, Terry presents the topic with a lot of humor.

Humor

As described above, children in Terry's class laugh together on the 1st day. Such shared humor can be the foundation for feelings of community as children begin to have feelings of belonging together. Terry made it a point to cultivate laughter by reading humorous poems and singing silly songs. On the 3rd day of school, she taught the class the "Garbage Song," which she made up when her young son's homework was put in the garbage by mistake. The son was upset, and Terry tried to get him to laugh by singing in exaggerated country-western style while playing air guitar:

"I was put in the garbage one morning by mistake;
They thought I was a rotten banana;
I sat there all covered with the crumbs of a cake;
Just me in my yellow pajamas;
Oh, lonesome; oh, lonesome; oh, lonesome me;
I'm getting all soggy;
I miss my doggy;
And it's almost a quarter to 3."

Children were delighted and shared their amusement as they giggled at the silliness. Terry succeeded often in appealing to the group's cognitive level of humor appreciation.

We hope this gives the reader a flavor of what it means to establish a constructivist sociomoral atmosphere. Through countless situations in which children experience sympathy, community, and clashes with others, the child constructs ideas of reciprocity among persons.

5

Conflict and Its Resolution

Conflicts are inevitable in an active classroom where free social interaction occurs. In many schools conflict is viewed as undesirable and to be avoided at all costs. Our view is rather different. Although our goal is a harmonious atmosphere in which productive work can occur, we see conflict and its resolution as essential to children's development and learning, especially in the construction of mental relationships. In this chapter, we discuss the role of conflict in development; review research on conflict resolution ability among children from the Boot Camp, Factory, and Community classrooms described in Chapter 1; outline the constructivist teacher's general attitude toward conflicts; present principles of teaching with examples; and examine the situation of conflict between teacher and child.

THE ROLE OF CONFLICT IN DEVELOPMENT

It is easy to recognize the practical value of ability to resolve interpersonal conflict. If all adults had this ability, we might have world peace. Aggressive children often suffer from poor peer relationships, peer rejection, and friendlessness. Children who are rejected by their peers are at high risk for later problems, including poor academic achievement, dropping out, and delinquency. Practical conflict resolution ability is thus an important goal in itself.

In Piaget's theory, the value of conflict for development is more complex, and the constructivist rationale also goes beyond the obvious value. In constructivist theory, conflict takes two forms: intraindividual and interindividual. Piaget viewed both as critical for development although his main research focus was on the first form, intraindividual conflict—conflict within the individual. This conflict is evident, for example, with regard to a physical phenomenon when Devon has the idea that the location of his shadow depends on his action. Having seen his shadow when he walked up to one wall, he is surprised not to see it when he walks up to another. The contradiction between expectation and result (disequilibrium) can lead to a search for spatial and causal relations among object, light, and screen. Thus internal conflict can lead an individual to make new and more complex mental relationships.

An example of intraindividual conflict with regard to counting and number is observable when young children play board games involving rolling a die to find out how many spaces to move on a path. As we explained in Chapter 2, at a certain point in constructing number, many children apply their knowledge of one-to-one correspondence in an erroneous way. They believe it is correct to count the space they are on as "1," rather than moving forward one on the count of "1," as plus-1 logic dictates. Many children show obvious mental conflict when they roll a 1, say "1," and make no forward movement. What usually happens is a sort of stuttering "1—1" as they count the space they are on and then stumble forward one. In the course of such repeated experiences, children may profit from their internal cognitive conflict and restructure their mental relationships. When children make this error, we recommend using a die with only 1s and 2s (or even 1s, 2s, and blanks to represent 0) so that they will have more opportunities to experience the conflict between their logic of acknowledging the starting space and their conflicting logic of addition.

The second form of conflict is interindividual—conflict between individuals. In his early work, Piaget (1932/1965) argued that such conflict can promote both intellectual and moral development. This occurs through decentering from a single perspective to take into account other perspectives and is prompted by confrontation with the desires and ideas of others. Piaget (1965/1977) stated, "Social life is a necessary condition for the development of logic" (p. 80), and argued that when the child has the experience of others who react to the content of what he or she says, the child becomes conscious of others as having feelings, ideas, and desires. Increasing consciousness of others and efforts to coordinate self-other perspectives result in higher-level interpersonal understanding (see the discussion of Selman's developmental levels in Chapter 2). That is, efforts to resolve conflict can lead to the construction of new understanding of others and of oneself. For example, when a child grabs the dice in a board game and takes two turns in a row, the child may be focused only on self-interest in moving the marker, or the child may not understand the turn-taking rule. Not anticipating the resultant outcry from the other players, the child may be shocked that these actions result in protest. He or she may be motivated to figure out how to play (make a new mental relationship between the order of one's turn and those of others) so that relationships with peers continue harmoniously.

Interindividual conflict can lead to intraindividual conflict. For example, a child making the logical error of addition described above may play the game with another child who objects and demonstrates how to proceed correctly. Children often respond with greater openness to correction by children than correction by adults. However, as we see in Chapter 2, correction of counting spaces in a board game may not be enough to convince the child who reasons that the occupied space must be acknowledged. In fact, sometimes the child making the logical error tries to correct the child who counts correctly! Interpersonal conflict can lead to motivation for thinking (and making new mental relationships) about how to proceed in a situation of differing opinions.

Conflict plays a special role in Piaget's constructivist theory. It serves to motivate reorganization of knowledge into more adequate forms. Piaget (1975/1985) stated that conflict (disequilibrium) is the most influential factor in acquisition of new knowledge (new mental relationships). Experiences of conflict prompt individuals to change how they think and feel. Conflicts may thus be viewed as a source of progress in development.

Children's desires for good relationships with peers can motivate them to persist in solving their problems. By experiencing over and over the resolution of negative feelings, children become committed to the value and possibilities of negotiation. However, we must emphasize how difficult conflict resolution may be for young children. In fact, resolving conflicts is hard work! When children experience conflict, especially with someone for whom they care, they can feel just as deeply about these ruptures as do adults when a relationship is broken.

THE SOCIOMORAL ATMOSPHERE AND CONFLICT RESOLUTION

In the study described in Chapters 1 and 2 (DeVries, Haney, & Zan, 1991; DeVries, Reese-Learned, & Morgan, 1991), we wanted to find out whether children experiencing very different sociomoral classroom atmospheres would differ in their ability to resolve conflicts. Comparing children from Boot Camp, Factory, and Community classrooms in the game situation, we found that children from the constructivist Community classroom demonstrated greater interpersonal ability by resolving significantly more of their conflicts than children from Boot Camp and Factory classrooms. Without adult help, Community children resolved 70% of their conflicts (54 out of 77), Factory children resolved 33% (16 out of 48), and Boot Camp children resolved 40% (15 out of 37). Boot Camp children tended to end their conflicts by overwhelming the other physically or emotionally, whereas Factory children tended to ignore their playmates' grievances. Community children tried to work out their differences.

We studied these conflicts further and found that even within conflict periods when interpersonal understanding was most challenged, Community children still used significantly more Level 2 negotiation strategies than either of the other groups. In addition, they had many more shared experiences in the course of their conflicts. This means that the tension of their conflicts was moderated by friendly overtures. We think the Community children were more successful because they had learned negotiation attitudes and strategies in their classroom and because they cared more about preserving their relationships.

THE CONSTRUCTIVIST TEACHER'S ATTITUDE TOWARD CHILDREN'S CONFLICTS

As a result of observing and talking with teachers about handling conflict, we distinguish three aspects of the teacher's attitude with regard to children's conflicts. These underlie the 15 principles presented in the following section.

1. Be Calm and Control Reactions

It takes practice, but the teacher should learn to appear calm even when children are extremely upset. Even when the teacher does not feel calm, it is important to communicate calmness to children. This means controlling body language, facial expression, and tone of voice. The teacher should avoid acting on the first impulse or rushing to the rescue, except to prevent physical harm. Children will come to welcome this calm strength as a support for working through their difficulties.

2. Recognize That the Conflict Belongs to the Children

The constructivist teacher believes that it is important for children to take ownership of their conflicts and therefore does not take on children's problems and impose a solution. This attitude leads to the principles of teaching that support and facilitate children's resolution of their own conflicts.

3. Believe in Children's Ability to Solve Their Conflicts

Success in working with children in conflict situations depends on believing that children can solve conflicts. We are continually impressed with the competence of young children who have had the support of a constructivist sociomoral atmosphere, but every teacher will have to construct his or her own confidence out of experiences that reveal children's potentials.

PRINCIPLES OF TEACHING IN CONFLICT SITUATIONS

The following 15 principles of teaching can provide guidance in working with children.

1. Take responsibility for children's safety
2. Establish an expectation in the classroom that children will engage in conflict resolution
3. Acknowledge/accept/validate all children's feelings and perceptions of the conflict
4. Help children verbalize feelings and desires to each other and listen to each other
5. Clarify and state the problem
6. Give children the opportunity to suggest solutions
7. Propose solutions when children do not have ideas
8. Uphold the value of mutual agreement, and give children the opportunity to reject proposed solutions
9. Teach impartial procedures for settling disputes where a decision is arbitrary
10. When children are no longer upset and lose interest in the process, do not pursue
11. Help children recognize their responsibility in a conflict situation
12. Offer opportunity for restitution, if appropriate
13. Help children repair the relationship, but do not force children to be insincere
14. Work toward children's emotional resolution
15. Encourage children to resolve their conflicts by themselves

In the following discussion of these principles, we give examples from Freeburg and Human Development Laboratory School (HDLS) classrooms that reveal ways in which teachers express respect for children in effective interventions that promote conflict resolution ability.

1. Take Responsibility for Children's Safety

Clearly, the teacher should prevent physical harm whenever possible. When a child is trying to hurt another, the teacher must restrain the aggressor to prevent harm. The teacher should express how strongly he or she feels about the importance of keeping everyone safe. Emotional safety is also sometimes at stake in conflict situations. The teacher can use non-verbal methods to calm and comfort extremely upset children. If children are too upset to talk, it may be necessary to give them time to pull themselves together before insisting on conversation.

Consider the following examples when a teacher upholds the value of physical safety.

In Peige's (T) Investigators class at the HDLS, Kayesha is crying.

T: What's up, Kayesha?
K: Steve pushed me down.
T: Steve pushed you?
K: Yes.
T: Perhaps you should go talk to him about that. Tell him how it makes you feel. Do you feel ready to go talk?
K: (Seems to agree)
T: Let's go get Steve so you can talk to him about how you feel. Steve?
S: What?
T: We need you.
S: (Comes over and sits on the teacher's lap)
T: Okay, Kayesha.
K: I don't it like when you push me down. That makes me sad.
T: She doesn't like it when you push her down. It makes her sad. Was there a problem that made you upset?
S: (Nods)
T: What happened that made you upset? Were you upset with Kayesha?
S: (Shakes head)
T: No, okay. But I have to tell you, Steve. If you are upset with Kayesha, if she does something to make you mad, you can talk to her. You can come and get my help, and I will help you talk to her or I will talk to her, too. But you know what, Steve? (Turns him to face her) Steve, I'm not going to let you hit the children, but I won't let the children hit you, either. So if you're making the choice to do some talking in the classroom, then I can help you with that. When you're making the choice to do some hitting or pushing in the classroom, it's not going to work because I can't let you do that. Were you finished doing the play dough, or do you want to do play dough some more?

After giving this clear message, Peige then helps Steve move from the conflict into positive activity. In this situation, Steve has the possibility to make many mental relationships, such as between hitting and the negative reaction from the person he hit, and between talking and feeling less angry.

In another situation in the same class, Rob is crying and Kayesha stands by. They have been keeping score in a beanbag toss game. Peige (T) sees the incident from across the room. While comforting Rob, she explores the problem in the following way, in a matter-of-fact, nonjudgmental tone.

T: (Holds Rob) What's up, Kayesha?

K: I wanted to write my letters [score].

T: You wanted to write yours? Well, I have a question. When you started scratching him and pushing him down and all that stuff, did that help to decide who was going to write on your thing?

K: No, but I wanted to write my letter.

T: You wanted to write your letter. When you pushed him and kicked him, did that let him know that you needed to write your letter? Did pushing him down help you to write your letter?

K: No.

T: Maybe you could tell him with your words. He's right here. What do you want to tell him? She has something she needs to tell you. Okay, he's ready, and we're all ready.

K: I want to do my letters.

T: She wants to write her own letters. What can he write?

K: He can write his letters by himself.

T: You can write your own letters by yourself. But when it's your time to write your stuff, who do you want to write it?

K: I remember I got 2 in.

T: You got 2 in? She got 2 in and she wanted to write all about it.

R: No.

T: No?

R: She didn't get 2 in.

T: Oh, he says you didn't get 2. How many did she get?

R: She got 1.

T: Oh, Kayesha, he says you didn't get 2. You got only 1. So can she write 2?

R: No.

T: How many can she write?

R: She can only write 1.

T: Kayesha, he says you can only write 1.

K: (Seems to agree)

T: What do you [Rob] have to say to Kayesha?

R: Nothing.

T: Nothing? Do you want to tell her how you were feeling about being pushed? Yeah? How did that feel? Or, no, you don't want to talk about it? No? Are you feeling better? Ready to do some activities? Maybe you guys could get it together and play beanbags some more now that you know what each other needs. (The children start over with a bean bag game.)

Here, Peige discovers the root of the problem in a disagreement over how many points Kayesha got. Peige gives an opportunity but does not press Rob to talk about his feelings. She inquires into whether he feels better, in order to be sure both children feel resolution. Satisfied that resolution has occurred in children's feelings, Peige orients the children back into cooperative play. Taking responsibility for children's physical safety is only the first step in working with children in conflict. In this case, both children had the possibility to recognize the difference between their ideas about the number of points.

2. Establish an Expectation in the Classroom That Children Will Engage in Conflict Resolution

Conflict resolution is highly valued by constructivist teachers. They communicate to children their concerns about interpersonal problems and their interest in having children resolve conflicts. We saw this expectation in the foregoing examples involving safety issues. Typical situations in which teachers express an expectation that children will engage in conflict resolution include those in which children complain about others, group time discussions, and use of the Peace Chairs. We comment on these below.

Complaints About Others

When a child inexperienced in conflict resolution comes to a teacher and complains about another child, the teacher can say, "Let's go talk with him/her." If a child has experience in conflict resolution, a teacher can provide coaching that suits the child's competence: "Did you talk with him/her about it?" "What did you say?" If the child did not talk to the other, the teacher might say, "What could you say to him/her?" "Tell him/her how you feel, that you don't like that," and so on. If a child seems unable to engage with the other, he or she might ask, "Do you want me to come and help you talk with him/her?" If the teacher cannot get away at the moment and the conflict is not violent or disruptive, he or she can say, "I can help you talk with him/her at [time]." The teacher's attitude says to the child: "I understand that this problem is important to you, and it is also important to me." This kind of situation occurs at every age level, but it is particularly typical of younger children who do not yet know what to do in conflict situations. When a child complains about another, it is a special opportunity to begin to foster conflict resolution.

Group Time Discussions

Community gatherings offer opportunities for discussion of conflicts that involve the entire class. Conflicts involving only two or three children should be handled privately. Reading stories involving conflicts, acting out conflicts, using puppets to show problems and conflict resolution, and so on, can help children think about how to resolve conflicts (see Chapter 6). When a teacher observes general problems with activity time or when children complain of problems, group time discussions can provide a time for children and teacher(s) to work on a problem. A teacher might introduce a conflict topic by saying, "I saw a lot of children having problems in the block area during activity time. Did any of you see that?" After a short time for children's observations, the teacher can say, "We seem to agree that we have some problems. What do you think we could do about these problems?" and write children's ideas on chart paper that can later be posted in the block center and revisited at a later group time. This should be a cooperative process where the teacher's attitude is helpful and sympathetic.

Peace Chairs/Bench

Peace Chairs or a Peace Bench are simply the designated furniture used exclusively for conflict resolution between two (or sometimes more) children. The general rule is that if someone wants to take you to the Peace Chairs, you have to go and talk with the other person(s) about the problem. In the Freeburg School, 4-year-olds were able to use the Peace Bench, although they usually needed a lot of teacher support. In the following transcript, Beth Van Meeteren conducts a review of the Peace Bench with 6- and 7-year-olds. She comes prepared with chart paper showing the "Peace Bench Rules" and a book with photographs of children at the Peace Bench the previous year. She places on the floor the removable top from the bench with two cushioned seats. (In this transcript, "C" refers to individual children calling out comments.)

T: Sometimes in the classroom if you have a problem, I'll ask you, "How did you handle it?" In 1st grade, in 2nd grade, in kindergarten, how do we expect you to handle it?

C: Peace Chair.

T: (Nods) At the Peace Bench. Now you will notice that we moved the

Peace Bench back over there to give you some privacy. On the Peace
Bench, there are some things that you need to do like (reading from
chart) "The Peace Bench." First you have to face—

C: Face each other like this (seats herself on one side of the Peace Bench
at the front of the group).

T: . . . face each other, and I drew a picture (shows drawing of two heads
facing one another beside the rule). Yes, and if Kariah and I are having
a problem, we're facing each other like this (seats herself on Peace
Bench facing Kariah as children gather around them). So you sit with
one leg over, and so you're facing each other. Now does that mean you
go like this (turns head away)?

C: No.

K: That means you can't go like this, either (puts her head down on
bench).

C: Or you can't look in your shirt.

T: Yes (imitates child looking in shirt). Face each other. See how they're
looking right at each other? Okay? (Reading) "And then, one talks, one
listens."

C: (Reading from chart) "Talk about one thing."

T: And so, if I had a problem with Kariah, maybe I want to talk to Kariah
first. And what's Kariah going to do?

C: Listen.

T: Listen. And so then, after I say what I need to say, then whose turn is it
to talk?

C: Kariah, and you listen.

T: And then who has to listen?

C: You.

T: Now, can I interrupt and say, "No! No! (antagonistic tone)!" Can I
interrupt?

C: No.

T: What do I have to do?

C: Raise your hand.

T: (At same time as child above) Wait until she's finished . . .

C: Wait for your turn.

T: . . . and then I can say what I need to say back. Do you want to
pretend, Kariah?

K: (Nods) You [start].

T: What should we pretend?

C: That like, Beth kicked Kariah, and Kariah slapped you. (Children
giggle.)

T: Oh, okay. Should we pretend that?

K: (Nods)

T: Okay. All right. Okay, who's going to talk first?

K: You.

T: (In strong tone) I don't like it when you slap me, Kariah, and I don't want you to slap me any more.

K: I don't like it when you kick me.

T: Well, you made me mad, Kariah, and I kicked you 'cause I was mad.

C: Go, Kariah, talk.

K: You—well, you could've just told a teacher.

T: When you make me mad, I should just go tell a teacher?

K: (Nods) Or you should just talk about it.

T: I should just tell you when I'm mad at you?

K: No.

T: You don't want me to kick you when I'm mad at you?

K: (Shakes head and seems self-conscious)

T: Oh. So if I'm mad at you, I can't kick you?

K: (Shakes head)

T: Well, when you're mad at me, you can't slap me, either. When you're mad at me, I don't want you to slap me. I want you to just tell me that you're mad. Okay?

K: When you mad, I don't want you to kick me.

T: Well, I won't kick you if . . . when I'm mad at you anymore. I'll tell you. I'll use my words, okay? All right. And (to the class) what goes by the Peace Bench?

C: The book.

T: Okay. All right. So, the rule book will be here. Oh, one more thing. One more thing here. (Reading) "Talk about one thing or one problem."

C: It says, "Face each other, one talks . . . "

T: So (reviews scenario) I kicked Kariah and she slapped me. I can't say, "Well, Kariah, I remember in kindergarten, you said that I had dorky hair and, and I remember one time 6 weeks ago that you pushed me off the swing and, and I remember last Christmas around Christmastime, you thought you got a better present."

T: One thing. Talk about what just happened.

C: (Chiming in with teacher) Just happened.

C: Where the other paper that was right over there (at Peace Bench)?

T: It kind of got torn up. Do you think we should add that? Talk about one thing. Talk about what just happened? Should I add that?

C: Yeah.

T: Okay. (As she is writing) Talk . . .

C: Talk about what just happened.

T: . . . about . . . (continues to write as children try to anticipate what

will come next). . . . Huh, huh, huh (sounding out *h*) what just . . .
happened. Okay? And the reason why this is so important is so that
you learn to solve your own problems. And so when there are adults
that aren't around, you're going to have good things, good ways—
K: Is this [at] the end of the day?
T: Oh, this is all day long.

The 2nd-graders in this group already know about the Peace Bench from
their experiences the year before, but one can imagine a similar introduction to an uninitiated group. The teacher takes a strong leadership role in
reviewing the rules for the Peace Bench that were used the previous year,
but engages children's participation. Beth shows that she is thoroughly
in tune with the culture in her classroom as she moves seamlessly from
engaging as a child to teaching. Her imitations of some of the children's
behaviors make them laugh at the idea of a teacher turning her head away
or interrupting. However, they watch and listen expectantly as Beth and
Kariah, a 2nd-grader, pretend with feeling to discuss a conflict. Children's
attention and emotional engagement provide a favorable context for con-
solidating and constructing mental relationships concerning resolving
conflicts peacefully.

When some children are new to the idea of Peace Chairs, they may
view them as punishment. In this case, we have heard teachers explain,
"Going to the Peace Chairs is not a punishment. It is where we solve our
problems." As children experience the Peace Chairs a number of times,
this view of it as punishment simply disappears. At group time, the teacher may make a point to congratulate children who solved a problem and
to talk about working on conflicts in a matter-of-fact way. Going to the
Peace Chairs and trying to resolve conflicts becomes part of the culture of
the classroom.

How does this play out as children go to the Peace Bench by themselves? A revealing transcript of 2nd-graders Kariah and Lorraine shows
that they have to invent their own ways of talking to each other that take
account of what the other says. The real issues children discuss are spoken
in their own personal ways that reflect their childhood culture. Although
each refers to a rule when the other seems to violate it, the conversation
is not at all scripted. The context is that Lorraine thinks that Kariah has
told other children to move away from Lorraine at group time. It is clear
that the two girls have progressed in their interpersonal understanding
to the point where they are able to care about what the other thinks. The
video recorder does not catch the beginning, so the following transcript
begins after the two girls have already begun talking, obviously with
some difficulty.

K: Stop interrupting me! The reason why I said you starting stuff is
     because I didn't tell nobody to move away from the . . . [unintelligible]
     . . . and then, I was like, "Lorraine's starting stuff because she said I
     made everybody move away." That's starting something.
L: Well, I didn't know, okay?
K: I'm not done. And, um . . . stop! Oooh (frustrated tone)! And when you
     had . . . when you said, "Kariah, you made everybody move away from
     me," I didn't, and I already told you that I didn't like it when you said
     that. And you was like, "So, well, you telling a fib." And then I said,
     "No, I wasn't," and you said, "Yes, you did," but I really didn't. And
     you kept saying that I did, and I didn't. And then I just said, "I don't
     like it when you say I'm fibbing."
L: Well, . . . well, I thought you did because I didn't know that.
K: I didn't tell her to move away from you.
L: But I thought you did.
K: I didn't.
L: I know now (frustrated tone)!

Lorraine is persuaded by Kariah's vehement protest of innocence, and the
former's anger disappears, replaced by frustration because Kariah does
not seem to hear her acknowledgment of the mistaken idea that Kariah
was trying to ostracize her. Kariah continues to restate her innocence and
vent her outrage. Lorraine appears to think that her explanation of how
the misunderstanding occurred should have settled the problem. Having
reached an impasse, Lorraine slips off the bench and lands on the floor,
laughing. (It is unclear whether this is deliberate or accidental.) They continue to argue until Lorraine pleads that she's just trying to be her friend.
This sincere declaration enables Kariah to take a more friendly tone. Lorraine then asks, "Well, is it settled?" She appears to understand that both
parties need to agree for the conflict to end and for the friendship to be
preserved. Both children have the possibility to make or consolidate mental relationships among communicating intentions and feelings, understanding another's, and preserving friendship.

   Constructivist teachers consistently communicate the expectation that children will work to resolve conflicts, and children in their
classrooms become accustomed to engaging in conflict resolution. The
teacher's support in individual conflict resolution and guidance during
group time discussions serve over time to increase children's productive negotiations. Moreover, some children take the role of the teacher
as a third party to others' conflicts, facilitating resolution through asking
questions, enforcing the rule of only one person talking at a time, and

making suggestions concerning possible solutions. As children become more competent in conflict resolution, the sociomoral atmosphere becomes more cooperative.

3. Acknowledge/Accept/Validate All Children's Feelings and Perceptions of the Conflict

Children have a right to feel the way they feel. Even when the teacher believes a child is guilty of violating the rights of another, it is important to respect that child's feelings. From his or her point of view, the actions may be justified. In addition, the adult should not assume understanding of a situation until hearing both sides of the story. "I can see that you both are upset. Can you tell me what happened?" After hearing what children have to say, the adult can acknowledge specific feelings. "You are sad because Kelly took your car, and you are sad because Jake hit you." The reader will find many examples of this principle in transcripts illustrating other principles of teaching.

4. Help Children Verbalize Feelings and Desires to Each Other and Listen to Each Other

It is important not to take sides but to help each child understand the other's point of view, recognize the other's feelings, and empathize. The verbal communications of young children are often not very coherent, and children thus often have difficulty understanding each other. Listening is not always easy for young children who have egocentric attitudes or who are caught up in their own emotions. Nor is talking always easy. Teachers are frequently heard saying to children something like, "Use your words" when children get into disagreements. However, often, children do not know what words to say, and they talk to the teacher instead of to each other. The teacher plays an important role as mediator, helping children to clarify their ideas by repeating or paraphrasing them, suggesting words to say when the children cannot think of any, and showing children that by exchanging ideas and feelings they can feel better afterward. This is illustrated in the following example from the 1st afternoon in Terry Anderson's 1st grade. Becky does not understand that each person's drawer is for personal belongings. Ronnie comes to complain that Becky has taken a bottle of liquid "white-out," or correction fluid, from her drawer. Ascertaining that Ronnie has already told Becky it belongs to her, Terry offers to go talk with her. When Ronnie is too shy to speak her mind, Terry continues as follows:

T: How about if I help you with it, okay? Say, "Becky, that is my white-out." Let's start with that, okay? Look her in the eye (puts arm around Becky).

R: That is my white-out, Becky.

B: After you got it, there was another one in there, and I got it.

R: (Now emboldened) I know—because my mom gave me two, in case I ran out.

B: Oh (turns around).

T: Becky, come here just a second. Do you know that Ronnie is a really nice girl, and if you wanted to use it, then the next time you could go to Ronnie and say, "Ronnie, can I borrow your white-out?" Okay, why don't you try it now. Ask her that.

B: Ronnie, can I use your white-out?

R: (Nods)

T: That was pretty easy, wasn't it?

B: (Nods)

T: Okay, she is going to let you use it, and when you are done, you put it back, but that is her private drawer. So you can't get in her drawer. Only Ronnie can get in her drawer, and Ronnie can't get in your drawer because that is your private drawer.

B: Okay. (The two girls return to the art table and resume working.)

In this intervention, Terry provides children with basic instruction in how to go about resolution of a conflict. She even gives words when a child needs help in engaging with a peer. She emphasizes the importance of verbally communicating one's feelings and considering others' feelings.

The following example occurred in Gwen Harmon's classroom at Freeburg when 4-year-olds needed the teacher's help to talk with one another and come to an understanding. Isaac is a particularly impulsive child who frequently has problems interacting with peers. Because the teacher so often had to intervene when children complained about Isaac, it was particularly important to support him when he felt wronged by Karl.

I: Then he just hit me with it.

K: No. I trying to play with it.

T: You were trying to play with what?

K: I trying to help people.

T: You were trying to help people?

K: No. I doing it myself.

T: I don't understand. Tell me what happened, Karl.

K: I put it like that in the flour.

T: Oh, you were banging it down in the flour? Is that what you're saying?

K: Yeah.

T: Uh huh, and?

K: I trying to get it out.

T: And you were trying to get it out. So was Isaac's hand in the way?

K: Yeah.

T: So you didn't mean to hurt him? It was an accident.

K: It was a accident.

T: Well, you know what? You know what? You may use your words and
    tell Isaac that "it was an accident, Isaac. I didn't mean to hurt you."
    Karl if you did not mean to hurt him, you can use your words and tell
    him it was an accident. Karl, do you want to tell him or would you like
    me to tell him? You want me to tell him? (To Isaac) Isaac? Isaac, look
    at me. Karl is saying that he was trying to get the thing out of the flour,
    and your hand was in the way, and he hurt you on an accident.

I: It was on purpose.

T: Karl, Isaac's saying you did it on purpose. Is that true, yes or no?

K: No.

T: Well, Karl seems to say that it was an accident, Isaac, and you're still
    saying he did it on purpose, so I need to know how we're going to
    work this out because Isaac was hurt, and he was crying. Isaac, listen. I
    need you to listen. How did it make you feel when he hurt you?

I: Bad.

T: It made you feel bad, and you were crying. So would you like to tell
    Karl that—that it made you feel bad?

I: It feels bad.

T: Karl, are you hearing what he's saying? It made him feel bad. (To Isaac)
    So what could Karl do? What could Karl do to make you feel better?

K: Give a hug.

T: Okay. Karl's saying he could give you a hug, but what do you need
    Karl to do, Isaac?

I: Play with me.

T: You need Karl to play with you. So, Karl wants to give you a hug, and
    Isaac wants you to play with him. Karl, do you think you could do
    that?

K: (To Isaac) Let's play marbles with that right there.

T: Okay. Isaac, he says you guys can play marbles. Would that be okay?
    Isaac, he says you guys can play marbles, if you want to play with him.
    Are you willing to play with Karl, play marbles with him, Isaac? Okay,
    and he wants to give you a hug.

I: (Isaac hugs Karl)

T: All right, and you guys are going to go play marbles? All right.

It appears that what Isaac wanted all along was to play with Karl, and Isaac finally succeeds in communicating this when the teacher asks what Karl can do to make him feel better. Both children had the possibility to make mental relationships between intentions and consequences and among talking, changes in feelings, and reconciliation.

Consider also the following argument between two 5-year-olds over use of materials. The teacher (T) is Karen Amos at the Human Development Laboratory School.

(In a boatbuilding activity, Nolan takes a wooden board that is near Ethan.)
E: I need it also. You are going to give it back to me.
N: (Runs away with board)
E: Hey, Karen, he won't give me that board back.
T: Did you use your words?
E: Yeah.
T: Maybe I'll go with you and you can use your words to him.
E: (To Nolan) I need your wood back.
N: I've been using it.
E: I wanna put it next to me (grabs wood)—
T: Wait. Can I hold it? (She takes the board.)
E: —so I can make my boat.
T: Is this the last piece of wood left?
E: No, there's some more, but I need that.
T: But I wonder if Nolan had this piece of wood and you just wanted it.
E: No, no.
T: Did you have it?
E: I have it.
N: No, I didn't see it in his hand.
E: I had it first.
N: I had it first.
T: You know, I heard Nolan's words saying that he didn't see you holding this.
E: See, I'm putting it next to me because I couldn't hold all of it and put 'em all together.
T: I see. Was it right here, Nolan?
N: Somewhere over here.
E: But it's still mine.
T: Ethan had this next to his boat. He was going to use it. He said he couldn't hold on to all the pieces. (At this point, another child, Jacob, hands a board to Ethan.)
T: So who should we give this [board in contention] to?
E: Nolan.
T: Okay. Thanks for sharing, Jacob.

Young children may not know that a toy lying on the floor is being used by someone who has just put it down. Thus Nolan said he did not see the toy in Ethan's hands. The teacher tries to support Ethan's reasonable explanation that he could not hold all the pieces at once, but this is not persuasive to Nolan. Finally, a resolution comes from an onlooker who offers Ethan another board. Conflict resolution does not always result in children's decentering. Yet we believe that many conversations such as the preceding eventually enable children to resolve conflicts on their own. The teacher takes advantage of Ethan's satisfaction with the new board and consults him about who should have the board that was in contention.

5. Clarify and State the Problem

When the teacher is clear about the problem, he or she should state it so both children understand what the other sees as the problem. This is sometimes difficult because children may not talk about the same issue, and sometimes their descriptions of what happened are distorted by desires to present their own actions in a desirable light. In the following example, the teacher (T), Gwen Harmon, only becomes aware of a problem when she sees two 4-year-olds chasing one another. She thus enters the conflict with no idea of what precipitated the problem but attempts valiantly to clarify what it is about (in this case, for herself as well as for the children).

T: Explain to me what's going on. John, I noticed you were running around, you chasing Ellen, and both of you look kind of sad and unhappy.
J: I was working.
T: You what? You were working?
J: (Nods)
T: And what happened?
J: She take my thing away from me.
T: Okay. So Ellen, what John is saying is that he was working with these, with the screwdriver and the screw, and you took it from him. Is that true, Ellen?
E: No.
T: What happened?
J: Yes, you did. Yes, her did. Her take both mine away from me.
E: It's not nice grabbing away from people.
T: So what happened? I don't understand.
E: He just took it from me.
T: He just took it from you?
E: Yeah.

T: He did? John, Ellen's story doesn't sound like yours. (To Ellen) So you
    had it first. Is that what you're saying?

E: (Nods)

T: (To John) She says she had it first. (To Ellen) And he took it from you?

E: (Nods)

T: And then what happened?

E: I was mad.

T: So, did you take it back? Did you chase him? What?

E: I ran away.

T: But you had it in your hand. So how did you get it back in your hand?

E: I caught it.

T: You caught it?

E: (Nods)

T: How? He threw it?

E: Because he threw it on the floor.

T: Okay. Okay.

J: Oh, no! I didn't throw it on the floor! That was you!

T: Now, Ellen said you threw it on the floor, John.

J: No, I didn't! Her threw it on the floor and took it.

E: He wasn't playing with it and threw it on the floor.

T: So, he threw it on the floor, and you picked it up? Is that what you're
    saying to me?

E: (Nods)

T: Okay. All right. Now, John said he was working with this. Let me get
    it right. He was working with the screwdriver and the screw, and you
    took it from him. (To Ellen) You're saying that's not true. You said it's not
    fair to take things from people, that you had it first, right?

E: (Nods)

T: Okay. I have a problem because I don't know what story to believe.
    John said he had it. (To Ellen) You said you had it. Okay. John, Ellen
    said you took these and threw them on the floor.

J: No I didn't! Her take them and threw them on the floor.

T: Okay. So what you're saying is she threw them on the floor and then
    picked them back up and started running around the room.

J: Yeah.

T: I don't—I can't figure out how come she would throw them on the
    floor.

J: Her was running around the room.

T: Yes, she was running around the room. Why do you suppose she was
    running around the room, John?

J: Because her want that.

T: Because she wanted it?

J: Yeah.

T: Then why do you think she threw them on the floor if she wanted them?

J: (Shrugs his shoulders)

T: You don't know.

J: (Shakes his head)

E: I know.

T: Why?

E.   I just picked them up, and he just threw them on . . .

T: He threw—You're saying he threw them on the floor.

E: He did.

T: Did what?

E: Somebody just picked them up from we two guys.

T: Okay, so how did you—You both wanted to work. (To Ellen) Okay, so how did you get these?

E: Because somebody threw them on the floor.

T: And you picked them up. Okay. Now, I—I don't know how we're going to solve this. (To John) You want the tools. (To Ellen) You want the tools. (To John) You said you had them first. Ellen said she had them first. Okay, we have two children, one screwdriver, and one screw.

E: And there's two over there.

T: There's two what?

E: Two screws over there.

T: Go get them, would you, please? Would you mind getting them?

E: (Runs away and brings back three plastic screws)

T: Oh! There's, let's see, there's one. That makes how many, John?

J: Two.

T: Two, and this one makes?

J: Three.

T: Three. There are three screws. So I think we have the problem of the screws fixed because (to Ellen), you could get one. (To John) You could get one. There's one left over.

E: Yep. Then we could go get another screw and we both can take turns with the screwdriver.

T: You could both take turns with the screwdriver? That sounds like an idea. What do you think, John? Ellen is saying you both can share with the screwdriver. (To John) I didn't hear you, I'm sorry.

J: I said I don't care.

T: You don't care. So you're willing to work with Ellen?

E: Maybe we could get a different screw, 'cause this one doesn't fit.

T: It doesn't fit? (To John) I didn't hear you, I'm sorry.

J: I don't want to do that.

E: Here you go. You can have all three of them. (She starts to leave.)

T: Well, wait, wait, wait, wait. We're not finished here. You know, first Ellen said you could share, then she turned around, and she gave it to you. What do you suppose you could do now?

E: He can have his turn now.

T: That was very nice of you to do that. That shows that you're willing to share and that you will take turns. So what is something, John, you might be able to do now?

J: I can take it and go over there.

T: Yes, but I mean for Ellen. I have an idea. You could either say, "Thank you," or "Ellen, you can come and play with me." Another idea: "Ellen, when I'm finished, I will give this to you." What could you do for her?

J: [When] I'm finished, I will give it to you.

T: Okay, well, you know what? You can use your words and tell that to Ellen. You can look at Ellen and say those very same things. Okay, well, there she is right here. Which one are you going to say? I can't hear you.

J: (To Ellen) You can have it.

T: Now or when you're finished?

J: (To Ellen) When I'm finished.

T: Okay. You hear what he's saying? When he's finished, he will give it to you, okay?

The children then return to the pretend center, where they play together without further conflict.

When children's stories are inconsistent, the teacher confronts them with this and holds up the value of truth when she says she does not know which story to believe. After lengthy discussion, the teacher determines that sorting out the two stories and arriving at what actually happened is not likely to occur. However, the teacher does manage to articulate the problem of both children wanting the screwdriver materials and moves on to what to do about it. A breakthrough comes after John (perhaps wearying of the wrangle) says he does not want the materials. Ellen decides she also is no longer interested and concedes that John can have his turn. Contrary to his professed lack of caring, John is all too happy to end the discussion and go on with his turn.

This is an example of how an impasse becomes softer through discussion of the problem itself. However, the point is not just to get rid of the problem. Gwen pursues the resolution by calling upon John to reciprocate by doing something for Ellen after she has given him the first turn. As he has no idea, she suggests several possibilities, and John decides she can have the materials after he is finished. A mental relationship these two children have the possibility to make is between lying or misstating facts and others' disbelief. They thus confront the value of truthfulness in this situation.

6. Give Children the Opportunity to Suggest Solutions

Teachers have confided that one of the most difficult things to learn with regard to constructivist teaching is to give children time and opportunity to express their ideas—rather than telling them what they should think and what they should do. In the case of conflict resolution, constructivist teachers ask children to suggest solutions as part of giving responsibility to children to resolve their conflicts. Wait time is extremely important here, as suggesting solutions may be new to young children whose language is yet developing. An example of this is Gwen's intervention in the conflict between Isaac and Karl, recounted above in Principle 4.

Children sometimes suggest solutions that do not seem like solutions to us. What is important is that we take their ideas seriously and help them try out the ideas whenever possible. Teachers therefore do not veto children's ideas but pursue the discussion in the direction of a solution. That is, if a child suggests an impossible idea, the teacher might ask, "How would you do that? Would you have any problems doing that?"

Other questions teachers can ask to help children figure out how to solve a problem include the following:

- What can you do to solve this problem?
- What else can you do [if one child vetoes the other's idea]?
- What can you do so that it will be fair for both of you?
- Which solution [of several discussed] do you think might work best?

7. Propose Solutions When Children Do Not Have Ideas

Children do not always have ideas about solutions. In this situation, the teacher can propose ideas for children's consideration, as Gwen did in the screwdriver conflict. Note that she suggested several ways in which John could do something for Ellen. Offering more than one solution is important because if the teacher gives only one suggestion, children can sometimes think that they must do what the teacher suggests, and lose a sense of autonomy or choice in the matter. Suggestions should be proposals, not impositions.

Consider the following situation with 4-year-olds Gina, Chuck, and Katy in the pretend center. Peige (T) employs other principles of teaching until she sees that the children are at an impasse. As she notices Marlan and Gina arguing, she approaches.

T: What's up, you guys?
G: This daddy's rocking chair. This daddy's rocking chair. (To Marlan) You don't live here, and you don't live in that chair (tries to pry Marlan out of chair).
T: Marlan, I don't think it's ever going to be solved if you sit there and not talk. You'll probably have to talk to tell her what you think about it.
M: Um, but you got out of the chair and I got in.
G: Well, you're not supposed to live here. We do. We're supposed to live here. You don't live here. This daddy's rocking chair.
M: I'm sorry. I—you got out and I got in.
T: He said you got out and he got in.
G: Well, this was daddy's rocking chair.
T: Well, but did daddy get out?
G: Well, we went to go out to eat, and then we came back to the home.
T: And so—
C: And when—where—when he goes out to eat, I don't come and get his things.
T: When you go out to eat, she doesn't come and get your things.
M: Because I don't live here.
C: But we live here.
G: Well, we live here, yeah.
T: They say they live here and you live somewhere else.
K: Because I'm the sister.
G: Yeah, yeah, and I'm your mommy, right?
M: Then what's Chuck doing here? Chuck's not supposed to be here.
T: Maybe he's a brother. Would you like to be a brother?
M: (Nods)
T: He said he would like to be a brother.
C: Okay, and this will be another sister, and then we're gonna have another brother, and that's the last one.
M: (Jumps out of chair to join Chuck as a brother).

This typical intervention—to suggest that an excluded child participate in a new role in pretend play—is offered in the context of children's discussion that questions Marlan's participation. The teacher supports the excluded child and helps him gain entry to the play.

Sometimes more direct instruction may be required. In one example, Peige notices that Damon is trying to grab the basketball from Yanna. Damon has some autistic-like behaviors and has great difficulty relating to other children. To create an opportunity for Damon to experience the reciprocity of turn taking, Peige says, "You know what, Yanna? You could have a turn at throwing, and you could give it to Damon, and Damon could have a turn at throwing, and then Damon could give it to you, and you could have a turn at throwing." To Damon, she prompts, "If you would like to have a turn, why don't you ask Yanna. Say, 'Yanna, you have a turn. Then I have a turn.'" The children are able to reciprocate in taking turns for a while, and the teacher helps Damon appreciate his social success, "You did it! You and Yanna took turns!"

In the following example, 3-year-olds at Freeburg need help in communicating with one another, and their teacher (T), Kathy Thompson, acts as translator and mediator. Jason is working at the water table, which is filled with beans. He is scooping the beans and pretending to cook. Seth comes to the beans table and takes a container that Jason had been using. Jason protests.

J: I need some eggs. No! Stop! He's dumping my—
S: Mine! (Runs with container to the other side of the room)
J: That was mine!
T: (Following Seth with outstretched hand) Come here. Let's go figure out a solution to this problem. Okay?
S: I had this. He didn't have it, so I picked it up.
T: Oh. Well, why don't you explain that to him?
J: That's mine!
S: You didn't have it. I had . . . You didn't have it. You was playing with those two and I picked these up . . . this one up.
J: I was making this stuff.
T: Well, you can do that, Jason.
J: He camed over here and snatched that away from me!
T: And how did that make you feel?
J: Sad!
T: Well, so what do you want him to know about this?
J: He didn't even use his words.
T: Oh. (To Seth) Maybe he wants you to ask him if he was finished with it.
S: (To Jason) Are you finished with it?
J: No.
T: Well, is there a jar that Seth could use with a lid? 'Cause he would like a jar with a lid, too. Is there one that he could use?
S: I want this one.
T: Well, wait. You can't just take it. (To Jason) Could you give him a jar with a lid that he could use?
J: He already got a lid.

T: Well, is it okay for him to keep this one then?
J: Yes.
T: Oh. He says you can use that one.
S: (Picks up a jar) I can't open this.
T: He needs help. Jason says he'll help you. (Jason removes lid from jar and gives the objects to Seth.)
S: Thank you, Jason.
T: (To Jason) Thanks.
J: I'm gonna dump it all out.
S: No! Here we go. I'm dumping it into the . . . the trash can.
J: Seth's having some cereal.
S: I want some milk. Give me some milk. Give me some milk. I need some milk.
J: (Simultaneously with line above) Here comes the milk. Milk milk milk milk milk milk.

With the teacher's help, children find a resolution of the conflict and a new way of being together.

When children cannot agree on a solution or do not have ideas, the teacher might offer ideas:

- When some other children had a problem like this, the ideas they had were to _____ and to _____. What do you think about those ideas?
- I wonder if it would work for you to do _____ or _____. What do you think?

8. Uphold the Value of Mutual Agreement, and Give Children the Opportunity to Reject Proposed Solutions

An important part of the constructivist teacher's role is to insist on the importance of working out agreements. Sometimes, it is tempting to accept the first solution offered without making sure the other child agrees. However, it is crucial to seek mutual agreement. For example, in a typical conflict over a toy, the teacher asks Harold for his idea. Then she turns to Marcus, asking, "Did you hear his idea?" After making sure that Harold hears Marcus's idea, she asks, "Does that sound like a good idea?" Consider also the following example in which two 5-year-olds, Yan and Colter, both want to be first in a game at the Human Development Laboratory School. Here, it becomes clear that competing in the game rests within a framework of cooperation. The teacher (T) is Rebecca Krejci.

T: Who should go first?
Y: Me.
C: Me.
T: You both want to go first.
Y: Bubble Gum, Bubble Gum (begins rhyme, pointing alternately to himself and Colter).
C: I don't like to do "Bubble Gum, Bubble Gum."
Y: Let's take a vote.
C: No, there aren't enough people who want to vote.

The strategies of both children are above the bald insistence on what they want. They focus on the method for deciding. The teacher moderates to keep the discussion going.

T: Okay, so far we've talked about "Bubble Gum, Bubble Gum" or voting, and you don't like either of those. What do you think, Colter?
C: I think that I'll just pick who goes first.
T: Yan, do you like that idea?
Y: No.
T: No?
C: I'll just pick.
Y: No, I said that first. And then you came and speaked when I was speaking. So, I'm just gonna do "Bubble Gum, Bubble Gum."
C: Okay, but that sure does disturb me.

Yan's insistence on what he wants brings another impasse, with each child repeating his solution. Colter grudgingly agrees to go along with Yan, but expresses his unhappiness. The problem for the teacher is to respect Colter's feelings but try to move to an agreement.

T: Do you think "Bubble Gum, Bubble Gum" would be all right with you, Colter?
C: It's not all right with me, but if he wants to do it (shrugs).
T: Do you think your picking would be fair, Colter?
Y: No, I don't think Colter should pick.

With the impasse reasserted, the teacher continues to give the responsibility to the children for coming to agreement. By respecting the ideas of both children, she expresses the idea that conflict resolution should consider everyone's feelings.

T: Let's see if y'all can decide on something that you both like.

C: I just wanna pick somebody. I don't like "Bubble Gum, Bubble Gum."

Y: All right. (He decides to try voting.) Who says to do "Bubble Gum, Bubble Gum"? (He raises his hand.)

C: Nobody. I don't.

Y: (Turns to teacher) Do you wish to do "Bubble Gum"?

T: Well, if I vote, then whatever I say will happen because you both disagree.

C: It's okay with me if you do whatever you want because you're the adult.

The teacher tries to move the children's thinking beyond identifying fairness with whatever the adult authority wants by upholding the idea of the importance of agreement among players.

T: But y'all are playing the game, too. I think y'all should decide, too.

C: Well, I'd just like to pick.

T: Do you have any other ideas, Yan?

Y: Well, you need to vote, too.

C: Well, Yan, the only thing that doesn't disturb me is "Eenie, meenie, miney, moe." You can say that, but not "Bubble Gum, Bubble Gum."

Y: Okay. Eenie, meenie, miney, moe. (Yan begins the rhyme and alternately points to Colter and himself.)

Thus it is decided, with both children in agreement.

Some of the questions teachers can ask to help children come to mutual agreement include the following:

- What do you [child hearing another's suggestion] think of that idea?
- Is that okay with you?
- He/she doesn't like that idea. Can you think of a different idea?
- Do you (both children) want to try that?

9.   Teach Impartial Procedures for Settling Disputes Where a Decision Is Arbitrary

As shown in the example above, some of children's disagreements involve privileges that can be decided only arbitrarily. It is helpful to teach children ways of making arbitrary decisions in an impartial way such as in Rock-Paper-Scissors or Bubble Gum, Bubble Gum. In the following example, Peige (T) teaches Adam and Noah to play a board game. These

4-year-olds know that saying "Eenie, meenie, miney, moe" is a method for settling disputes, but they have constructed only part of the form and understanding of the procedure.

T: Who goes first?
A: Me!
N: Me!
A: I never get—
N: I want to—
A: You always say that! I never get a turn (folds arms and pouts).
T: (Imitates Adam by folding her arms) Oh, I don't, either. How shall we decide?
N: Just go, "Eenie, meenie, miney, moe." (Demonstrates pointing).
T: Okay.
A: Eenie, meenie, miney, moe (simply recites the rhyme without pointing).
N: You're not pointing!
T: You're not pointing!
A: (Starts over) Eenie, meenie, miney, moe. Catch a monkey by the toe. If he hollers, let him go. My mommy told me to pick the very first one and it is me. (As he recites, Adam points vaguely, then obviously waits to point to himself at the end.)
N: (Looks at the teacher with doubtful expression)
T: Is that okay?
N: Maybe.
T: Maybe. Okay. And then you'll go next and I'll go after you.
N: Yeah.

Peige offers Noah an opportunity to protest, recognizing that he is not quite satisfied. However, in the interest of moving the game forward, she does not probe his grudging agreement.

We should point out that teachers can observe developmental levels in children's use of rhymes to decide who goes first. Initially, children simply view them as a sort of ritual. Then they seem to try to use the procedure to get their own way and use their intelligence to figure out how to make the procedure favor their own interests. At a certain point, they "wise up" to others' similar efforts and argue over who will administer the rhyme procedure, since whoever says the rhyme gets the privilege! When children no longer view rhyme procedures as an impartial mechanism, the teacher may propose (and in some cases, teach) other procedures such as drawing a number, choosing red or black and drawing from a bag of checkers, Rock-Paper-Scissors, or others.

10. When Children Are No Longer Upset and Lose Interest in the Process, Do Not Pursue

Dora Chen, a teacher of 4-year-olds at the Human Development Laboratory School, receives a complaint from Marc, but she cannot immediately go with him. When she is able to follow him, she finds the problem has either dissipated or been solved. "Did you talk to Carl about it? Is your problem solved or not? Are you all done? Yes? Okay." Making sure the children are both satisfied with their resolution, Dora also lets it drop.

11. Help Children Recognize Their Responsibilities in a Conflict Situation

Frequently, an aggrieved child has contributed in some way to a conflict. It is helpful to children to realize their role in a misunderstanding or altercation. Consider the following example of a conflict in which Karen Amos (T) intervenes at the Human Development Laboratory School. For some reason, the children think it is interesting to put adhesive tape over their mouths. Michael jerks the tape off Dantavious's mouth and hurts Dantavious, who responds by pinching Michael.

(Michael and Dantavious, both 5 years old, are running. They fall over each other, with Michael grabbing Dantavious's shirt.)
T: Michael, what's wrong?
M: He pinched me.
D: Because you [inaudible], and I had—because he took the tape off [my mouth], and I didn't want to. I didn't take the tape off of you when you put the tape on you.
T: Did he pinch you?
M: Right here.
D: No, no, except he—he—he did that first.
T: He did what first? Put the tape over your mouth?
M: No, he took it off.
T: And so when he took it off your mouth really hard, how did that feel?
D: Not fun because it scratched my face up.
T: It scratched your face, so what did you do after that?
D: Pinch him.
T: Hmmm. Do you know why he pinched you, Michael?
M: Yeah, I didn't pull it off hard (demonstrates).
D: Nuh uh. That's really hard. That's fast. Fast is hard.
T: How did it feel when you pulled your own tape off?
M: I pulled it off soft.

T: Hmmm.

M: I pulled it off hard.

T: How did it feel?

M: I didn't feel anything.

T: You didn't feel anything? Well, Dantavious did, and it really made him angry, and that's why he chose to pinch you. It's not really okay. What could you do instead of pinching?

D: I don't like [inaudible].

T: You don't like what? What did he do you didn't like?

D: I didn't like when he took that tape off hard.

T: So can you tell him that now?

D: I don't like when you took that tape off hard.

M: I don't like it when you pinched me.

T: Can you understand why he did that? I know he probably should have used his words, but do you understand why he did it?

M: (Nods)

T: You didn't use your words. So what could you do, Michael, the next time if you see that Dantavious has tape on his mouth again? What could you say to Dantavious?

M: Take the tape off.

T: Is it okay now? You guys are not angry any more? Is it okay?

(The boys assent, and return to their play.)

In a situation at Freeburg, Sherice Hetrick-Orton (T) works with two kindergartners. Cory had called Jaylon "Pink," and Jaylon had reacted by calling Cory "Pink." Cory then put his hand over Jaylon's mouth, and Jaylon bit Cory's hand. It is unclear exactly what the word *pink* means to the children, but it is evident that it is used here as a taunt. After a conversation to clarify the sequence of events and to have each child say what he wants to be called, Sherice moves to focus the children on their intentions in name-calling.

T: Cory, when you called Jaylon "Pink," did you want him to feel good (pauses for answer, but receives none)? Jaylon, when you called Cory "Pink," did you want him to feel good (pauses)? Or was that something to make him feel not good? Did you want to make him feel bad when you called him "Pink"?

J: Because he called me "Pink" first. He made me want to call him ["Pink"] so he could be mad. (More discussion of what children want to be called.)

T: Cory, I want you to really think about what you want to be called, something that you want someone to call you that's respectful. The

        word *pink* sounds to me like it was not respectful—that it was meant to
        make someone feel bad.
J: Yeah, but it was just a color.
T: It was a color, but nobody said that when they said it they wanted the
        other person to feel good about it.
J: I didn't want him to feel good about it because he made me feel mad
        about it.
T: Cory, what do you want to be called?
C: Cory.

Although Cory is avoidant during the discussion, Jaylon is conscious of
his intention to make Cory feel bad. However, this does not mean that
Jaylon views his own intention negatively as he continues to blame Cory
for what he himself did.

    Some of the ways a teacher can help children take responsibility in a
conflict include the following:

- Call the child's attention to the victim's specific hurt body,
  feelings, or property ("Come look at her knee. See where it's
  bleeding?" "When you called her that, it made her sad. See, she's
  crying.")
- Call the child's attention to what he or she did to antagonize
  another ("She knocked down your block structure because she
  was mad that you said she was dumb.")

    As evident in the examples in this chapter, one does not stop with help-
ing children recognize their own responsibilities in a conflict as this might
run the risk of a child's simply feeling blamed. The goal is to arrive at an
agreement and emotional resolution as well as to give children the possibility to make mental relationships among words, actions, and feelings.

12. Offer Opportunity for Restitution, If Appropriate

    When one child has hurt another, it is important to make restitution
possible. If the offending child can do something to make the other feel
better, feelings of guilt and resentment will be less likely. Restitution paves
the way for reestablishing a friendly relation after the conflict ends and
also helps the perpetrator maintain a positive image—in the eyes of both
self and others.

    In the following example from Peige's Investigators class at the Hu-
man Development Laboratory School, children plant flower seeds in small
containers. Some children take their seeds home while others leave them

at school in order to watch them grow. Steve pulls up Carol's plant, breaking it off at the roots. Carol cries, and Peige (T) takes both children aside to talk with them. What follows is an edited recounting of a long discussion among Steve, Carol, and Peige. Because Steve has difficulty decentering and taking responsibility, Peige insists that he figure out something to do to solve the problem that he created when he destroyed Carol's plant.

T: All right, Steve, you pulled her flower out of her flowerpot. You didn't pull the root up with it, so it will not grow now. What will you do about this?

S: I don't know.

T: Hmmm. Do you have a flower?

S: No.

T: No? Why not?

S: My mom must have took it home.

T: Well, since your mom took your flower home, does that mean that you can rip up other people's flowers?

S: Yes.

T: Do you think you would like it if Carol went to your house and ripped up your flower?

S: No.

T: So you have your flower. The problem is that you have pulled up Carol's flower. What will you do about this?

C: I want to put this back in so it will grow. (Peige accepts Carol's desire to replant the flower as a worthwhile experiment but explains that without roots, it probably will not grow.)

S: I want to go clean up.

T: But, Steve, you have not come up with a solution. You have pulled up Carol's plant, and now she doesn't have a plant. What are you going to do about it?

S: I don't know.

T: Carol, do you have any ideas about what he could do?

C: I don't know.

T: I don't know, either.

C: He's not supposed to do that.

T: He was not supposed to do that.

C: It's gonna take a long time for another one to grow. (They talk about how long it takes for plants to grow.)

T: Well, Steve, I can't think of what you can do, either, to make this better for her. I'm out of ideas.

S: How about more seeds?

T: Put more seeds in there?

S: Yeah.
T: If we have more seeds. We'll have to ask Coreen [kindergarten teacher] because she used the seeds. Why don't you guys go ask Coreen if there are any more seeds? (This solution satisfies Carol, so the two children leave to try to find more seeds. They succeed and replant them for Carol.)

Peige places the responsibility for making restitution squarely on Steve's shoulders. She does not blame him but merely states matter of factly that since he pulled up Carol's plant, he must do something to make it better for Carol. Eventually, when Steve thinks of finding another seed and replanting it, Carol is happy with the solution. Steve is restored to favor in Carol's eyes as they become collaborators who work together to create another plant for her.

Two possible ways to lead children to restitution include the following:

- Asking the victim: "Can you think of anything [the aggressor] can do to make you feel better?"
- Asking the aggressor: "Can you think of anything you can do to make [the victim] feel better?"

When physical hurt occurs, the teacher should show concern and appeal to empathy. When dealing with children who have difficulties recognizing emotions in others, the teacher might ask, "What do his tears show us about how he's feeling?" If the child cannot answer, the teacher can be more direct, stating, for example "His tears show us that he is sad." If the child suggests something to make the victim feel better, the teacher should ask the injured child, "Would that make you feel better?" Constructivist teachers are careful in this discussion to make sure that a particular restitution is satisfactory to both children in a conflict. Children should never be placed in situations in which they are forced to unwillingly accept restitution from someone who has hurt them. Sometimes a victim is not ready to forgive and therefore will not accept a proposed restitution. In this case, one can leave the discussion open by saying, "She's not ready to do that. Maybe you can ask her again later." Once an injured party agrees, the teacher can help the perpetrator carry out the restitution. At the Human Development Laboratory School and at the Freeburg School, favorite restitutions were to take the injured child to the kitchen to get some ice or an adhesive bandage to put on the injury. Sometimes, a hug is healing when angry feelings have dissipated. When property is damaged, the teacher focuses on how the child can repair or replace an object.

13. Help Children Repair the Relationship, But Do Not Force Children to Be Insincere

A number of principles come together in this goal to help children repair their relationship through a coordination of minds, feelings, and attitudes. The seeds for repair are planted as children say to each other how they feel and listen to each other, focus on the problem and suggest and hear possible solutions, begin to recognize their own responsibilities in a conflict, consider restitution, and try to reach mutual agreement. In short, repair of the relationship is based on how the children come to understand each other in the course of the conflict resolution.

We would like to point out that we never ask children to apologize. This view is a reaction to the prevalence in homes and schools of such insistence that leads children simply to say the words in order to get the adult to be quiet. Forced apologies are usually insincere and operate against decentering and the development of empathy. Apologies do occur in constructivist classrooms, but resolution, restitution, repair, and so on, can occur without any apology. Constructivist teachers are primed to recognize the insincere apology and to challenge it when necessary to help a child deal with a conflict.

Coreen Samuel (T) at the Human Development Laboratory School encounters a seriously ruptured relationship between two 5-year-old best friends, Rianna and Nancy, during cleanup. She does not see how the problem began. As we learn later, Nancy accidentally caused a bump on Rianna's head. In this abbreviated account, we see efforts of several children to assist Rianna and Nancy. Gail, in particular, shares insights based on experiences of her conflicts with a friend.

N: It was a mistake. My hand [inaudible].
R: Shut up!
N: Now you stop that!
G: Are you guys fighting?
T: Yeah, what's—
R: I'm not your friend.
G: You guys, stop fighting.
R: (Walks over to Nancy and hits her)
N: Don't hit!
T: Okay, Rianna, I need you to use your words. You can just choose to not be her friend, but you can't hit her. That's not okay. Would it be okay for teachers to let her hit you when she's angry at you? Sometimes you get angry with your friends, but you can tell them with your words that you are angry.

R: She doesn't want to solve the problem! That's okay with me.

T: She doesn't?

N: Yes, I do.

R: No, she doesn't.

N: I do, but—

R: She does not, either! She does not because she's covering her ears. So that's why I'm not going to talk to her.

T: You're covering your ears?

N: I first did, because I did not want to [inaudible].

T: Oh, maybe that's why she feels like you don't want to listen to her. But if you want to listen to her, you—

N: I want to solve the problem!

R: Well, I'm not solving the problem with *you*!

T: Hmmm.

N: You got to.

R: Well, I'm not solving it.

T: I think Rianna is really upset now, and she's not ready. Do you need some time, Rianna? She's not ready right now. Maybe she could have some time. Is that okay, Nancy, if she has a few minutes? It's not okay? You want to solve it now?

R: Well, I'm not even solving it, even if you don't give me a little bit of time.

T: Does this mean you're never going to be friends again?

R: (Shakes head)

G: (Strong, skeptical tone) Ah, well, Rianna, I don't know about that. Sometimes friends get into big fights, like me and Carol get into big fights, but we get over it.

T: Yeah, they do.

G: Don't we, Carol?

T: And you guys [Rianna and Nancy] get over it, too. You got over it in the past. Maybe you can try what you did last time. What did you do last time?

N: What we did is we stayed away from each other for a while. And then one day, Rianna came up to me and [inaudible].

T: Well, maybe that will work again. Why don't you try that again? She looks like she needs some time. I don't want to force her to talk right now.

N: Sometimes I come up to Rianna and I say sometimes, "Why don't we play?"

T: So it happens both ways?

G: Sometimes Nancy gets mad with Rianna.

R: Look! Why don't you just leave me alone, Nancy!

G: Sometimes Nancy gets mad with Rianna, and then Rianna tries to make Nancy feel better, and now, Rianna got mad with Nancy, just on the case of the bump on the head. And Nancy is trying to make Rianna feel better. So I guess they both really love each other a whole lot, but sometimes friends can get into fights.

T: Yeah.

G: Like me and Carol are best friends. Sometimes we get into fights, don't we, Carol?

C: We fight like cats and dogs sometimes. (Children ask to go outside, and the teacher gives permission. Rianna leaves the room. Coreen and Nancy remain in the room and put blocks away together.)

T: I'm so glad you have patience and are able to wait on Rianna.

R: (Comes back just inside room) Nancy, I'm going outside. (Nancy follows Rianna outside and joins a game of "Mother, May I?" Rianna watches Nancy but does not join game. She looks unhappy.)

N: You want to be in the game? It's fun. You go 1, 2, 3 (kicks up her legs in imitation of giant steps, causing sand to fly up). (Both laugh, and Nancy puts her arm around Rianna and steers her toward the game.)

In this case, the teacher clearly has in mind the goal of the girls' repair of their relationship. However, when she sees that Rianna's attitude makes a discussion fruitless at the moment, the teacher advocates for giving Rianna time instead of insisting on talking immediately. She respects Rianna's right to say so when she is unready to forgive. When the two best friends express a negation of their friendship, the teacher raises the question of whether they are ever going to be friends again. The strength of the friendship, with a little time for cooling of tempers, does lead the girls to repair their relationship in the context of playing a game, without a specific resolution of the original conflict. We cannot know for certain how the discussion led to reflection and aided in the repair, but the teacher and children clearly give importance to the conflict. We are particularly impressed with Gail's skepticism at their denial of the friendship and her advice from experience with her best friend, Carol. This kind of concern for each other's problems is one of the hallmarks of a successful sociomoral atmosphere.

In another situation, two kindergarten boys at the Human Development Laboratory School get into an intense conflict over what occurs in a checkers game. Jordan legitimately jumps one of Kerrick's checkers, but Kerrick honestly believes Jordan had illegitimately taken two turns in a row. They cannot agree, and their argument deteriorates into upsetting the board and sweeping pieces off the table onto the floor. When the teacher intervenes, Jordan and Kerrick cry and scream at each other incoherently.

The teacher tries to talk with each one individually, but this does not work, as the boys continue to scream at each other while putting their hands over their ears. A bystander, Evan, comments, "They're not listening to each other." The teacher asks Kerrick and Jordan to stay apart until they are ready to talk, and Jordan goes to the bathroom while Kerrick sits at a table. Amazingly, Kerrick immediately begins watching until Jordan reappears. From across the room, Kerrick begins a kind of peekaboo with Jordan and imitates Jordan's stiff-legged side-to-side rocking. Upon catching Jordan's attention, Kerrick blows on his arm, making a rude sound. When Jordan laughs, Kerrick approaches him. Intercepting Kerrick, the teacher asks, "What do you think we should do first, talk or clean up?" Kerrick replies to the teacher, "Clean up," and to Jordan proposes, "Let's clean up." The teacher asks Jordan if he wants to clean up with Kerrick. Kerrick and Jordan grin at each other and start picking up checkers from the floor. Kerrick continues to blow on his arm, to Jordan's shocked delight.

The interpersonal relationship is thus repaired by silliness that enables the boys to reestablish a positive interaction. With this story, we simply want to call the reader's attention to the fact that children may have their own ways of repairing a relationship. Similarly to Nancy and Rianna, above, they could not resolve the argument itself, but the strength of their friendship and desire to be back on good terms led them to their own solution of simply moving past the disagreement.

When trust is absent, it is difficult to repair a relationship. One 1st-grader at Freeburg protested the idea of becoming friends again. He said he had given the other child many chances, and he did not trust him any more because he always repeated the offense. In such a situation, the teacher might ask, "What would he have to do so you would trust him again? Is there something he can do that will show you he wants to be friends?" If the other child states that he does want to be friends, the teacher might offer to help the offended child make a proposal: "Would you like me to help you think of some ideas?" If not, the teacher can simply say to the offender, "He really does not trust you because you _____." The feeling of trust or mistrust reflects a complex mental relationship that conserves past experiences in the present.

14. Work Toward Children's Emotional Resolution

Children's emotional resolution of a conflict is necessary in any conflict resolution. If any party to a conflict still feels angry, resentful, and so on, then the conflict has not been resolved. Therefore, constructivist teachers try to make sure at the end that all parties feel comfortable about the final point of agreement. They ask each party a question such as "Do you feel okay/better now?" "Is it okay with you to [statement of agreed-upon action]?" Some of the earlier examples in this chapter show teachers following this principle. If one child expresses a lack of resolution, the teacher calls the other's attention to this, and continues to work on the problem with the children.

When a teacher assumes a resolution and forgets to check on children's emotional resolution, children may correct the teacher. For example, one teacher said, "You look much better, and I know you are buddies, so that happens sometimes [that people have fights]." A kindergartner responded, "We ain't buddies still 'cause he made me more mad, but I'm just a little angry." The teacher realized her mistake and supported the child's effort to resolve his anger by saying, "But you're trying to get over it? Do you need to talk to him again?"

It is not always possible for children to find emotional resolution and forgiveness of another's wrong. When this is the case, the teacher can acknowledge any progress made and state a lack of resolution. For example, one teacher said to the aggressing child, "He is still angry. Maybe he will change his mind later, but right now he does not want to play with you because you [state what child did to the other]."

We could talk about emotional resolution as *emotional equilibrium* that is a counterpart to the cognitive equilibrium discussed in the introduction. Every equilibrium has both cognitive and emotional aspects. The understanding that one can change one's negative feelings toward another through talking, expressing feelings, and negotiating conflicts can contribute to more positive and satisfying interpersonal relationships.

15. Encourage Children to Resolve Their Conflicts by Themselves

The long-range goal is for children to be able to resolve their conflicts without teacher intervention. Constructivist teachers therefore refrain from intervening if children are solving or can solve their problems. When children come to complain about another child's actions, teachers encourage children to deal with the problem themselves. "What could you say to him?" "Can you use your words and tell him you don't like that?" "Can you figure out how to solve that problem?" If children need help, the teacher, of course, responds.

In a cooperative sociomoral atmosphere, children develop an attitude of wanting to resolve conflicts, and they use a wide variety of negotiation strategies. The pleasure and intimacy of shared experiences provide a general context for the ripening of close relationships and the desire to maintain them. Consider the following conflict at the Human Development Laboratory School among three close kindergarten friends, Monty,

Diane, and Naomi, who are playing a game of Concentration. Many pairs of tiles are turned face down, and they take turns turning up two tiles at a time, trying to get a match. Naomi pretends to play the guitar and sings. Monty is an exceptionally bouncy and exuberant child whose piercing screams when he is excited have disturbed everyone. This problem has even been the subject of a class discussion where the teacher and children tried to help him by giving suggestions about how to do something different, besides screaming. Here, he is excited about the game.

M: (Turns two tiles and screams) Look, I got a match! Look, I got a match!
D: Monty, don't scream.
M: (Sticks out lower lip and pouts)
D: Doesn't that hurt your ears, Naomi?
M: (Turns his back on the girls and puts his head on his folded arms)
N: No.
D: It hurts my ears. Naomi, does it hurt yours just a little bit?
N: Ah, you made him sad, that's all.
D: (To Monty) I'm sorry, you can be my friend. You were just hurting my ears a little bit.
N: Well, he didn't hurt my ears. I didn't make him cry. You did. But that's all right 'cause I can make him feel better (goes to Monty and looks into his face).
D: He was just hurting my ears a little bit.
N: Monty, do you want to play, Monty?
M: (Turns with a cheerful look) Do you know what, Naomi? Look, I've got a match!
D: And I've got a match! (Shows Monty)
M: Yeaaa!
N: I've got a hundred match.
M: And I've got a match! (Shows Diane)
D: And I've got a match! (Shows Monty)
M: You've got a match!
N: Let's don't play this game. (The children put away the game pieces in the box and carry it together to a storage shelf where they find another game to play.)

This is an example of the kind of caring that can occur in the context of an atmosphere where people's feelings are highlighted on an ongoing basis. Monty hears Diane's protest at his excited screaming, hears her affirm the friendship, and, to his credit, is able to regain a cheerful attitude when Naomi tries to make him feel better. Monty repeats, without screaming, that he has a match, and everyone shares his joy. This sharing resolves the conflict and reestablishes the friendly dynamic. Although the teacher had talked with Monty about his screaming, he may have made the mental relationship between screaming and others' pained protests in a more meaningful way in this context of caring friendship.

What Not to Say in Conflict Situations

Teachers can shut down a child's openness to conflict resolution or even escalate a conflict. What not to say can include the following:

- "Do you want me to put that away?"
- "How many times have I told you not to do that?"
- "Why did you do that?"
- "You need to apologize."
- "What do you need to say?"

Perhaps the readers of this book would never say such things. However, we have heard this kind of talk in classrooms where teachers are striving to be developmentally appropriate. Some teachers have told us how difficult it is to refrain from threats, punishments, and forced apologies that they say come almost automatically. It is not easy to cultivate caring relationships with children who are prone to frequent conflicts. However, a feeling of psychological safety is necessary for children to be open to the teacher's efforts to promote conflict resolution abilities.

CONFLICT PREVENTION

Although conflict resolution is an important component of the constructivist curriculum, preventing conflicts is also important in creating a cooperative sociomoral atmosphere in the classroom. It is particularly necessary to try to avoid conflicts in classrooms with children who struggle with self-regulation or exhibit challenging behaviors.

Materials can be a source of preventable conflicts. Earlier, we discuss how to prevent conflicts that arise over scarce materials. When children are ready developmentally for these sorts of conflicts, then they can be productive in providing occasions for constructing cooperation. But when younger children are not capable of sharing scarce materials (for example, staplers and tape at the art center, hats and coats at the pretend center, marbles at the ramps center, etc.), it is better to provide multiples so that children do not lash out in frustration when they cannot do what they want to do.

Careful furniture arrangement can prevent conflicts by providing enough space for activities so that overcrowding does not occur. When children's ability to control their bodily movements is still developing and not completely under control, insufficient space in certain activity centers can lead to conflicts. For example, too little space in the block center can result in children accidentally knocking down others' structures. Although an occasional accidental knock-down can lead to productive conflict resolution, frequent occurrences can detract from children's opportunities to be productive in the block center. In such a case, the teacher might consider finding ways to expand the size of the center or discuss with children whether to limit the number of children there at one time.

Some classroom situations actually make conflicts and misbehavior likely to occur. These include crowding in a particular part of the classroom, activities that do not engage children, and too much time spent waiting (discussed in Chapter 10).

CONFLICT BETWEEN TEACHER AND CHILD

Conflict between teacher and child is not unusual. It occurs when a child becomes angry with a teacher for actions the child sees as unfair or for actions the child simply dislikes. Conflict also occurs when the teacher becomes angry with a child. We discuss these situations below.

When the Child Thinks the Teacher Is Unfair

A perception of unfairness often results when a child's desire is not fulfilled. This problem is avoided when the teacher makes concerted efforts to understand children's perspectives and refrains from judging and blaming children. The principles of teaching discussed above include safeguards against feelings of being treated unfairly. Such feelings do not usually develop when the teacher is careful to accept children's feelings and perceptions, clarify and state problems from all points of view, and engage children in focusing on how to solve a problem. When a child does feel angry or hurt over perceived unfair treatment, the teacher should acknowledge and accept this feeling, then let the child know he or she is concerned about how the child feels.

Sometimes children do not, or cannot, understand the adult's actions. This is sometimes the case despite the teacher's best efforts to explain. In these rare situations, the teacher may be able only to communicate regret that the child is upset. It is then important to find a way to reestablish the relationship.

When the Child Dislikes What the Teacher Does

The teacher is sometimes surprised to find that a child is upset with him or her. In such a situation, the comments above also apply. Efforts to explain and reestablish the relationship are important. We remember one occasion in a kindergarten when a child could not accept the group's vote to act out a different story from the one he wanted. He began to cry. In this situation, the teacher had to uphold the majority rule. She acknowledged his disappointment and tried to console him by indicating that they would be able to act out his story on another day. It is important for the children in the majority to empathize with the minority's feelings. In the face of severe disappointment, the teacher may wish to consult the group about whether they want to plan a compromise. In some cases, however, it is not possible to carry out what the minority wishes. One of the goals is for children to overcome egocentric attitudes and accept majority rule for the sake of being a member of the group.

When the Teacher Becomes Angry with a Child

Most of the time, teachers can manage their feelings and take a professional attitude in relation to children. However, being human, teachers sometimes feel angry with children, despite all professional efforts to keep such emotions under control. We know of cases in which teachers have expressed anger with a child for hurting another. We also know of situations in which a teacher has become angry at being hit or kicked by a child.

When a teacher becomes so upset with a child that he or she has difficulty staying in control or being with a child, two options are open. One method is for the teacher to explain to the child that he or she is too angry or upset to talk and wants to wait until he or she is more in control. Then, the teacher should follow through and find a time to talk with the child about the problem calmly when anger will not be destructive to the child. The second option is to seek another adult to serve as mediator. Then the teacher can express his or her point of view, listen to the child's view, and try to come to a resolution.

CONCLUSION

How best to deal with conflicts in a classroom is often a topic of intense discussion among constructivist teachers because each conflict is unique, and teachers are challenged to tailor interventions to particular situations and particular children. Conflict resolution calls upon a teacher's ingenuity and willingness to engage in the emotional concerns of children. We have given many examples in this chapter of how teachers have intervened, in the hope that we can help the reader develop an attitude of openness toward the educational possibilities in conflict resolution, some ideas about intervention, and perhaps the courage that it takes to enter into the heat of such highly uncertain situations as children's conflicts.

6

Group Time

Of all classroom activities, group time may be the most critical in terms of the sociomoral atmosphere. For many teachers it may also be the most difficult and challenging time of the day. In this chapter we discuss constructivist objectives of group time, types of group time, leading group time, and some common problems teachers encounter. In addition, we give examples of actual group times. The reader may notice that we do not include show-and-tell, or share time, a nearly universal group time activity in early education. We discuss this controversial activity and explain why we do not include it in our list of group time activities. Finally, we tell a story of one class's experience with problems during group times.

OBJECTIVES

Objectives for group time fall into two broad categories: sociomoral and cognitive. We discuss these two domains separately, but remind the reader that they are in fact inseparable.

Sociomoral Objectives

Objectives of group time are to promote identity with the group and caring about group members. Young children are notorious for their egocentrism that makes it difficult, for example, to feel an obligation to the needs of the group, including a need to stay in a given space on the carpet, refrain from talking, accept a friend's different vote for a field trip, or consider another's reasons for why a character in a story should solve a problem in a certain way. Long-term aims of identity and caring lead constructivist teachers to work toward building a sense of active community among children through activities whose purpose is to focus on the common good of the group. Examples are self-governance and involving children in thinking about specific social and moral problems that arise in the course of life in the classroom. In these and other group time activities, children have the possibility to construct knowledge, feelings, and values with regard to living as part of a group. Many teachers are accustomed to thinking about these goals in specific behavioral terms such as having children sit in a circle on the carpet, listen to the teacher read a story, and raise a hand to talk when called on by the teacher. Our goals go beyond these behaviors.

To build community, teachers use activities that promote a feeling of belonging together and a recognition of common purposes. Favorite songs and finger plays engage young children in a repertoire of shared rituals that lays a foundation for group identity. Discussing and planning shared experiences (such as a field trip to an apple orchard) and projects (such as re-creating a radio station in the classroom) contribute to a feeling of common purpose and mutual interests. Group cohesion can also arise from group identity symbolized in class names. At the Human Development Laboratory School, for example, classes are called (in order of age) the Explorers, the Experimenters, the Investigators, and the Inventors. These names are especially meaningful to the older children, who discuss what it means to be investigators or inventors. Through frequent recognition of children's work, the teacher fosters in children a certain sense of pride in characterizing themselves as having a lot of ideas, being able to figure out how to make certain things happen, and so on. This is different from the goal of group identity in many high schools and colleges where it is linked mainly to competitive sports.

Children experience group purposes that transcend the needs and wants of the individual as they plan how to share responsibility for taking care of their class. As children participate in making rules (see Chapter 7), proposing and choosing from options for class activities, and making other decisions (see Chapter 8), they learn numerous lessons in democracy. They learn that all voices are given the chance to be heard, that no one opinion is given more weight than another, and that they have power to decide what happens in their class. Children practice mutual respect and cooperation as they work together, listen to each other, exchange ideas, negotiate problems, and vote to make decisions that affect the whole group. They think together about what can be done when mutual respect and cooperation break down, and they solve classroom problems. Through discussion of both real-life and hypothetical social and moral dilemmas, constructivist teachers try to help children develop feelings of necessity about what is right and wrong, good and bad, fair and unfair (see Chapter 9).

Underlying all these sociomoral activities is the general goal of decentering and the development of perspective-taking (see Chapter 2). This leads to concerns with fairness and justice in a community in which people care about each other. Children who come from families where they experience compassionate caring may easily transfer a feeling of trust and caring to the teacher and then to other children. Children without this advantage may require focused effort on the part of a teacher to develop a relationship of caring and trust. How this contributes to the child's construction of a self who respects and is respected by others is discussed in Chapter 3.

Cognitive Objectives

The overall cognitive objective for group time is to promote the general development of reasoning and intelligence. Decentering to consider and coordinate points of view is an intellectual as well as a social, emotional, and moral endeavor. Specific cognitive goals are to promote children's construction of mental relationships in subject matter knowledge.

TYPES OF GROUP TIME

Types of group time include rituals, story times, class meetings, and large-group instruction.

Rituals

Traditionally in early education and also in constructivist classrooms, a morning group time welcome includes shared experiences of songs or finger plays, attendance, and introducing the day's special activities. Some teachers have a flannel board (or other device) with children's names on cards they or the children move from the "Not in School" column to the "In School" column. Some classes identify a "special helper" who is called upon to assist classmates and the teacher in various ways throughout the day. Opening group time is a good time to intrigue children with new activities that can be pursued during activity time (see Chapter 11). A feeling of community develops through shared experiences of rituals.

Story Time

Story time is an important occasion for facilitating the development of attitudes and competencies related to literacy, but it is also an important occasion for establishing and enlarging shared knowledge. When children listen to a fictional story, they share the emotions of suspense or expectation about what is happening and what is next. When the teacher is sensitive to the social and moral issues in the story, rather than just focusing on comprehension, children have opportunities to think about the story, reason about the characters' intentions, and make predictions. After children have heard a story many times and know it well, they may cooperate to act it out, with all the sociomoral advantages entailed. When the teacher reads nonfiction, the children have opportunities to acquire shared knowledge about topics of interest to the class. In all these ways of using books, teachers foster interest and mutual engagement.

Class Meeting

The class meeting is a group time in which the focus is on how the classroom operates with regard to interpersonal relationships. The Developmental Studies Center's (1996) book, *Ways We Want Our Class to Be*, supporting videotapes, and lists of recommended books are excellent resources. A class meeting to discuss the topic "How We Want Our Class to Be" near the beginning of the year can be very helpful in establishing a culture of caring and cooperation. When children have an opportunity to say how they want to be treated, they often state that they want people to be kind, not to embarrass or make fun of them, and so on. Follow-up group times can be planned as opportunities to revisit the list made by children and evaluate how the class is doing. Rule making, decision making, and problem solving are other class meeting topics that relate to interpersonal issues.

Large-Group Instruction

Instruction often takes the form of mini-lessons at group time. These might include thinking about number and mathematics in varied activities such as attendance, voting, and mental math. Beth Van Meeteren regularly challenged 1st- and 2nd-graders at Freeburg to do mental math during group time. For example, she wrote a problem (such as $19 + 32 =$) for children to do mentally, without paper or pencil. After all children raised their hands indicating they were finished, they took turns explaining how they got their answer (typically, making combinations of tens from numbers in the ones column, adding the tens, then adding the number less than ten remaining).

The teacher might convene a group time with the purpose of having children share with the group what they had figured out during activity time about a physical phenomenon, such as how to construct a ramp structure that allows a marble to jump from one ramp segment to another.

Literacy is promoted through methods such as reading names of children in a class, reading charts of familiar poems or songs, and calling attention to conventions of writing in books and in writing dictated to the teacher by children about their discoveries and inventions. Conventional or societal knowledge is involved in learning vocabulary in stories; learning about different traditions associated with holidays; and learning about special topics such as a bakery, insects and other animals, or handicapped-accessible buildings. Within every topic, constructivist teachers plan possibilities for children to construct specific mental relationships such as grouping of similar items sold in a bakery project or classification and comparison of various materials used for parachutes as unworkable or workable. These are examples of virtually unlimited content objectives that constructivist teachers may pursue during group time.

Although group times involving instruction emphasize cognitive objectives, the constructivist teacher also aims to foster mutual respect and community, and children's interactions provide them with opportunities to construct mental relationships between their own and others' efforts to be heard, their ideas and the ideas of others, and so on.

FORMAL ASPECTS OF GROUP TIME

Formal aspects of group time include seating arrangements and length of group time.

Seating Arrangements

We recommend that group time be conducted in a circle so that children can see each other. Sitting on the floor is typical and convenient, but if for some reason one or more members of the class cannot physically sit on the floor, then everyone can sit on chairs. The important point is that everyone (including the adults) should be at the same level. This serves as a tangible symbol that everyone is part of the group. The exception to this would be during story time, when it is appropriate for the teacher to be higher than the children so that children can see the book.

When seated on the floor, some teachers insist that children sit with their legs crossed and their hands folded in their laps. We find this unnecessarily controlling. As long as children are not hurting others, interfering with others' ability to see, or disrupting group with flailing limbs, we believe that it is more respectful to allow children to sit in the position they find most comfortable. It also makes better use of children's (and the teacher's) time by not devoting large amounts of time to telling children how to sit.

Whether children's places in circle should be determined by the teacher or by children depends on children's self-regulation ability. We have seen classes where the teacher needed to determine places because some children could not control themselves when seated next to certain others. One way to do this is to use carpet-sample mats (or chairs) with children's names taped on them. The teacher can decide where to place them in a circle before children come to group time. Another approach is to discuss the problem with children privately. The teacher can say something to the effect of "I know that you and _____ are special friends and like to play together, but when you play at group time, it disturbs us, and you miss out on what we are doing. What can we do to solve this problem?" With teacher support and appreciation, children often decide not to sit together. The general constructivist goal is for children to be self-regulating, so allowing children to decide where they want to sit is a reasonable long-term goal.

Length of Group Time

The length of group time is a practical decision that depends on children's interest and ability to focus. We simply encourage teachers to be sensitive to the needs and abilities of the children. Generally, group times will be 5–10 minutes for children under 3 years old, 10–20 minutes for 3- and 4-year-olds, and 30 minutes for 5-year-olds and older. These times are only approximations. If children are engaged and interested in a topic and are not becoming restless, group time can last longer. We have seen 30-minute group times with 3-year-olds, and 45-minute group times with 4-year-olds on occasion, when they were very interested in a topic. If children are restless, the teacher can end group time and tell the children that they will resume talking about the topic at the next group time.

LEADING GROUP TIME

As stated earlier, the role of the teacher during group time is somewhat different from what it is at other times of the day. During activity time, children generally take the lead in pursuing their play and work. The teacher's role, as we discuss further in Chapter 11, is to support, suggest, and facilitate children's purposes and to strive to reduce the exercise of adult power in interactions with children. During group time, however, the teacher must be a leader. Some constructivist teachers have told us that they felt uncomfortable in the leader's role because it felt heteronomous. They found it difficult to shift from facilitating to leading and thought it was not easy to balance these two seemingly contradictory roles. Let us simply say that leadership at group time is a legitimate role for the constructivist teacher. The teacher should not be timid about leading group. We have seen teachers who, confused about how to balance equality with leadership, raise their hands when they wanted to talk. Such actions confuse children. It is necessary to be clear about who is leading group. If a child is taking the leadership role (we have seen this done very effectively with kindergarten children), then the teacher should act like a member of the group and follow the customary practices such as raising hands. But if the teacher is leading the group, then he or she should lead without feeling apologetic.

Having in mind the general goals and objectives of constructivist education will help the teacher keep the leadership role in perspective. The role of the teacher is to facilitate the children's development by creating an environment that fosters the goals of self-regulation, perspective-taking, and cooperation.

The exercise of leadership does not need to become coercive. Effective leadership relies on appeals to reason, mutual respect, and shared responsibility. Adults recognize that it is much easier to follow a respectful and reasonable leader than a controlling and punitive one. Children are no different from adults in this respect. They will be much more inclined to cooperate with a leader who is reasonable and respectful.

If possible, the teacher should be in place before the first child comes to circle so that group time can begin when the first few sit down. Favorite songs, finger plays, and other rituals give the children already at circle something to do while others arrive, and provide an attraction for the stragglers. This also focuses attention on the teacher as leader from the beginning. Some teachers have songs that are sung only to bring children to group time; whenever the teacher begins to sing the song, children know to come to circle.

We have noticed that teachers who are most successful with group time often bring a written agenda that includes an alternative or two in case children do not respond to something that is introduced. Agendas will vary, depending on the many types of group time, each with differing goals.

Group time is fragile in terms of group dynamics, and the teacher's role is to maintain group focus and continuity. The most effective thing the teacher can do to prevent problems is to keep group time moving. Pacing is critical to maintaining children's interest and attention. A long gap of silence should be avoided whenever possible because it invites children to fill the void, and the teacher thus loses the lead. Lengthy activities that can be done by only one person at a time should also be avoided. When children are not actively engaged, they may become bored and restless and initiate their own activities.

COMMON PROBLEMS AT GROUP TIME

Despite the teacher's best efforts to prevent problems at group time, sometimes children become restless, and no one wants to sing or sit still or listen. We address what teachers can do when interest in group time wanes, when children all talk at once, when children talk only to the teacher, and when external regulation directed to one child is necessary.

When Interest Wanes

When interest wanes, the teacher should avoid disciplinary remarks and use indirect means to recapture lost interest. Experienced teachers know that if attention wanders, starting a song or finger play can regain the group's focus. Generally, minor restlessness of one or two children can be ignored. The teacher can go on with group time as long as most children pay attention. However, if many children are restless, the teacher should take this as a sign that children have lost interest. Losing interest is not a punishable offense! When this happens, the teacher should drop the rest of the plan and wrap up quickly or move to an alternate group time activity such as a group game (for example, Musical Chairs or Simon Says).

When All Talk at Once

Often, a topic interests children so much that they all want to talk about it at once. This occurs for a number of reasons. Children's general egocentrism and impulsiveness causes them to be unable to think of something without saying it out loud. Children may feel they have to compete with others for a chance to talk. When more than three or four children have something to say on a topic, the teacher should set up a sequence and assure children that everyone will get a turn to talk. "I'll start with_____ and go around the circle. Everyone will get a chance, so you can put your hand down." By allowing each child a turn (with, of course, the option to "pass"), the teacher avoids problems. Children do not feel compelled to wave their hand in the air while exclaiming, "Call me! Call me!" Children can relax about getting a turn to talk, and so can listen to each other, rather than concentrating on trying to get the teacher's attention.

We urge teachers not to follow the approach of calling on children who quietly raise their hands. If many children are being quiet and raising their hands, the choice of whom to call on becomes arbitrary. We have watched many group times where one child sits patiently in circle, hand raised quietly, and never attracts the teacher's attention. It is easy to neglect the quiet, undemanding child. Going around the circle and giving every child a turn to speak prevents this from happening.

When children all talk at once, and the circle becomes noisy, the teacher should avoid shouting over the din. Some strategies that work include sitting quietly and waiting for the noise to subside, holding one's hands over one's ears and looking pained, and whispering. The goal is to get back to taking turns. Nagging children to be quiet does not usually work and undermines the teacher's leadership role. In extreme cases, starting a song or clapping rhythm can bring children back to a common focus.

The ultimate goal in regulating conversation at group time is that there be no need to regulate talking. That is, we would like children to be able to talk at group time with neither hand raising nor turn taking but with the casual give-and-take of polite conversation. However, this is sometimes a difficult task even for adults, and therefore some form of regulation by the teacher may be necessary. Children can be encouraged to discuss the problem of people wanting to talk at the same time, and their solutions can be tried.

When Children Talk Only to the Teacher

The teacher should encourage children to talk to the entire group, not just to the teacher. This is difficult, because children will always direct their comments to the teacher. It may be necessary to be obvious and say something such as "Tell this to everybody. Class, Rianna has something she wants to tell us."

When External Regulation Is Necessary

External regulation in response to misbehavior should be used sparingly. When necessary, however, it should be clear, concise, nonjudgmental, and direct. For example, when a child was making noises at circle, we heard one teacher very matter of factly state, "Sean, please take the 'Ah-ah-ah' noise out of the classroom. When you are finished making that noise, then we would like to have you back in circle." (An assistant teacher was available to supervise.) This same teacher, when one child was walking around in the middle of the circle pretending to be a dog, said, "Tom, do you want to be a dog, and leave circle, or do you want to be a boy, and sit on your mat?" When he chose to sit down in circle, she replied, "Oh, I'm so glad you decided to stay. We like having you in circle."

Sometimes one child will be seriously disruptive. Each child is unique, with different reasons for the disruptive behavior, and we can thus offer no hard and fast rules for working with difficult children. The teacher must respond to the individual child's entire history, needs, and circumstances. Sometimes it helps if an assistant teacher can sit beside a disruptive child, put an arm around him or her, and whisper encouragement. Having said that, a logical consequence of seriously disrupting circle is for the child to leave circle until he or she is ready to come back and participate. If a child must leave, the teacher can still show respect for the child by stating, "Can you leave circle by yourself, or do you need help?" Giving children choices is a good way to show respect while at the same time setting clear limits. This places the responsibility for regulating behavior on the child. Children often respond to the chance to be self-regulating.

THE ISSUE OF SHOW-AND-TELL

Many early childhood classrooms assign a day a week for each child to bring a prized object to school and show it to the class or tell the class about something he or she did recently. While we do not want to convey the message that we think children should not share these personal interests with the group, we would like to point out the problems we have seen with this type of institutionalized sharing. First, children often forget when it is their "Share Day," do not bring anything to share, and then become very upset when they get to school and discover their mistake. We have seen children so upset that they had to leave the class with an assistant in order to calm down. Second, sometimes children do not have anything they want to share but feel compelled to share something. They stutter and stammer and feel awkward and inadequate. Third, some children are quite shy and find sharing painful and embarrassing. Sharing for them is simply an occasion to suffer embarrassment and be reminded of their shyness. Finally, some children dominate sharing, going on and on about their trip to the circus or the snake they found in the backyard. It is difficult to get these children to be brief without cutting them off and making them unhappy, and group time can become much too long, causing children to become restless and cranky.

What can be done about the problems with show-and-tell? We recognize the benefits of having children share things from home. Children feel special, they have an opportunity to be "on stage," and they develop good public-speaking skills. First, we suggest letting sharing occur spontaneously. By its not being institutionalized, sharing will probably occur less frequently and involve more meaningful contributions. When only one or two children have something special to share, it can be incorporated easily into group time. When more than one or two children want to share, we suggest moving sharing to activity time. If children tell the teacher before group time when they have something to share, the teacher can announce this opportunity as part of the description of activities. A sharing table, shelf, or other space can be designated where children can place things they bring from home. The children can stay at the sharing table during the beginning of the activity period and tell children who come to look all about it. They may make signs describing it and can decide whether others are allowed to touch or not. Some children may even prefer to share during activities rather than during group time. This system of sharing can eliminate the problems in conducting sharing during group time, while not depriving children of the opportunity to share things from home. It can also promote children's oral language, as the more relaxed time frame and smaller group structure fosters conversation about the object or event being shared.

EXAMPLES OF GROUP TIME

The following examples illustrate how constructivist teachers used group time to plan a field trip, serve as a resource to a child with a problem, discuss a physical-knowledge activity time, and celebrate birthdays. Finally, we tell the story of how in one classroom, group time was lost, then regained.

Planning a Trip

Planning group projects, parties, and trips can be fruitful group time activities. The teacher will have to decide how much planning children can do and how much must be done by the teacher. In the following example at the Human Development Laboratory School, Peige (T) provides extensive guidance as she discusses with her class of 3- and 4-year-olds their proposed field trip to the zoo, with the purpose of finding out whether turkeys can fly (see Chapter 8 for the full story about children's question of whether turkeys can fly). She listens respectfully to the children's ideas and draws out and elaborates their ideas so children participate fully in the planning.

T: Now we had an argument, remember, about whether or not turkeys fly. So we were going to go to the zoo and check out this thing, right? Now, I guess these are the things we'll need to go to the zoo. We'll need to get permission from the moms and dads, and we'll need at least two other moms or dads to go with us.
D: I have one mom.

M: I have one mom.

T: You have one mom? And we'll need some people to drive their cars.

G: I have a mom.

K: My daddy would drive us.

T: He would drive, do you think? (Children continue to volunteer their moms, dads, and cars.)

C: Peige, I have an idea!

T: Oh, Clark has an idea. What's your idea, Clark?

C: If we call all the moms and tell them that we're going to the zoo, and we need two more moms, then they'd want to come.

W: But my dad can't come because he's got to go to work.

T: Oh, you guys, listen. Wayne said his dad can't come because he has to go to work. Now, I was thinking. Maybe we could write a letter to the moms and dads, and then we'll have Jane [the secretary] make copies so that each mom and dad can have a copy.

Z: Maybe Jane could come with us.

T: Oh, maybe Jane could come with us.

Z: Or maybe Ann (the assistant director).

T: Maybe Ann could. We could ask them, too. What do you think about writing a note so that the moms and dads will know we want to go to the zoo? And then they could try and take time off work to take us. Do you think that's a good idea?

Children: Yeah, me, too. And we could get lots of moms and dads.

T: We could get lots of moms and dads. (Peige asks the special helper to get paper and a marker.)

C: And we could ride on the train. And we could see some animals and different animals.

T: Clark was saying we could see different animals. Not just a turkey but different animals too.

G: And they have birds. (Children suggest animals they want to see at the zoo.)

T: (Begins to dictate while she writes) Dear Moms and Dads. What do we want to tell them?

Children: We want to go to the zoo. That we want the moms and dads to come.

T: (Writing) We want to go to the zoo. Do you know how to spell zoo?

Children: Zee-oh-oh!

T: *Z-o-o.* We want to go to the zoo. What do we need to tell them that we need?

Children: Some money . . . We need some money to go on the train ride . . . And, you know, we need tickets.

T: We need tickets to go on the train, so we have to pay money to do that. And we need money to go to the zoo, too. Right? Now we also need moms and dads to drive their cars. So how should we ask them to do that? Does anyone have an idea?

C: Please drive your car.

T: Please drive your car. Okay. And we need some moms and dads to come with us. How should we ask them about that?

N: Nicely.

T: Nicely? What's a nice way to ask them?

N: Please.

T: Please what?

C: Please come with us. How's that? Please drive your car. Please come with us.

T: Let's see, we have to decide on a day to go.

Z: Are we going today?

T: Would you like to go—no, we can't go today, because the moms and dads need to be able to get the note.

W: Because they're at work.

T: They're at work. They have to be able to give us the money and come back and all that. How about if we go on next Monday?

Children: Yeah! No! I have a great idea. We could go on Thursday.

T: On Thursday? Do you think that would be enough time for the moms and dads to get the note and all that?

C: Yes, because on Tuesday they'll put the note up, and then on Wednesday you get the note, and on Thursday you come.

T: I have an idea. Why don't we go on Friday, and then that would give them 2 days to get themselves together.

C: Why?

T: Well, because sometimes it takes a long time for moms and dads to ask for time off.

D: What do you think about going on Friday?

C: How about Monday?

T: Okay, so we'll go on Friday or the next Monday. We have to take a vote, you guys. Okay, today is Tuesday. The earliest we could go is Friday, but we might get more moms and dads to be able to participate if we go on the next Monday. So the vote is, should we go Friday, or should we go the next Monday? (They vote, and decide to go on Friday.)

T: Okay, so now our note says, "Please come with us and we want to go on Friday."

C: What time?

T: Oh, Clark said, "What time?" Should we go in the morning?
C: Seven o'clock.
T: Uh, we're not in school at seven o'clock. Our circle time starts at 9
    o'clock. Maybe we could leave at 9:30.
Children: Yeah!
T: Okay. We want to go on Friday at 9:30. Okay. Oh, do we want to take
    our lunch and eat it there?
Children: Yeah!
T: Okay, this is what it says. (Reads) "Dear Moms and Dads, We want to
    go to the zoo. We need some money to ride the train and to get into
    the zoo. Please drive your car. Please come with us. We want to go on
    Friday at 9:30. We want to take a picnic lunch." Okay, now who is this
    from?
T: So should we write Investigators down here?
Children: Yeah!
T: (Signs) Investigators.

This edited segment of a group time illustrates how teachers can involve
children in planning a field trip. The teacher listens to the children, solicits
their opinions, and respects their decisions, even when they do not vote
for the day she recommends. When she had to veto the idea of leaving at
7:00 A.M., she explains why this will not work and suggests a realistic time.
Although the teacher could have made all these decisions, the children's
involvement gives them ownership of the plan and engages their investment in the trip.

Children Using Group Time as a Resource

In Chapter 4 we mention that problems of concern to only one or two
children should be handled privately, rather than in the group. We gave
an example of the exception, when a problem with one child concerns
the entire group. However, when children consider their classmates as a
resource, it can be appropriate for group time to focus on one child's problem. In the following example from a kindergarten class at the Human
Development Laboratory School, Sheila brings to the group her problem
of always getting to school too late to be special helper in the first group
time. (In this example, T1 stands for the lead teacher, Coreen Samuel, and
T2 for the assistant teacher, Karen Amos.)

S: I was just wondering if anybody had some ideas of a way that we
    could see how I could get to school earlier.

C: Um, why don't we send a note to your mom and dad and then they could read it and then they could bring you more earlier.

S: No, no, no, no, no.

T2: Why won't that work?

S: 'Cause I've already talked to my mom about that.

C: Umm, I think, tell your mom to wake you up more earlier.

T1: You know what? I just spoke to Sheila's mom, and she was telling me there was a problem because she wakes up early but sometimes it's hard to get Sheila up.

S: (Nods)

T1: So if it's really hard for her to wake you up in the morning, what can you do, Sheila?

S: Because, because my sister keeps on playing with me in the night.

C: Do you have bunk beds?

S: No.

T1: You guys, Andrea is really willing to give an idea.

S: Andrea?

A: I have an idea. Do your mom and dad have like an old alarm clock up in the attic, or down? Well, maybe you could, like, get somebody to, like, buy you an alarm clock, and you could—

S: (Interrupts) No, we already—

A: —you could ask them to put the time on it, and then the alarm clock would ring, and then you could get up earlier.

S: I have an alarm clock already. It's brand new, I got it for Christmas, but my daddy will never set it up.

C: Ask your mom.

S: My mom can't do it because she's growing a new baby.

T1: So she can't set the alarm, huh? Okay, but, Sheila, . . .

S: It's not plugged in.

T1: Maybe that's something that you can think about, setting the alarm.

S: I can tell my dad to do it 'cause he's never done it. My mom told him to do it, but he hasn't done it since, like, a long time ago.

A: Well, why don't you have a big meeting with your parents, and tell them what you've been missing in school in class.

S: (Talks while holding her nose; cannot be understood.)

T2: Say it again, I can't hear your words like that, Sheila.

Children: (Laugh)

T2: We want to help you, but you seem to be playing, Sheila.

A: If you're not really serious about this, then we'll just cancel it.

T2: We can go on to something else. Do you want us to help you?

A: Then stop being so silly.

T2: Okay. Well, what were your words? About having a meeting?
S: Maybe at suppertime I could talk to my parents about it.
T2: That's a good idea.
A: You could write down, like, some rules.
T2: What's your idea, Emily?
E: When your mother gets her baby out of her stomach, she could, like, set the alarm clock.
S: That would be too much time, because then I can't wake up early enough for my time for the special helper. Then I'll have to be last on the special helper list.
T1: Well, let's see. Clark?
C: Well, how I get early is I wake up a little bit early enough, and I get dressed real fast, and then my mom can come to school real fast.

The children continue to give Sheila suggestions about how she can get up and get to school earlier. Throughout the discussion, they are engaged, interested, and concerned about Sheila's problem and genuinely want to help her. When Sheila acts silly, her classmate Andrea even rebukes her mildly, reminding her that this is her problem, and if she wants help in solving it, then she must take it seriously. Discussions such as this contribute to the feeling of community by involving everyone in helping a friend with a problem. The teachers do not pass judgment on children's ideas, even Sheila's idea that her mother cannot set the alarm because she is pregnant.

Discussing Good Game Partners

Group time is also, of course, a good time to engage children in generating solutions to problems that affect everyone. During a group time in Beth Van Meeteren's 1st- and 2nd-grade Freeburg class, a child complained that his partner was lazy and did not stay with their math game. The teacher broadened this into a discussion of what makes a good game partner and wrote what the children said on the board.

T: You said he was lazy and that he doesn't stick with it. Do you like to play with someone who gets up and quits?
Children: (In unison) No!
T: Or do you like to play with someone who stays in the game?
Children: (In unison) Yes!
T: (Writes on whiteboard) Okay. No quitting. Stays in the game. What else do you like about someone who works [unintelligible]? Norman?
N: I don't want to play with somebody who says I cheat.

T: Okay, you'd rather not have them say, "You cheated." You'd rather have them say, "I disagree with that"? You want them to say that?

N: Yeah.

T: Okay (writes), you'd rather have them say, "I disagree," not "You cheated." And then if they disagree, you work it out? Jack?

J: I don't play with anyone who says (shouting), "You cheat, you little [unintelligible]!"

T: So you agree with Norman. You'd rather have them say, "I disagree."

C: No, I don't want them to say, "You cheat!" if I won.

T: Oh, so you'd rather for them to be happy for you if you won?

C: Yeah.

C: I want to play with Waynette.

Children: I want to play with Waynette.

T: Why does everyone want to play with Waynette?

Children: She doesn't cheat, and she [unintelligible].

T: Let's talk about games you want out.

Children: (Call out) Pick-Up Sticks, Tapatan, Bingo [and several other games].

T: (Writes names of games on board)

(Children group themselves and select a game to play.)

In this short, spontaneous discussion just before children play math games, they have the opportunity to think for a moment about what kind of partner they want and what kind of partner they need to be.

Celebrating Together

Group time is a good time for celebrations such as birthdays. We witnessed a particularly endearing birthday ritual at the Human Development Laboratory School, invented by Peige Fuller, in a class of 3½- to 4½-year-olds. Usually, parents would bring cake or cupcakes to school on their child's birthday, and there would be a party after morning activities. (We should note that this event occurred before the initiatives to ban birthday cakes and other sugary sweets from schools.) Peige (T) puts the cake in the center of the circle, holds the child in her lap, and tells this story.

T: Once upon a time there was a man and a woman and their names were Velma and Michael. And they loved each other very, very much so they got married. And before long, Velma's tummy started to grow bigger and bigger, and do you know what she was growing in there?

N: What?

C: A baby.

T: She was growing a baby in there. And one day that baby was born.
     And they named that tiny little baby Marcel.
C: Marcel!
T: They did. And he was so little, you could hold him in your arm
     (pantomimes holding a baby) and he had tiny little fingers and tiny
     little toes and a tiny little nose. And before long he started making
     noises that sounded like (makes baby noises). Just like that. Little baby
     noises. Well, then he grew and grew and when he was 1 year old, do
     you know what he could do?
Children: What?
T: Walk. He could walk a little bit. Just baby steps. And when he wanted
     something, he said, "Aw baw," and that meant "I want a ball."
C: Why?
T: He'd say "Aw awa," and that meant "I want water."
C: Agua!
T: Uh huh, he did. When he was a baby. And before you knew it, he
     grew and grew and he was 2 years old. And he could do many, many
     things. He could speak more regularly now.
C: He was a big boy.
T: Then he grew and grew some more. He came to school. He made
     friends, like Kurt and Nina and Carson.
C: And like me.
T: And he made friends like Danny and Nate and Kiko, and like Wilson
     and Shelly and Monte and Sophia and Paulo. And then he was 3. And
     then one day do you know what happened?
Children: What?
T: One day this boy who used to be a little baby, and who used to be 1
     and who used to be 2 and who used to be 3, turned 4 years old.
C: And Marcel!
T: That's right. (Peige then lights birthday candles, they sing "Happy
     Birthday," and Marcel blows out the candles.)

Peige told a birthday story for every child, customizing it each time
for the particular child, including names of siblings and other relevant
information. Sometimes, she showed pictures of the child as a baby or
pictures of the mother with her big tummy. The children loved these
stories and never grew tired of them. This example illustrates how celebrations provide an opportunity at group time to provide individual
children with recognition in the group and at the same time make children known to one another, further developing the sociomoral atmosphere of mutual respect.

Group Time Lost, Group Time Regained

The following story describes a constructivist kindergarten class at the Human Development Laboratory School experiencing problems with group time and the steps taken by the teachers as they tried to deal with their problem.

Once there was a kindergarten class that had two group times every morning. During the first group time at 9:00 A.M., they had many things to do. They usually started with a song or two. They figured out who was the special helper for that day. The special helper counted to see how many people were in the class. Sometimes, the special helper had trouble counting, and had to start over, again and again, while the class waited. Then, the children who were scheduled to share that day shared what they brought to class. Sometimes, four or five people shared, and it took a long time. Then the teachers introduced the activities for the morning and discussed some of them. That, too, took a long time. Sometimes the teacher read a story or a poem. Sometimes, they had problems to solve, and they voted to make decisions. They often did not begin activities until 9:50 A.M.

Many children found it hard to sit still and listen for such a long time. They were restless, and they talked out, forgetting to raise their hands. Sometimes there were conflicts between children at group time, and this upset the teachers, who wanted children to listen to each other and respect each other.

After the morning activity time, the class had another group time. At second group, they talked about what they did during activities. Sometimes they had stories and songs. If the children scheduled to share did not get a chance at first group, they shared at second group. Soon, second group, too, became very long. Children were restless and eager to go outside and play. Teachers were frustrated because children seemed not to listen to them or to each other.

Finally, one day, the teachers decided that they had had enough! Children did not like group time, they thought, so they would just quit having group time. When children came on Monday, teachers told them there was not going to be a group time. "Just go straight to activities," they said. "We're not going to have group time unless children want it." Children were pleased. They cheered and said they did not like group time. For 2 days they did not have group time.

On the 3rd day, one child decided that they needed to plan their Halloween party. But how could they plan if they never had group time? She went around the class, gathering names of children who wanted a group, to plan their party. All but four children signed the paper. So all those who wanted to plan stayed inside and had a group time.

Slowly, they started having group time after activities again. Children had the option of staying for group time or going outside. At first, many children went outside, but soon, they were all staying for group. They liked being together, talking about what they did during activities, singing songs, hearing stories.

After about 3 weeks, they started having group time regularly again. However, teachers changed group time. They did not spend a long time doing attendance, and they quit doing sharing. Teachers talked about having short groups and getting to activities quickly. With shorter groups, children were paying attention better and not getting so restless. They still forgot to raise their hands sometimes, but not as much as before. Teachers were not spending so much time telling children to be quiet, raise their hands, or take turns. Everyone seemed to enjoy group time more.

Doing away with group was fairly dramatic, but the teachers thought it was necessary. They hoped that children would recognize the usefulness of group time and would come to miss it. Children did, and when they found their own reasons to participate in group time, they suggested having it again. However, the teachers also learned something in this experience. They learned that the important part of group time was wanting to be together as a community of people who listen to each other, plan things together, and make group decisions.

7

Rule Making

A unique characteristic of constructivist education is that the teacher shares with children much of the responsibility and power to make rules, insofar as children are able to do so. We refer to *rules* as formal agreements between teacher and children and among children about how to organize and regulate the operation of the classroom, including interpersonal relationships. In the constructivist view, rules are not just a means to the end of smooth classroom organization. Although they do serve this function, children's experiences in rule making fulfill developmental goals. We hope to convince the reader that rules made by children are better accepted and more conscientiously followed than rules given ready-made by adults. In this chapter, we present the objectives of involving children in rule making and discuss principles of teaching. Finally, the role of norms or teacher-made rules is discussed.

OBJECTIVES

The overarching objective of involving children in rule making is to contribute to an atmosphere of mutual respect in which teachers minimize the use of external control, and children practice self-regulation and cooperation. Inviting children to make rules and decisions is one way the teacher can reduce heteronomy and promote autonomy (see Chapter 3).

Three specific objectives of involving children in the rule-making process are (1) to promote feelings of necessity about rules and fairness, (2) to promote feelings of ownership of classroom rules and procedures, and (3) to promote feelings of shared responsibility for what happens in the class and how the group gets along together.

Through reflecting on the problems of classroom life together children can be led to realize the necessity for rules. By participating in the determination of rules, children will have the chance to understand why they have particular rules. Piaget (1932/1965) commented that "every rule, whether it be imposed on the younger by the older child, or upon the child by the adult, begins by remaining external to the mind before it comes to be really interiorized" (p. 185). We want children to follow rules because they understand their meaning and agree with their necessity.

Rule making presents a clear opportunity for children to exercise autonomy. Many teachers feel nervous at first about sharing the responsibility for rule making with children. They may believe children cannot make rules. They may fear that children will make unacceptable rules or, worse yet, no rules at all. These fears have not been realized in our experiences of observing young children participate in rule making. Of course, the constructivist teacher does not turn all rule making over to children, but rather, makes decisions based on what children are able to do. The teacher exercises leadership in guiding the rule-making process and the development of children's attitudes and knowledge about rule making. We suggest some principles of teaching for conducting rule making, offer some ideas for how to record and post rules that children make, and discuss involving children in enforcing rules and determining consequences for failure to follow rules.

PRINCIPLES OF TEACHING

Teachers who have never involved children in rule making may be tempted to start out with a few of their own rules and simply invite children to add some of their own. We urge teachers to refrain from this course. Although we recognize that teachers do feel that certain rules are necessary, we hope to convince the reader that with careful guidance, children can propose these. We suggest nine principles of teaching:

1. Conduct rule-making discussions as a response to a particular need or problem
2. Emphasize the reasons for rules
3. Accept children's words, ideas, and organization
4. Lead children toward "do" rules
5. Cultivate the attitude that rules can be changed
6. When children suggest unacceptable rules, respond with persuasion and explanation
7. Emphasize that teachers also must follow rules
8. Record and post rules
9. Encourage children to enforce rules

We discuss these rule-making principles below and give classroom examples.

1. Conduct Rule-Making Discussions as a Response to a Particular Need or Problem

The most productive rule making occurs when a problem exists in the classroom. A rule-making meeting might begin with the introduction "I have noticed that we have been having a problem with [children hurting other children, children taking turns with the blocks, being able to hear each others' words at circle, etc.]. What can we do about this problem? Does anyone have a suggestion about how we can solve this problem?" Young children's attention spans for rule discussions can be fairly short, so it is practical to discuss rules for one problem at a time. Sometimes the discussion of even one problem takes a considerable amount of time, and this makes it even more important to keep the focus on only one problem.

For example, in the constructivist Community described in Chapter 1, Mary Wells confronts the problem that a few children are mistreating the guinea pig. Other children are upset and complain. Mary makes this the occasion for asking, "Do we need to make rules about how to treat the guinea pig?" The following rules were made by the children.

- Ask Mrs. Wells before you get the guinea pig out.
- Be careful—no hurting the guinea pig.
- Don't squeeze, drop, or throw him. Hold him gently.
- Don't put him on the floor. Hold him.
- Don't pull his hair. Be gentle.
- Don't pull his hand or sit on him.
- Don't let him down in the house. Hold him in a blanket.
- Hold him like a baby.

A similar problem arose in Gwen Harmon's classroom at Freeburg with regard to treatment of the chicks they hatched. When Gwen brought to group time the problem that some of the chicks were being hurt, her 4-year-olds made the following rules.

- Pick them up safely.
- Don't push them.
- We don't squeeze them.
- Don't put things in their box.
- Don't punch them.
- Don't put them on the lightbulb.
- Don't drop them.

- Don't pick them up by their wings.
- Don't color on them.
- Don't pull their heads off.

These examples illustrate how important it is for children to create their own rules. They also show that the rules that make sense to children include many that adults would never think of proposing.

After children are accustomed to rule making, they often express the need to make rules when they observe a problem. Sometimes they reveal surprising competencies in making very precise rules so that children will know exactly what to do. In Dora Chen's classroom at the Human Development Laboratory School, a 4-year-old saw another child eating snack during cleanup and felt this should not occur. He told Dora, who raised the issue at group time. A 17-minute discussion followed in which children suggested various possibilities. The teacher clarified the choice between "No snack during cleanup; throw it away" and "Finish snack before going outdoors," and children voted. The new stringent rule, to throw away unfinished snack when cleanup begins, was driven by children's interest and concern that went beyond what the teacher would have suggested.

If a teacher believes that a particular rule is important, then he or she must figure out how to present the problem to the class in such a way that children will also see the necessity for the rule. For example, consider a common elementary school rule: "Walk in a straight, single-file line in the hallways." This usually seems arbitrary to children, and it often does not work without coercive consequences. Imagine yourself as a teacher, trying to convince children to accept this rule as necessary. What is the justification for the rule? Is it a problem in the school? Do children make so much noise in the halls that it disrupts other classes? If so, it is still possible to avoid arbitrary imposition of a rule. Instead, the teacher can present the problem: "I have noticed that sometimes children make a lot of noise when we walk through the halls, and it bothers the other classes. Other teachers have told me that their children can't hear each other when our class walks past their room. What can we do about this problem?" Children may think of solutions different from walking in a single-file line, such as making the rule that children must be quiet in the halls or that children should walk through the halls with their hands over their mouths, to keep from talking. If everyone agrees, the group's solution might solve the problem while allowing children to be self-regulating. If other classes are not actually being disturbed, and children feel that a bit of talking should be acceptable, then perhaps the teacher should be open to a rule that soft talking in the hallway in acceptable. After all, adults in a similar situation seldom walk together without talking.

Generally, it is not a good idea simply to ask children to suggest rules without connecting the need for rules to specific problems. With teacher colleagues we have experimented with rule making at the beginning of the school year. The results of these experiments have been mixed when the teacher simply asks open-ended questions such as "Can you think of any rules we need in our classroom?" This invitation is too broad and usually leads to long litanies of "don'ts" that often do not have any relation to needs in the life of the classroom. For example, we have heard children suggest rules to address problems that had never occurred in the classroom, such as "No throwing blocks at the fish tank" and "No throwing chairs." We have also heard young children repeat rules they knew from other contexts, such as "Never talk to strangers." They may interpret the teacher's request as "Tell me the rules you know." In one instance, we saw children enter into a competition for the most outrageous or elaborate rule. We realized that children were suggesting rules only because the teacher asked them to, not out of any personal need to figure out how to regulate themselves. If a teacher wants children to make rules at the beginning of the year, we suggest focusing the children's attention on areas of potential problems. For example, the teacher can provide leadership by asking, "Can the whole class fit in the block center at the same time? What rules do we need so everyone can have a fair turn with blocks?"

2. Emphasize the Reasons for Rules

Constructivist teachers convey the message that the purpose of rules is to make the classroom a safe, comfortable place for everyone. When they raise a problem of physical, intellectual, or emotional safety, they talk about their responsibility to make sure all children are safe, have an opportunity to participate in activities, and feel good about being in the classroom.

When children suggest a rule, the teacher can ask, "Why do we need that rule?" or "Why is that a good rule?" If they cannot answer, the teacher might ask, "What would happen if children [do whatever the rule forbids]?" Generally children answer that hitting and kicking hurt. To emphasize the purpose of a rule, the teacher may want to include the reason in the statement of the rule. For example, "Don't hit, because hitting hurts," "Don't kick the door, because you might hurt the door and you might hurt your foot," and "No throwing sand, because it might get in someone's eyes." It is important to have sufficient discussion so that all children are clear about the necessity for a rule. If the teacher simply writes a rule without discussion of its reason, children may not feel the need to follow it.

Sherice Hetrick-Orton discovered in her Freeburg kindergarten classroom that when rules are made about activities children are invested in, they care about the reasons for rules. Her children were passionate about block building and created complex structures of which they were justly proud. When children became concerned about problems in the block area, they were eager to make rules and post them. The rules they made were the following:

- No knocking people's stuff down ("stuff" was later changed by the children to read "structure" when they learned that word)
- Keep hands off other people's stuff ("stuff" later changed to "structure")
- Three friends in the block area at one time (later changed by the children to four friends)

Sherice reported that the children cared about and referred to these rules more than other rules made at her initiative.

3.   Accept Children's Words, Ideas, and Organization

Even if children's wording is awkward, it is important to use it anyway. The grammar matters less than the spirit of the rule. Children will remember and respect the rule more if it is in their own words. In the following example at the Human Development Laboratory School, Peige Fuller (T) is preparing to have a group time discussion because her 3- and 4-year-old children have been hurting each other. Before the discussion begins, Zelna calls Carol a name, and Norma calls this to the teacher's attention.

N: Carol is sad.
T: I can see that. Do you know why?
C: Zelna called me "a naughty girl."
T: Are you a naughty girl?
C: (Crying) Nooo! (Peige suggests that maybe some of the children near Carol could hug her and make her feel better. They do, and Carol starts to cheer up a little bit.)
T: Oh, I see a smile! I think she feels loved! Okay, now Carol, what do you want to be called?
C: My name.
T: Your name. So should we have a rule about calling people by their names?
Children: Yeah!

T: How should we write that? Tell me how to write that.
C: Write "Call them your name."
T: (Writes and repeats) "Call them your name."
C: Don't call them "naughty girl" or "naughty boy."
T: (Writes and repeats) "Don't call them 'naughty girl' or 'naughty boy.'"
   Okay, so that takes care of kids using hurtful words. What about people using hurtful hands and feet?

The suggested rule contains questionable grammar, but the meaning is clear to the children. The wording helps to remind the children of why Carol wanted to make the rule and why they need that particular rule.

It is also important to accept children's organization of rules. Imposing an organizational structure on the rules may result in children's failure to understand them and lack of acceptance. Consider the rule discussion in Angie Quesada's class of kindergarten and 1st-grade children at the Sunset-Pearl Elementary School in Houston, Texas, where a child tries to impose an organization. This is an example of what happens when children's logic does not permit them to accept one child's more sophisticated organization. Earlier in the discussion, children suggested five rules: "No slapping in the face," "No hitting in anybody's eye," "No pinching," "No kicking," and "No fighting." Then Eldon suggests that they simply make the rule "Don't hurt anybody," and erase all the other rules. He explains, "'No hurting anyone' would be the same as writing all of that that's already on there." It is clear that many children in the class do not understand Eldon's logic that the category "No hurting" includes all specific types of hurting (an example of class inclusion). Children suggest additional rules that Eldon thinks are included under his no-hurting rule. He objects, "It doesn't make sense to have some things and other rules that mean the same thing. That's just a waste of paper." Angie suggests that they vote about whether or not to erase rules. She starts by having children vote on whether to keep the rule "No slapping in the face," since Eldon claims that the no-hurting rule includes slapping. The children vote to cross out the slapping rule, and Don exclaims, "We can slap people's face! We don't have a rule!" The more children discuss, the clearer it becomes that the other children do not understand the inclusive meaning of Eldon's rule. The rest of the children feel a need for each specific rule. Finally, Angie suggests that they vote on whether to keep all the rules or just have Eldon's rule. Despite Eldon's protests, children vote to keep all the rules, including Eldon's rule, "Don't hurt anyone." The resulting list is thus not a neat logical form, but it makes sense to most of the children. In such a situation, the teacher can say, "That's a good idea, Eldon, but the other children don't agree today."

4. Lead Children Toward "Do" Rules

Young children, when first invited to generate rules for the classroom, tend to suggest "Don't" rules. The preceding examples from Angie's class are typical. Children find it much easier to think of rules as prohibitions. The teacher should not reject "don't" rules. These are often useful and appropriate. However, children can be led to think of things that they *can* do. At the end of the example from Peige's class (above), the teacher asks children what they should do about children who use hurtful hands and feet. The discussion continues.

C: That hurts people, and it's not nice.
T: That hurts them, and they don't like it. So what should we tell children to do?
C: Use their words.
T: Tell them to use their words? (Writes and repeats) "Use their words."
C: And if the words don't work, go get the teacher.
T: (Writes and repeats) "And if the words don't work, go get the teacher." Okay. Is there any other guideline that we need to be able to have friendly people in our class?
C: Friendly hands.
C: And friendly words.
T: (Writes and repeats) "Friendly hands and friendly words." Is that how everyone wants their friends to treat them? With friendly hands and friendly words? Okay.
C: No hitting.
T: Okay. (Writes and repeats) "No hitting." Investigators, would you like to hear what you wrote? Let's read this so you can hear what it is that we said are the guidelines for having happy people in our class. Okay. (She reads the rules.)
T: That should about do it. That's it, only four little guidelines. Four little rules will help us to be very happy people in the Investigators class.

Assisted by Peige, the children create a mixture of do rules and don't rules that expresses how they want to be treated in the classroom.

5. Cultivate the Attitude That Rules Can Be Changed

Sometimes rules need to be changed. In the following example from Coreen's kindergarten class at the Human Development Laboratory School, an occasion arises in which the teacher (T) thinks perhaps the rule about block structures might need to be revised. The rule, made by children, states that block structures can remain standing for 1 day and then have to be taken down during cleanup time. However, Sheila is sad because her block structure was knocked down according to the rule, and she wanted it to remain so that her father could see it when he picked her up that afternoon. Coreen raises the problem at group time.

T: So should we still keep that rule, Sheila, of the 1 day?
Children: Yeah. No.
S: I think . . . I'd rather . . . mostly I prefer that it would be for 3 days.
T: For 3 days?
C: No.
T: Well, if you have another idea, then raise your hand and we'll come to you. So Sheila thinks we should have it for 3 days. Harry wants to say something about that.
C: I want to say something. If she gets 3 when she gets her structure, then we can keep ours for 3 days.
C: If Sheila gets 3 days and we don't, then it won't be fair, so 3 days.
S: You guys are gonna get 3 days if you want to.
T: So you think 3 days. Connie, what do you think? Is there any problem with that?
C: Well, what I think we should do is we should keep our structures for 5 days, and after 5 days we have to knock it down.
T: But you know what? Five days is kind of like a whole week. You think kids should keep their structures up for a whole week?
C: (Nods yes)
Children: Yeah. No.
T: It seems like you really want to keep your structures up for a longer time. Does anyone see any problems with kids having it 3 and 5 days? That's no problem? Norma, what do you think; what could be a problem if we kept them up that long?
N: If we keep it up 5 days, then that would mean a whole week. And then after a whole week the other kids would have to keep their structure up for a whole week and if they built a big structure and it was blocking the walkway, then how would people walk through? And how would people walk through the walkway? Would they have to bam it down?
T: Okay, yeah, you know, I do see a problem too, Norma. The other problem is that we have how many kids in our room? We have 18 kids. The problem is, would everyone be able to have a turn if you guys keep it up for 3 days? That's why we made the rule of 1 day—because there were a lot of kids in the room. (The class votes and decides to allow block structures to remain up for 5 days.)

T: Okay. It seems like a lot of people want to keep their structures up for a long time. And most people don't have any problems with that, so we'll try it and see what happens. If it doesn't work, then we'll need to come back and try and make a better solution. Okay. So it's going to be that kids who make a structure get to keep it up for the whole week.

Despite the teacher's objections and attempts to help children foresee the problems that might arise when blocks are left up for an entire week, the class votes for 5 days. The teacher's statement that they can always come back and reconsider the rule if it does not work helps children begin to learn that rules are not sacred and immutable. Rather, rules exist to serve specific purposes. When the rules no longer serve the purpose for which they were designed, or when the situation changes, the rules can change, too.

6.   When Children Suggest Unacceptable Rules, Respond with Persuasion and Explanation

During the course of considering solutions to many problems, children inevitably suggest unworkable rules. In the example from Coreen's class (above), the teacher did not veto the children's decision to leave block structures up for 5 days, even though she foresaw problems. Unless the teacher thinks the rule could lead to consequences that cannot responsibly be permitted, children should be allowed to discover for themselves that a rule is unworkable. In this way, when they revise the rule, they will do so with a more differentiated understanding of the problem they are addressing. More complex thinking reflects intellectual as well as sociomoral progress.

Children sometimes suggest rules that the teacher cannot accept. In Chapter 8, we see that Peige tells children why they cannot go on a picnic away from school with only one teacher to supervise. When the teacher must veto a suggestion, it is important to explain why it must be rejected. This can be done respectfully, treating children as reasonable human beings who may want to withdraw an idea whose unacceptability is explained.

7.   Emphasize That Teachers Also Must Follow Rules

Piaget (1932/1965) pointed out that it is useful for adults to stress their own obligations to others, in order to promote such feelings in children. We know one teacher who would on occasion intentionally violate a rule in order to give children the opportunity to remind her of the rule. She wanted to underscore the point that the teacher is a member of the group and must live by the same rules as everyone else in the class. For example, one rule forbade sitting on the tables. Occasionally, she would casually sit on a table while talking to a child. Inevitably, one child would notice and correct her, whereby she would exclaim, "Oh, I forgot our rule! We can't sit on the tables. We sit on chairs and on the floor." In Chapter 8, we present an example of group decision making in which the teacher explains that she has to follow guidelines that prevent her from taking the children by herself out of the building for a walk.

In one constructivist class, the teacher offered children the opportunity to suggest rules for her to follow. Understanding that the teacher must follow rules can be especially helpful to children who have had previous experience with a heteronomous teacher. Examples of rules for teachers include "Let us look at books during nap time if we are not sleepy" and "Don't throw away children's art." By opening this opportunity to children, teachers can learn about some issues that children would not be likely to raise without a special invitation. Teachers can also suggest rules for themselves. The teacher might propose the rule "The teacher will respect children by letting them choose their activities."

8. Record and Post Rules

Rules made by children become a familiar part of the constructivist classroom culture. One way to achieve this is to post written rules on a bulletin board or in the area of the classroom where certain rules are needed. We have found that even children who cannot read recognize and remember written rules when they have been involved in their creation. For this reason, rules should be written down and placed where children can find and refer to them easily. One teacher, Karen Capo, after making rules with her kindergarten class at the Human Development Laboratory School, made a book with each rule on a single page and asked the children to illustrate each rule. Each child signed the title page. Karen then laminated the pages and bound them in such a way that new pages could be added as needed. The rule book remained in the reading center of the classroom for the entire year, and many times she saw children dash to get the book, open it, point to a page, and say, "Look, it says right here that you can't do that. You gotta follow our rule."

Having the children's rules posted in the classroom also allows the teacher to emphasize that the moral authority of the classroom comes not just from the teacher but from the children themselves. About 2 weeks after the rule discussion (above) in Peige's class, she was concerned about an increase in violations, and started morning circle by reading the rules to children again.

T: Before we get started with morning circle, do you remember what
     these are about? These rules?

H: No.

T: These are rules that you guys told me to write. You told me the words,
     and I wrote your words down. They talk about how we want to be
     treated in our classroom. Do you remember that? Because some
     people were doing some hurting of feelings and of bodies, and we
     wrote these words so that people would know how to be friends in
     class. Do you remember what these are about?

C: The rules about so we can make happy children and some kids are not
     following them.

T: That is exactly it. Let's read them again so you can remember what
     they are. (Points to the written rules) This one is "Call them your name.
     Don't call them 'naughty girl' or 'naughty boy.'"

C: That's Carol.

T: So people want to be called their own name. Okay. (Reading) "Use
     their words. And if the words don't work, go get the teacher." If the
     words don't work, can you pinch and then go tell the teacher?

Children: No!

T: If your words don't work, can you hit them and then go tell the
     teacher?

C: Where's mine [his rule]?

T: Don, if your words don't work and somebody kicks you, can you kick
     them back?

C: No, I don't kick back.

T: What do you do?

C: Go tell the teacher.

C: You know what happened outside today? Bill throwed sand in my
     mouth.

T: Really? What did you do?

C: I telled the teacher.

T: Did the teacher help you talk to Bill?

C: Yes.

T: That's important. This one says, "Friendly hands and friendly words."
     So we want to use friendly hands and friendly words. Hey, you know
     what we could do? We could practice friendly hands.

C   What is that?

T: You cross your hands over (demonstrates crossing her arms). Now
     hold the hand of the person next to you. Now shake. That's the biggest
     handshake. That's friendly hands, huh?

C: Marvin doesn't have his hands crossed.

T: That's okay. Now this one says, "No hitting."

C: I did that.
T: Do you guys remember those rules?
Children: Yeah!
T: What do you think? Do you think we can remember them during outside time and during activity time?
Children: Yeah!

Especially with young children, it may be necessary to review the rules frequently, to help children remember them. This need not be an unpleasant task. As we see above, Peige made reading the rules an occasion for a friendly, shared experience.

9.   Encourage Children to Enforce Rules

Earlier we stated that one of the objectives of engaging children in rule making is to promote feelings of ownership of classroom rules. These feelings of ownership can develop into willingness to enforce rules fairly. Karen Capo's experience with the book of class rules, described above, is one example of this. When children feel the rules are theirs, they turn to the rules when they need them or when they need others to follow them. Young children can develop the ability to take responsibility for regulating their own behavior with the help of rules.

In the following example, Peige (T) and two other children help David remind Gavin of one of the rules. A rule in the class states, "No touching when people say no." Children made this rule in response to the problem of some children touching others in ways that they did not like.

G: (Puts his hand on David's leg)
D: Stop it, Gavin.
G: [Unintelligible]
D: (To the teacher) Gavin touched me.
T: (To David) And what will you do about this?
D: I don't . . . (to Gavin) I don't want . . . No! (To T) You gotta say, "The rule says ____," to Gavin.
T: Oh, you can tell Gavin what the rule says.
D: (To Gavin) The rule says, "No touching."
L: "When they say no."
W: "When they say no."
L: "No touching when people say no."
D: Yeah.
T: "No touching when people say no." Okay.

Peige does not take responsibility for reminding Gavin of the rule but supports and encourages David's reminding Gavin. She remains close by, if needed, but expresses confidence in David's ability to handle the situation.

Children can also be involved in helping to decide consequences for breaking rules, although this can be a little tricky at times. Young children's ideas about justice are often very harsh, and they can show a decided lack of empathy in dealing with rule infractions. For example, in a kindergarten class at the Human Development Laboratory School where there is a problem with children spilling water on the floor around the water table, a child slips on the wet floor and Coreen calls a class meeting about the problem. She explains that a wet floor is dangerous and asks the children what they think should be done. One child suggests that the children who make a mess at the water table should never be allowed to use the water table ever again. The teacher points out, "Never is a long time. I know sometimes I get careless and spill water on the floor accidentally." She suggests tempering justice with mercy: "I wonder if they could play at the water table again if they promise to be careful." Finally, the class decides that if a person makes a mess at the water table, they cannot go there for 3 days.

TEACHER-MADE CLASSROOM NORMS

One common misunderstanding of constructivist education is that teachers never make rules except in consultation with children. This is not entirely accurate. The responsible teacher also communicates norms— specific expectations for children's behavior—that are necessary for smooth operation of the classroom and for children's protection. Some teachers we know refer to these as "teacher rules" or "non-negotiables." Constructivist teachers always explain the reasons for norms and, as often as possible, give children the possibility to make these rules for themselves. Norms, like rules, become part of the culture of the classroom. Unlike rules made by children, however, these norms are not always written down and posted. Drawing from interviews of teachers at the Freeburg School about the norms and rules in their classrooms, we identify three kinds of norms that seem distinct from the rules that children make: safety and health norms, moral norms, and discretionary norms. We consider each of these types of norms and give examples.

Safety and Health Norms

Teachers must insist that children abide by certain safety and health norms that ensure children's well-being. Freeburg teachers mentioned the following norms of this type.

Indoors

- Stay inside the classroom unless accompanied by an adult
- No running in the hallways
- No climbing up the outside of the loft
- Wear safety goggles at the woodworking bench
- Keep water in the water table
- Don't make the water fountain spray outside the sink
- Don't go into the storage closet
- Puppets don't bite
- No weapons play
- Lie down at rest time
- Wash hands before eating or cooking
- Don't lick the stirring spoon in cooking
- Ask a teacher to plug in appliances

Bathroom

Christina Sales discovered that she had expectations about use of the classroom bathroom at Freeburg that were not shared by her 3-year-old children. When she discovered a dirty bathroom with paper all over the floor and in the sink, water on the floor, and so on, she decided that in some matters her children needed instruction. She posted the following list in the bathroom, and gathered all the children at the bathroom to demonstrate and explain these norms:

- Boys, lift the lid
- If you sit down, you don't need to lift the lid
- Put the lid down when you are done pottying
- Wipe your bottom
- Flush
- Put soap on your hands and wash them
- Wipe your hands with one or two paper towels
- Throw paper towels in the garbage

Outdoors

- Stay inside the fence
- Keep shoes on
- Don't climb on the fence
- Don't climb on top of the trapeze bar
- Don't throw sand
- No crashing trikes or other vehicles

- One at a time on the slide
- Wear plastic shower cap when playing in the sand
- On a field trip, stay with the group

Although these norms are written in rule form here, they are not necessarily presented to children in this form. Instead, the teacher is likely to say to a child, "I can't let you _____ [run in the hallway, climb up the outside of the loft, throw sand, etc.], because it is dangerous and someone could get hurt."

Moral Norms

Moral norms are those that pertain to respect for people, animals, and the environment. They often relate to fairness of treatment and fairness in distribution of goods. Like the health and safety norms, teachers can enforce these norms even if a formal rule does not exist by simply treating them as expectations in the classroom.

People

- No hurting others' bodies (also a safety norm)
- No hurting others' feelings
- Don't call people names
- Take fair turns by using a sign-up list or other method
- Talk through a conflict until resolution
- You have to go to the Peace Chairs if somebody has a problem with you
- Be honest; no making up stories about what happened in a conflict
- Don't disturb others at rest time
- Cooperate with others in the use of scarce materials
- Don't talk over others at group time; be quiet unless you have the floor
- Wait while someone finishes using something you want
- No rolling eyes at people

Animals

- If you bring something alive into the classroom, try to make it comfortable
- Return an animal to its habitat after studying
- No hurting animals; take care of them

Environment

- Handle materials carefully; take care of them so all can enjoy
- Put materials away at cleanup time
- Put trash in trash can

Discretionary Norms

Discretionary norms pertain to routines and procedures to make the classroom run smoothly and make learning possible. They also include norms for politeness and individual responsibility that children need to know.

Routines

- Follow the daily schedule
- Sit with group at group time
- Wear a smock when painting or experimenting with water
- Do *have-tos* by required deadlines
- Don't use the bathroom or drinking fountain during group time (unless it is an emergency)
- Sit on your bottom at group time
- If you bring something to group time, put it behind your back

Manners

- When introduced to adults, don't call them by their first names without permission
- Wait until all are seated at lunch before eating
- Ask others to pass dishes
- Say "please," "thank you," and "excuse me"
- Push your chair in when you get up from a table

Individual Responsibility

- Clean up your place after lunch/snack
- If you take your jacket off, put it in your cubby

The reader can undoubtedly add other discretionary norms that are important in a classroom. We caution that these norms in classrooms can be extended beyond the "acceptable and necessary," resulting in a heteronomous classroom atmosphere. We simply want to point out that children in constructivist classrooms live in a society having numerous reasonable norms they are expected to follow. The existence of such norms does not contradict the general constructivist sociomoral atmosphere of mutual respect when accompanied by explanations children can understand. As children become more and more self-regulating, the norms become a part of the culture of the classroom.

Frequently, the focus of rule making involves a norm. If possible, it is always better for children to suggest a rule than for the teacher to give it to them ready-made.

8

Decision Making and Voting

A constructivist teacher can involve children in many other group decisions besides rule making. We discuss decision making about classroom activities, classroom procedures, and special problems that are common in constructivist classrooms. Next, we present principles of teaching, including issues concerning voting. Although voting is seldom necessary in rule making, it is often necessary in decision making because children disagree and suggest competing ideas. Finally, we share a story about voting gone awry when children learned that voting does not determine truth.

OBJECTIVES

The sociomoral rationale for encouraging children to make classroom decisions rests on the discussion of objectives of group time (see Chapter 6) and of rule making (see Chapter 7) that emphasize promoting children's decentering, perspective-taking, autonomy, mutual respect, and cooperation. Those details will not be repeated here, but we emphasize that when children exercise initiative to make group decisions, they feel ownership of what happens in their classroom. They are motivated to formulate and express opinions. Through exchanging points of view, children may be persuaded or make efforts to persuade others, thereby developing their interpersonal understanding. When teachers encourage voting as a tool in decision making, children have the opportunity to construct the idea of equality as they see that each person's opinion is valued and given equal weight in the decision-making process. In the process of voting, children can come to terms with the idea of majority rule yet develop sensitivity to minority positions.

In addition to these sociomoral objectives, children have opportunities to think about writing and number. Through conceptualizing and recording issues and votes, conviction is cultivated about the usefulness of written language. Similarly, as children count and compare votes, the teacher can help them decide which is more and predict how many more votes are needed for a particular decision. Thus, they construct number in a personally meaningful context.

DECISIONS ABOUT CLASSROOM ACTIVITIES

Young children are capable of many group decisions about activities in their classroom. They can sometimes be involved in deciding issues about the arrangement of the classroom, placement of materials, and choices of activities in the class. In Chapter 4 we describe Peige's experience of asking children what they wanted to learn about and then designing lesson plans around the children's interests. We recognize that curriculum is often mandated in schools. However, the teacher has considerable latitude in how to approach specific topics, and children's ideas can be solicited. When certain topics are mandated, constructivist teachers try to work children's ideas into the mandated ones. Or they provide the list and explain, "These are the things all 1st-grade children have a chance to learn about." The teacher can ask children which topic they would like to do first and how they would like to go about it. We have seen this approach used successfully with much older children. The idea is to engage children as decision makers, insofar as the teacher can do so. Children not only derive sociomoral advantages from this approach, but they also become invested in the teacher's academic goals.

Special class projects present an opportunity for children to make decisions. We have seen children design pretend center restaurants, plan a toy store for Christmas in which they build and "sell" toys to younger children, and plan parties for parents for which the children prepare all the decorations, food, and entertainment. These projects can be challenging for the teacher, who must work behind the scenes to make sure things run relatively smoothly, yet without taking over.

DECISIONS ABOUT CLASSROOM PROCEDURES

Children can take responsibility for deciding many classroom procedures, such as how to regulate turns being special helper, sharing privileges, and so on. Sometimes children themselves bring up problems regarding classroom procedures. In discussions about these decisions, the teacher must uphold values of fairness and equality because children may not yet have constructed these principles. In Coreen's (T) kindergarten class at the Human Development Laboratory School, one child, Wayne, objects to the way they regulate talking at circle, with the teacher calling on children whose hands are raised. He thinks there is a better way.

T: I knew that Emily wanted to talk because she raised her hand. Wayne, you don't want to raise your hand?

N: (Without raising her hand!) Then he shouldn't talk anymore.

T: Wayne, what would be a better idea instead of raising hands? What do you think? Does anyone know of any other way we could do it so everyone could talk and we won't talk at the same time?

W: I know.

T: What's another way?

W: Wait until someone else is finished.

T: Well, suppose two people decide to talk after someone is finished?

W: No, you see, the reason I wait until someone is finished is, like when Alice was talking, and she'd done, then I would talk, and then Carl would, and he would wait until I was finished.

They discuss this issue for quite some time. Wayne is convinced that children can take turns talking without raising hands. He has started to figure out the reciprocity of conversation. The teacher is skeptical that this will work and introduces the problem of what to do if more than one person talks at the same time. Wayne modifies his idea and the group agrees that if only one person has something to say, that person can speak out without raising a hand, but if more than one person speaks out, then they have to raise hands. This system works for the remainder of the year.

Kathy Thompson relates what happened at Freeburg when conflicts and chaos arose in her class of 3-year-olds over where to sit at group time. She suggested to children that they might like to have a place to sit that is just their place. After some discussion, they voted on two alternatives: (1) Sit where you like; and (2) Names on the carpet. Because they were so invested in the importance of this issue, these 3-year-olds were very attentive to the voting process and watched carefully as everyone took a turn putting his or her name card under the favored alternative on the magnetic board. More people voted for putting names on the carpet, and they then individually decided where they wanted their names. As days passed, another problem arose. Some children were pulling the names off the carpet. Kathy brought the problem to the group. They discussed how people did not know where to sit, and people became upset. At the end, all voted on the rule "Don't pull the names off." A child then suggested that they also needed a rule about pulling other people's names off. This was accepted unanimously. Kathy wrote all the rules and read them back to the children. She reports that group time transition went much more smoothly after children adopted these rules.

DECISIONS ABOUT SPECIAL PROBLEMS

Children can also be called upon to make decisions about special problems that arise in the classroom. In the following example at the Human Development Laboratory School, Peige (T) comes to the Investigators (3- and 4-year-olds) with a problem. She explains that workers are installing equipment on the playground, making it too dangerous for children to play there. Notice that Peige does not hesitate to inform children when an unworkable or unacceptable idea is suggested. However, when this is necessary, she explains the reasons clearly, in ways children can understand.

T: There are workers on the playground, and they have dangerous tools and stuff. So we can't be out there. What should we do instead?
S: Just play on the porch [concrete area on the playground just outside classrooms].
T: But we can't. Ann [the assistant director] said we can't play out there at all.
C: How about up in the booth [the large visitors' observation booth that sometimes serves as an early morning activity area]?
T: In the booth? I hear someone up in the booth already. Can you think of something we could do outside that would not be playing on the playground?
W: Maybe we could take care of this.
T: Take care of this? Like, could we go somewhere and do something interesting? What do you think?
C: We could go to the cougar's cage [the campus home of the university mascot].
T: We could go to the cougar's cage.
M: We could watch a videotape.
T: We could go to the cougar's cage and watch a videotape?
N: We could watch the water fountains.
T: You mean watch the water fountains on the walk?
N: Yes.
T: Okay, we could do that. We could go to the water fountains and the cougar's cage. What else, Sharon?
S: Take a little walk.

C: And watch a video, too.

T: Take a little walk and watch a video, too. Maybe we would have time for a video when we got back. What do you think, Gilbert?

G: Maybe a bus ride [on the university shuttle bus] would be good.

T: A bus ride would be good. What do you think, Zelna?

Z: Maybe we could go find caterpillars.

T: And you think we should find caterpillars while we're out there. Okay, what do you think about this? This might use everyone's idea. We could take a bus ride, then go to the cougar's cage. Then, on the way back from the cougar's cage, we could see the fountains. The whole time, we could be looking on the ground to see if we see caterpillars.

N: And some acorns.

T: And acorns. Then after that we can go back to school, and if we have time we could see a videotape.

Children: Yea!

T: What do you think?

G: We're gonna be hungry.

T: We are going to be hungry when we get back.

G: We could take our lunches on the bus ride.

T: Now that's an idea. What do you think?

C: And we could have them someplace at the water fountains.

T: Now the only problem with that, Gilbert, is that if we eat our lunches out there, we won't have time for a videotape. So we'll have to vote. Picnic or videotape.

H: You know what? I went on a bus and I saw a bus sign, and it said, "No eating on the bus."

T: If we carry our lunches and we keep them in the sack, could we take them with us?

H: No, I don't think so.

T: You don't think we could? But I've been on the bus before, Harlan, and if I keep my lunch in the lunch bag, they don't get mad. But if I eat it, they get mad.

H: You keep it in there?

T: You keep it in there and don't eat it.

H: You keep it in there and they didn't get mad?

T: No, they didn't get mad. It was okay for me to carry it on, but if I unwrapped it and ate it, then they said I couldn't do that. They said I had to put it away.

Z: Did you try to open it?

T: I tried one time because I didn't know the rule. And then the guy said, "You can't eat on the bus. Put it away." So I put it away and it was all right. Okay, let's see. Zelna, do you want to have a picnic or watch a video? Oh (to Elizabeth, the aide), what time do you have to leave?

E: 11:15.

T: Oh! We have a problem. This is not a possibility. Oh, this is such a serious dilemma.

H: What?

T: We cannot have a picnic this day.

G: Why?

T: Because Elizabeth [the aide] has to leave and go to her class.

(Note: This discussion is taking place at approximately 10:30. The problem is that the person scheduled to relieve Elizabeth at 11:15 would not know where to find the class if they took a walk, and that would leave one teacher with the entire class.)

C: Well, we could let her leave right now.

T: But then there's only one teacher, and what if somebody got out of control or had a problem?

C: We would have to wait for Ann [the assistant director] then.

T: Yeah, but see, I would be one teacher all alone with all these children, and do you know what? There are some rules that teachers have to follow. They are called guidelines for child care. Because we care for children, so we have to have guidelines for caring for children. And those guidelines say that we will have one teacher for every seven or eight children. That means that we have to have two teachers with this group. If we have only one teacher, we are breaking the rules, and I can't do that.

C: We could take Ann.

T: Elizabeth is going to see if there is someone else who can go with us. (Elizabeth returns with news that someone is available to go with them on their walk.)

Children: Yea!

T: Okay, great. Well, then let's make a decision. Zelna, picnic or video? (They vote by polling individuals in the circle and decide to go on the picnic.)

Peige wanted to involve the children in deciding what to do. However, she did not think it necessary to put every idea to a vote. Children's ideas were flowing freely, and for the most part, all fit together nicely. In this case, if Peige had put every idea to a vote, they would have spent their entire time deciding and would have had no time left to take their walk. Peige knew this, and so exercised leadership over the discussion, without dominating it.

PRINCIPLES OF TEACHING

Observation of decision making, as well as experimentation with voting in the classroom, led us to conceptualize six principles of teaching that can guide teachers in conducting decision-making discussions and voting on decisions where everyone does not agree. We present them here, along with examples taken from our observations and research.

1. Choose appropriate issues
2. Encourage discussion, accept differences of opinion, and define the alternatives
3. Suggest a vote only when differences of opinion exist
4. Use voting procedures understandable to children
5. Participate as a voter
6. Foster acceptance of majority rule and respect for minority views

1. Choose Appropriate Issues

How does the teacher decide what issues are appropriate to bring to a class for a decision? As in rule making, not all issues can be submitted to children. First, an issue should be of interest to children and affect the entire class, bearing on their life together. If an issue belongs to an individual child, or to two children, it is best handled with the parties involved. However, in Chapter 7 we describe an incident in which the distress of one child brings the attention of the entire class to the problem of whether block structures can remain standing in the block center for only 1 day. In the end, the group members become engaged in the issue and vote on what they want the rule to state. The teacher supports them in their spontaneous desire to make a group decision.

In choosing issues, the teacher must keep in mind that he or she does not have veto power after the fact. Once given, the power to make decisions is difficult to retract. Therefore, if a teacher knows ahead of time that he or she cannot live with what the group might decide, then this issue should not be offered to children for decision making.

2. Encourage Discussion, Accept Differences of Opinion, and Define the Alternatives

It is important to conduct a thorough discussion of the pros and cons of the children's alternatives. The teacher can ask children to share why they support their choice. If the alternatives are not already defined, children can help define them. Be sure that alternatives are stated clearly, preferably by children. The teacher can repeat a child's words, if necessary, to be sure the group understands them. Frequently, it is necessary to help a child articulate an idea so it is clear. If children do not understand what they are voting for, they will not make the connection between the process of voting and its result, and the outcome will seem arbitrary.

During this discussion period, it is important to write the alternatives on a chalkboard or a large sheet of paper, using language appropriate to the age of the children This helps children be clear on what they are voting for, even if they cannot read.

Notice in the following transcript how the teacher, Dora Chen (T), works to clarify exactly what children mean in a particularly difficult situation. In this class of 3- and 4-year-olds at the Human Development Laboratory School, one child notices that another is still eating snack during cleanup time. She believes this to be against the rule and raises the issue at circle. Some children suggest changing the rule.

T: So you think that when one light goes out for 5 more minutes, that's still time to finish up eating? Just like it's time to finish up writing names or finish up pictures and things. But when both lights are out for cleanup, then it's not time to finish up writing names and it's also not time to finish up snack.

A: Or you could, one day if you wanted to draw a picture that you didn't finish with, if you could start writing it, and finish it.

T: Can you say that again, Alton? I didn't really get that.

A: If you don't finish your picture at school, and it goes home, you could bring it back one day and draw the part of it.

T: You could finish it the next day?

A: Uh-huh.

G: Or you could finish it at home.

T: That's another good idea, Gabe. Anybody else have an idea about that? Chelsea?

C: I do. Well, first, after you, if you draw at that table there, and you do it before it's cleanup time or 5 more minutes, and when it's cleanup, then you clean up, and then when it's outside time, you can stay inside longer to do it.

T: You think that when it's cleanup they should clean up but then when children are going outside after group time, that they could stay longer and finish it up?

N: Well, if you leave your snack on the snack table, then we'll just think somebody is through and we'll just have to throw it away, and we'll just have to. We clean the snack table every cleanup time.

T: But Chelsea was saying that if they don't finish a drawing, or does this apply to snack too? If they don't finish snack, Chelsea, then after cleanup time and after group time, then if they save it, like on the shelf, then they could come and eat it, or take it outside on the bench and eat it, you think?

C: (Nods) Yeah.

T: Okay, so we can vote on whether they could save the snack that they have not finished eating, to eat during outside time, or that they will just have to clean up and throw it out. Is that right?

A: I know.

T: Yes, Alton?

A: What if the light goes off and someone has not taken a bite of their snack and someone takes it and—

M: Well, they can recognize the bite.

T: Let Alton finish his thought.

A: And if they, the people that want to eat it, and they didn't get a chance to bite it, and someone throws it away.

T: So if someone already took a bite of a snack, then it has to be thrown away, Alton, during cleanup time? So you are saying that when it's 5 more minutes,

A: No, cleanup.

T: When it's cleanup time. Well, if they were already eating snack or if they started eating snack, making snack at 5 more minutes, and the light goes off, they will have to throw it out?

A: And if they eat all their snack at cleanup, they can't do that.

T: Okay, so when the light goes out for cleanup time, they cannot eat their snack. They will have to throw it out, clean it up just like any other activity. Okay, that's Alton's idea. And Chelsea's idea was to give them a chance to come back and eat it after group, after cleanup. Right? Okay, Braden, you have something else to add about snack?

B: I thought maybe we might, we could bring it outside if they're not finished and they could eat it while some people are playing.

T: Okay, outside? So that Braden and Chelsea are saying that if someone has started to make snack at 5 more minutes and if during cleanup time they are not finished eating, then they could save it on a paper towel and maybe put it on that table there and save it until after cleanup and after group, and when everyone's outside and they could eat it outside? Give them a chance to finish eating that snack after group time?

B: (Nods)

T: Okay, then let's take a vote about that. (Stands up, writes on board) "No chance to finish eating snack during"—when it's time to clean

up? How about if I say "when the light goes out?" Does that make it
clearer?

Children: No.

T: (Reading) "No chance to finish snack when the light goes out." Well,
how about if I say, "Throw away snack during cleanup time?" Does
that make it clearer?

Children: No.

T: (Erases board) Let's try this again. I'm not saying it right today. Let's see.
How about "Children must clean up snack during cleanup time?"

A: No. No.

T: How shall I say it, Alton?

A: Say, if you . . . I don't know either.

M: I do, I do.

T: Yes, Malcolm?

M: Um, if the children take a bite of their snack and take a few bites, at 5
more minutes, and then the light goes out, you could just put it on the
shelf, not up there, but over there, and then—

A: That's the happy part.

T: That's the happy part, Alton says.

J: How about "No more eating at cleanup time?"

Children: Yeah, yeah.

T: That's great. (Writing) "No more eating during cleanup." That means,
this side here also means that you have to throw it away. That means
that you will not get to eat it, even afterwards, okay? (Writing) "Throw
out snack." And this side here, we will vote on Chelsea and Braden's
idea about getting a chance to finish it as part of outside, during
outside time, after group. Okay? So we will have (writing) "Get chance
to finish snack after cleanup and group time." Okay. Let's start with . . .
Think about which way you are going to vote for it, okay?

The teacher goes on to conduct the vote, and children decide the rule will
be that they must throw snack away during cleanup time. Children have
strong opinions about this topic, and they struggle to make themselves
understood by both the teacher and each other. We also want to draw
attention to the careful way in which the teacher makes sure that she cap-
tures on the chalkboard the exact rules the children suggest. She writes,
erases, checks with children, and rewrites, until she writes what the children want the proposed rule to state.

While helping children understand alternatives to be voted on, teachers should be alert to the fact that children often see no logical problem in
voting for two mutually exclusive possibilities. For example, if the field
trip choices are "zoo" and "farm," children may enthusiastically raise

hands for both. This is why we recommend voting with polling procedures (discussed below). When children are asked, "Do you want to go to the zoo or the farm?" the mutually exclusive nature of the choice is clearer to the child.

We have observed two types of errors in teachers' definitions of voting issues. One is failure to present alternatives, and the other is confusion of the nomination process with voting. Frequently, teachers who are inexperienced but committed to the idea of voting forget to present alternatives, and instead ask children to vote on a single activity. For example, we watched a kindergarten teacher ask, "Who wants to sing 'Down by the Bay'? Raise your hand." Without an alternative, children who raised their hands were not really making a choice but were simply responding to the teacher's enthusiasm. Voting should be employed to decide between two (or more) alternatives, such as "Sing a song" or "Hear a story."

We have also observed situations in which children thought they were nominating alternatives but teachers interpreted the nominations as votes. For example, in a kindergarten class in which a turtle had recently been added to the collection of animals, the teacher suggested at group time that they might want to name their turtle. She went around the circle, asking each child in turn his or her idea for a name and writing down every suggestion. Then, she looked at the list, noticed that two names had each been suggested twice, and declared that since those two names had got the most "votes," they would choose between those two names. The rest of the children's ideas for names were erased. This was very distressing for children whose ideas were discarded.

Similarly, in a kindergarten class, the children planned a picnic for Valentine's Day. [The previous day, they had made suggestions at group time about what foods they would like for their picnic.] The teacher had children vote on what foods to have. However, the teacher decided arbitrarily to limit the vote to the items that got the most "votes" (meaning nominations) yesterday. She looked at the list and saw four items that could be considered desserts: ice cream, popsicles, bubble gum, and hot chocolate with marshmallows. Ice cream and popsicles had received the most nominations, so she asked, "Who would like to have ice cream?" She did not specify that the vote is between ice cream and popsicles, and she ignored the suggestions for bubble gum and hot chocolate with marshmallows. She then looked for proteins on the list, and asked, "Who wants heart-shaped sandwiches?" without presenting another choice. When she got to the beverage, she asked "Who wants lemonade?" failing to mention the nominations of a soft drink and of milk.

In this teacher's defense, she wanted the children to make the decisions for the picnic, and she also wanted to ensure a balanced meal.

However, she could have done some organizing without being coercive or subtracting from the children's involvement. She might have had an easier and more fruitful class discussion if she had categorized, or enlisted the children's help in categorizing, the list of food ideas by food group (protein, fruit, dessert, beverage, etc.). Then the class could have voted on the choices within each category. In this way, children would have been involved in the process, while the teacher's concern for a well-balanced meal would have been satisfied.

3.   Suggest a Vote Only When Differences of Opinion Exist

Voting is a good tool for decision making only when a difference of opinion occurs or a choice must be made. We witnessed one group time in a kindergarten class in which the teacher suggested playing a favorite game. The children all cheered when the teacher made the suggestion. She then suggested that they vote. A vote was not necessary in this situation, as the teacher already had popular support for her idea. In contrast, in another kindergarten class at circle time, the teacher suggested doing a flannel board story. Some children called out, "The Three Bears!" while other children called out, "The Gingerbread Boy!" Under these circumstances, a vote was highly appropriate.

4.   Use Voting Procedures Understandable to Children

Voting is an integral part of the democratic procedures of the constructivist classroom. However, like so many constructivist activities, merely taking a vote is not enough to ensure that it promotes constructivist aims. Voting can be conducted in ways that defeat constructivist purposes. When preparing to conduct a vote, it is crucial to make sure that children understand the method of voting. If the children cannot follow the vote, the outcome will appear to be arbitrary, undermining the whole purpose. The particular method of voting used in any class will vary, depending on the age and developmental level of the children. Voting methods we review here include raising hands, polling children, casting ballots, and counting bodies in a line. We also discuss how to deal with tie votes and lobbying.

Counting Raised Hands

The most familiar method of voting, counting raised hands, has serious problems when used with young children. We cannot recommend it, for a variety of reasons. Often, very young children (4 years and under, and some inexperienced 5-year-olds) are so excited to raise their hands that as soon as the teacher says, "Raise your hand if —," hands shoot into the air. The fact that they have not heard what it is they are voting for does not bother them in the least.

Children often raise their hands halfway, or wave them around, or raise and lower them, making it difficult for the teacher to count. Sometimes children tease the teacher, saying, "I was just scratching my head." By the time the teacher has counted all the votes on the first option, some children may have forgotten that they voted and vote again for the second option. The teacher ends up having to exhort the children to keep their hands up, not to vote twice, and so on. Often everyone ends up confused about what happened.

Children who vote more than once may not understand the mutual exclusiveness of the alternatives. Children old enough to understand that one should vote only once still may believe that it is unfair for someone to vote twice because that way, it is as though that child's vote is worth twice as much. They have not yet grasped that if someone votes twice, and there are only two choices, the two votes cancel each other out. Therefore, the best way to deal with the problem of voting twice is simply to use methods where it cannot happen. Discussing the problem is not likely to be productive when children's understanding of the logic is not yet developed.

When the teacher counts hands from a distance, children often are not sure whether they have been counted. The teacher may look at children as he or she counts them, or point, or even name them (Billy— that's 1; Felicia—that's 2; Corinne—that's 3; etc.), but it is still possible that children do not realize that they were counted. Young children often need something concrete to assure them that their vote has been included. Also, if children are too young to understand number as representing quantity, simply announcing, "Five people want X and seven people want Y, so we will do Y," is not a good idea. When children do not know what 5 and 7 mean, this announcement may leave many children bewildered about what just happened.

Having said all that, if the situation arises where hand raising seems the only method of voting that is practical, there are ways to make it work better. The teacher can ask a child to do the counting so that the child is the authority. To emphasize the mutual exclusivity of the choices, the teacher can state, "If you want X and not Y, raise your hand," and "If you want Y and not X, raise your hand."

Polling Children

We consider polling to be one of the best ways to conduct a vote with young children. Although there are many variations, all polling methods basically involve asking individual children to state in some fashion how they vote.

One way to do this is to go around the circle systematically, asking each child individually how he or she votes. When children state out loud, "I vote for X," they become more conscious of points of view, their own and others'. They also feel more of a sense of ownership of class decisions. The vote is a concrete symbol of the child's participation in the group.

It is important to allow for abstentions. Sometimes children do not care which way the vote goes, and they should not be forced to make a choice. Young children easily learn that if they do not want to vote, they can say, "Pass." The danger of unreflective voting was constructed by one 1st-grader who passed when asked whom she wanted to be president of the United States. Questioned about why she "passed," she answered, "If you don't know who the best person is, you could accidentally help the wrong person."

Polling requires making a written representation of each vote. Teachers often use slash marks, but we recommend this representation only for older children experienced with voting. Young children understand polling best when their votes are represented by their names or initials. When the teacher writes a list of voters under a written option, children can see their vote and know that it has been counted for the alternative they chose. Teachers also use name cards when polling, with great success. The teacher can hold up a card with a child's name written on it, ask that child how he or she votes, and then place the name card in that choice's pile or line. It may be important to place the votes in physical one-to-one correspondence, either vertically or horizontally. This is very helpful to children who do not yet have a solid understanding of number. They can look at the lines or rows and see which one is longer, without counting. The teacher can point out the length of the two lists, asking, "Which one looks like it received the most votes?" Counting will make more sense to young children when combined with the strong visual/spatial cue.

When children are truly interested in the outcome of the vote, they will be interested in understanding the number aspect. As they become better able to reason about number, they will begin to predict outcomes. For example, if there are 15 children in the class, and the vote is 8 to 4, some children might say, "It doesn't matter now, 8 is the most. That one has 8, so it wins." We would not suggest that the teacher call off the vote at that point, because the children who had not yet voted might feel as though they did not "count." The teacher could stop briefly to ask, "How do you know? Why do you think that X will have the most? Let's see if that works out." The teacher thus capitalizes on the spontaneous arithmetic experiences that arise in voting.

Casting Ballots

One of the problems with the polling method is that it is conducted publicly, and peer pressure can become a problem. Sometimes children's attempts at persuasion can turn into bullying or a popularity contest. When this is a problem, some form of casting ballots can be used. This can be done with neutral ballots (pieces of paper, checkers, etc.) and containers for each choice. Or it can be done with a neutral container and paper ballots. It may need to be conducted in secret, depending on the needs of the group. Everything that we said about counting votes when polling children holds true here as well. It is important for the teacher to make sure that votes are counted in a way that children can follow and that is meaningful to them.

Counting Children's Bodies

In this type of voting, children vote with their bodies, by standing, sitting, or otherwise moving their bodies to the place designated for the voting option desired. This is a good method to use if the class is outside and the teacher does not have access to paper and pencil. However, we have not had good results using this method with children 4 years and younger. Although the teacher can see both lines in their entirety, the children may not be able to compare them. However, when children understand elementary number, this method can work. Another problem we have seen with this method of voting in the classroom is that when children are settled in a circle, having them get up to vote invites chaos and confusion.

Dealing with Tie Votes

Tie votes provide great opportunities to engage children in considering the feelings of others. "What should we do? Six children want X and six children want Y. What is the fair thing to do?" Some children suggest that the fair solution to a tie vote is to do both things, even with two mutually exclusive choices. Other children suggest voting again, and this sometimes, although not always, results in a different vote. In one situation, 4-year-olds voting on which of two books they wanted the teacher to read had a tie vote. The only solution the children could think of was to read four pages from each book! So the teacher read four pages from one book, put it down, and read four pages from the other book. The children were very surprised as they witnessed the inadequacy of their solution.

Dealing with Lobbying

As mentioned earlier, sometimes children can become vigorous in their lobbying efforts (for example, threatening loss of friendship unless a child votes a particular way). Mild lobbying can be a good thing, giving children experience in negotiating with others. It certainly shows that children understand the process and respect its power. The teacher's role is to make sure that the lobbying does not become destructive. In cases where children's lobbying appears to be getting out of hand, the teacher can step in with gentle reminders that "Kaylin can vote for what she wants, and you can vote for what you want. That's why we vote, so everyone can have a say."

Sometimes, children will cheer when votes are cast for what they want and boo when they are not. This can upset the children who are not voting with those cheering, and the best way to deal with this is to point out how the others feel when children cheer. Ask one of the children in the minority to tell those cheering how it feels. Remind them of other times when the children doing the cheering were on the minority side, and try to get the children to take the perspective of the minority.

5. Participate as a Voter

When teachers take part in the vote, it demonstrates that the teacher is also a member of the community and that the teacher's opinion is worth neither more nor less than any other person's opinion. The teacher's vote is one vote among many. The teacher can try to persuade, but in the end, he or she must accept the wishes of the majority, just as the children must. In the vote on how many days to leave block structures up (see Chapter 7), the teacher believed that 5 days was too long. However, she could see that no harm would be done by allowing children to experience the result of their decision. If 5 days is too long, that would become apparent to the children at some point, and then they could change the rule.

One teacher told us that she often votes last, or near last, and votes with the minority whenever possible. She explained that her purpose was to demonstrate being disappointed with the outcome of the vote but dealing with the disappointment. In this way, she offered a model for being in the minority and fostered sensitivity to minority viewpoints. By voting last or near last, the teacher also can sometimes manage to create a tie vote if he or she thinks children are ready to discuss what to do in the case of a tie. If the teacher thinks a tie vote would not be in the best interests of the group at that time, he or she can cast the tie-breaking vote.

Teachers can also demonstrate how to handle differences in opinion by voting opposite each other. If there are two adults in the class, one adult can make a point of respectfully disagreeing with the other adult by casting an opposite vote. Children have the opportunity to understand that disagreements do not mean that people are not friends, just that they hold different opinions.

6. Foster Acceptance of Majority Rule and Respect for Minority Views

After the vote has been conducted, the teacher should announce the outcome of the vote with an attitude of acceptance of the ideal of majority rule. The teacher can state something to the effect that "this vote means that more people want X than want Y, so we will do X." The language of fairness is helpful when the teacher points out that "since more people voted for X, the fair thing to do is X."

Constructivist teachers try to avoid the language of winning and losing. We recognize that this may be difficult because children use these terms spontaneously. We have often heard children erupt into a spontaneous chant of "We won! We won!" This is an opportunity to remind children gently of their friends who wanted the other choice and how those friends feel right now.

The teacher should show sensitivity to the minority viewpoint. In the Investigators' class at the Human Development Laboratory School (HDLS) after a vote over which book to read, Elizabeth raised her hand and was close to tears, saying, "My book always loses." The teacher, Peige Fuller, recounts that she struggled over what to do with the minority opinion. Children had strong opinions and declared, "This book won." Peige decided to act as Elizabeth's advocate. "Yes, but Elizabeth is sad. She says her book never wins." Some children just wanted to move on to reading the book. Peige recounts, "What we finally came to was a compromise solution where the book that got the most votes was read first and the other book was read at second group time. That was a powerful lesson in fairness. What does it mean to be just and to take everyone into consideration?"

In cases where a vote addresses a problem, the teacher can state that the solution voted on will be tried, and if after a certain length of time that solution does not work, they can come back together and try to find another solution. This leaves open the possibility of trying the other choice, the one that received fewer votes.

WHEN VOTING GOES AWRY

Voting went awry in a 4-year-old class at HDLS when children had an unexpected difference of opinion about whether turkeys could fly. Experienced in voting and convinced of its power, they suggested a vote! The teacher, Peige Fuller, related this story to us:

Children were arguing so vehemently over the question of whether turkeys could fly that I thought they were going to have blows. It was getting out of hand—screaming, "No, they can't!" "Yes, they can!" Someone jumped up and said, "Let's take a vote!" I'm sitting back, because it's their circle, and I want to see what happens. So they took a vote, and they voted that turkeys can't fly, which is the best of all outcomes when you carry the story to its conclusion. I raised my hand and asked, "Well, can turkeys fly?" The answer was no. They had voted, and it was a settled question. Turkeys can't fly. I said, "We voted and said that turkeys can't fly. But what if they really can?" I asked them whether you can vote about whether something *is* or not. I used "fish swim" to illustrate my point. Can fish swim? Yes. But what if we voted that fish can't swim? Could they still swim? The power of being 4 years old is overpowering sometimes. Some said of course they could still swim. But some of them just weren't sure. "How could we find out?" I asked. Well, we could go see turkeys. Then it was my job to find turkeys. Luckily, they had turkeys at the zoo. We were committed to following this through.

The class took a field trip to the zoo, where they asked the zookeeper if the turkeys could fly. Peige continues:

We were wrong—turkeys *can* fly! So some things you can vote about, and some things you can't vote about. Some things you have to find out by investigating the world.

Although the group's ability to vote is power, children found out that this power cannot be used to determine a fact about the world.

9

Social and Moral Discussions

Social and moral discussion is another type of group time activity aimed toward promoting sociomoral development. In this activity, teachers focus children's attention on social and moral dilemmas and problems. In this chapter we discuss how teachers use discussions to promote children's reflections about social and moral issues.

First, we provide a brief theoretical foundation for understanding the development of moral judgment, discuss two types of social and moral discussions, offer advice on sources of materials for these, and present six principles of teaching for conducting discussions. Finally, we give examples of moral dilemma discussions in classrooms at the University of Houston Human Development Laboratory School and at the University of Northern Iowa's Freeburg School.

MORAL JUDGMENT THEORY

Our work in sociomoral development has been informed primarily by three theorists—Jean Piaget, Lawrence Kohlberg, and Robert Selman. We discuss Piaget and Selman in Chapter 2. Here we review briefly Kohlberg's work on developmental stages of moral reasoning.

Using Piaget's work as a springboard, Kohlberg did extensive research on moral reasoning in children and adults. In interviews, he probed to uncover how people reason about moral dilemmas and identified 6 stages in the development of moral reasoning. These stages appear to be hierarchical and sequential, and the first 5 have since been confirmed in numerous studies (see Colby & Kohlberg, 1987; Kohlberg, 1984, for reviews). We present here an outline of the first 4 of these stages that pertain to young children.

Stages 1 and 2 are both very individualistic and are referred to as *preconventional* morality. In Stage 1, right is defined in terms of that which avoids punishment or is in obedience to a higher authority such as parents and other adults. Actions are judged in physical rather than psychological terms. That is, the child's concern is with material damage to persons or things rather than with intentions. Interests of others are not considered.

In fact, there is no recognition that the interests of others exist apart from one's own.

At Stage 2 (often called the stage of *instrumental purpose and exchange*), right is defined as that which is in one's own self-interest, but everyone is recognized as having self-interests, and what is right is simply relative. This is the stage in which we see an "eye for an eye" morality, and where children are concerned with strict equality—for example, measuring to make sure each one gets the same amount of cake. Children at this stage begin to cooperate with each other in order to get what they want, a sort of "You scratch my back, I'll scratch yours" mentality.

Stages 3 and 4 are referred to as *conventional* morality. Stage 3 is the stage of mutual relationships, and what is right is defined in terms of the immediate social system (family, class, circle of close friends, etc.). The child begins to act in terms of the expectations of people important to the child. Children in this stage are concerned about being a "good girl" or "good boy" and will act to gain approval. The Golden Rule is understood in a concrete way, as putting oneself specifically in one other person's shoes.

At Stage 4, the larger social system begins to enter the picture, and right is defined in terms of *societal norms, laws, duties, and expectations.* There is the recognition that everyone must submit to a system of shared laws for the common good.

To summarize, in moving through Kohlberg's stages, the child's social perspective becomes increasingly larger. The child moves from the position of looking out simply for the self, to considering one other person, then to considering a slightly larger group, such as the family or class, and then to an even larger group, such as the society as a whole. At the higher Stages 5 and 6, what Kohlberg calls *postconventional* morality, the perspective becomes even larger and considers humanity in general.

Kohlberg and numerous other researchers have demonstrated in research with older children that over time, dilemma discussions can foster stagewise development (reviewed in Power et al., 1989). When children are exposed to reasoning one stage above their current stage of development, they tend to prefer the higher-level reasoning to their own. When dilemma discussions occur in a classroom context emphasizing community, individual moral growth occurs as well as growth in the level of moral culture of the community.

MORAL DILEMMAS

Most moral discussions focus on dilemmas. Let us define what we mean by dilemmas, discuss the different types of dilemmas, and suggest sources of appropriate dilemmas for discussions with young children.

Definition of Moral Dilemma

A moral dilemma is a situation in which competing claims, rights, or points of view can be identified. For example, the classic moral dilemma used in Kohlberg's (1984) research is known as the Heinz dilemma. A poor man named Heinz has a wife who is dying of a rare form of cancer. A druggist in the town has discovered a drug that will save her life; however, he wants $2,000 for the drug. Heinz does not have that much money. Should he steal the drug? Here the competing rights are Heinz's wife's right to life and the druggist's right to property.

There is no clear right or wrong solution to a dilemma. Kohlberg examined the reasoning behind people's answers to the questions about what the actors in the dilemmas should do. He states that people can advocate the same action for very different reasons that represent different stages of reasoning. For example, a child might say that Heinz should steal the drug because if his wife dies, then he will not have anyone to cook for him—Stage 2 reasoning—or because if his wife dies, their children will be very sad and they will be upset with him—Stage 3 reasoning. In contrast, persons can advocate different actions using the same-stage reasoning. For example, a child at Stage 1 might say that Heinz should not steal the drug because he might get caught and get sent to prison, or that Heinz should steal the drug because if he does not, his wife's father might come over and beat him up. In assessing level of moral judgment, the emphasis is on the ways people reason, not on the specific actions they advocate.

Types of Dilemmas

A dilemma for discussion can take one of two forms—hypothetical or real-life dilemmas. Both types can be useful for the purpose of promoting children's development of social and moral judgment. We also discuss stories written in response to the need for moral dilemmas that are drawn from children's everyday lives, but can be discussed as hypothetical.

Real-life dilemmas offer certain advantages for discussion. Since they occur spontaneously, the situations are intimately familiar to children. The actors involved are themselves and fellow classmates, and the situations usually bear directly on the life of the classroom so children feel genuine concern about what happens. They also offer the advantage of having consequences children can recognize and evaluate.

Hypothetical dilemmas are not as emotionally laden as real-life dilemmas because children are not personally involved in the issue. There is some emotional distance between children and the story. No one stands before the class angry or hurt or bleeding. It is safer to express opinions when no one will react personally or suffer a real consequence. Children can discuss what is right or wrong without the risk of hurting someone's feelings by failing to take a particular side in the issue.

Sources of Good Dilemmas for Discussion

Children's literature is one source of hypothetical social and moral dilemmas. However, children's stories often have moral lessons but not moral dilemmas. For example, the moral of the story of the boy who cried wolf is that you should not trick people because then they will not believe you when you tell the truth. It is a good moral and may be a good story to read to children, but it is not a dilemma. In contrast, in a moral dilemma a character must choose between two equally undesirable actions. A dilemma story might portray the boy as trying to decide whether it is right to kill a wolf in order to avoid a calamity's befalling his village.

Everyday life in the classroom is another source of dilemmas. Children are often heard to complain, "That's not fair!" when something happens in the class that violates their sense of justice. Teachers can sometimes find good topics for discussion in these complaints. For example, if children complain that people leave the caps off markers and the markers dry up and are ruined, the teacher has a dilemma. The teacher wants children to be able to use markers, but cannot afford to buy unlimited markers. What should happen? Is it fair to deprive all the children of markers because some children are careless? If the class gets new markers, should the children responsible for ruining the old markers be allowed to use them? This dilemma can be brought to children to discuss and resolve. Children tend to feel strongly about such problems, and the answers are important to them.

One problem with conducting moral discussions about real-life events is that they are unpredictable. One never knows when an issue will arise or what it will be about. This problem led the first author and her mother, Lorraine Goolsby (a former 1st-grade teacher), to write several illustrated dilemma stories, drawn from actual experiences with young children. Unlike the dilemmas used in Kohlberg's research, which are too far removed from the experience of young children, the situations in these stories are ones with which young children can be expected to be familiar. Such stories enable teachers to conduct moral discussions without having to wait for problems to arise in the classroom and without worrying about children's rights actually being violated.

In *When a Friend Refuses to Share* (Goolsby & DeVries, 1994b), the classroom rule is that four children can play at the block center. Three children are there, building an elaborate zoo, with cages for the animals and a fence around it. Another child comes to the block center, sees that there is room for him, and starts to build a tall building. However, only four blocks are not being used in the zoo, so he asks the three children for some of their blocks. They refuse, saying that they worked a long time on their zoo, and now they want to play with it. The dilemma is between the right of the child to play with the blocks, and the rights of the children who were there first to use as many blocks as they need for their zoo. Other stories are *When a Friend Eats More Than Her Share* and *When a Friend Steals* (Goolsby & DeVries, 1994a, 1994c). We describe below some children's reactions to this story.

OBJECTIVES

Our goal in conducting social and moral discussions is that these experiences will contribute to children's progress with regard to the stages of perspective-taking and moral reasoning. Specifically, we want children to think about interpersonal issues in more differentiated ways, becoming better able to think beyond their own perspective to see and consider multiple perspectives. Social and moral discussions can help children construct moral principles concerning justice, welfare, and the rights of self and others. However, children do not construct these big, general ideas right away. It is important to realize that children often give socially acceptable or correct answers to questions such as "Is it okay to hurt others?" and then deliberately hurt someone. Actions do not automatically match words. Children must deal with many events (observed, experienced, and hypothetical) before they can coordinate all the relationships involved in the notion of the Golden Rule.

Before children can begin to make stagewise progress in reasoning about social and moral dilemmas, they have to recognize that a dilemma exists. This is more difficult than one might think. Because of their limited perspective-taking ability, young children tend to focus on only one side of the issue and fail to recognize the two perspectives that define a dilemma. Therefore, our goals are more modest than for older children. First, children must recognize that there are conflicting points of view in a situation. Having accomplished this goal, we then try to help children generate and evaluate possible solutions in terms of all participants and to think about resolving moral issues in ways that are fair to everyone involved.

PRINCIPLES OF TEACHING

Conducting sociomoral discussions is a delicate matter. We present six principles of teaching. Some of these pertain to only hypothetical dilemmas.

1. Choose an Issue About Which You Can Reasonably Expect to Find a Difference of Opinion

Disagreement among children is necessary for a dilemma discussion to be successful. In one sense, this is the test of a dilemma—whether or not there is a conflict of rights in the story and whether children have different opinions. For example, consider the old story of the boy who tricked villagers by crying, "Wolf!" when he saw no wolf. This happened so many times, the villagers no longer believed him, and when the boy really saw a wolf, his cries were ignored. If asked the question "Was it okay for the boy to trick the townspeople like that?" probably no child would say yes. However, the story of the three little pigs is much more likely to elicit differences of opinion. Even though the pigs are the good guys and the wolf is the bad guy, some children might be expected to sympathize with the wolf. If asked, "Was it okay for the wolf to blow down the pigs' houses to eat them?" some children might state that the wolf was hungry and needs to eat, too. The children's book *The True Story of the Three Little Pigs* (Scieszka, 1989) presents this familiar story from the wolf's perspective. This book can be a good basis for a moral discussion that inspires differences of opinion.

2. Read, Tell, or Act Out Dilemma Stories Many Times

It takes many hearings of a story to enable children to think about the perspectives of all the different characters and all the subtle nuances that may be involved. The children may not notice a dilemma the 1st, 2nd, or even 15th time they hear the story.

One children's book that constructivist teachers often use in moral discussions is *Heckedy Peg* (Wood, 1987). In this story, a witch has stolen a mother's children, with the intent of eating them. The mother goes to the witch's house to try to get her children and, in the process, tricks the witch. Peige Fuller at the Human Development Laboratory School states that she had read this book to one group of 4-year-olds at least a hundred times. They loved it and knew it by heart. Peige did not expect the book to be the subject of a moral discussion. Then one day, when they get to the part where the mother tricks the witch, a child says, "She's lying!" Peige (T) follows up on this comment. The dilemma in this story becomes the mother's obligation to tell the truth versus her obligation to save her children.

T: (Reading) "Let me in!" the mother called. "I want my children back."
     "You can't come in," said Heckedy Peg. "Your shoes are dirty." "Then

I'll take them off," the mother said. And so she did. "Let me in!" the mother called. "I want my children back." "You can't come in," said Heckedy Peg. "Your socks are dirty." "Then I'll take them off," the mother said. And so she did. "Let me in!" the mother called. "I want my children back." "You still can't come in," said Heckedy Peg. "Your feet are dirty." "Then I'll cut them off," the mother said. And she went away.

E: She's not. She's lying to her.
T: "She went away as if to do so. But instead—"
J: [Unintelligible] her feet. She's lying.
C: She's tricking the witch.
T: "—the mother hid her legs behind her and crawled back to the witch's door." I had a question. Carol says the mother is just tricking the witch, and Javon and Emily say the mother is lying.
L: I know! She's tricking the witch.
E: Huh-uh! (Shakes his head emphatically).
T: Well, Earl, I have a question. Do you think that what the mother is saying is okay?

We return to this example below in Principle 4 to follow how the discussion continues. Here let us point out simply that Peige listens to her children and picks up on the disagreement over whether or not the mother was lying. However, we have tried the same story with some children who could not even understand the question. It went right over their heads because they did not understand the concept of a lie. The lesson is to listen to your children closely and be prepared to discuss moral issues that children discover in familiar stories.

3. Help Children to Recognize All Points of View

A familiar theme in children's stories is that of a small or weak creature tricking a larger or more dangerous creature in order to save the weak creature's life or someone else's life, as in *Heckedy Peg*. Stories that take this form can often be effective in helping children to examine multiple perspectives. The book *Doctor DeSoto* (Steig, 1982) follows this theme. A fox has a toothache, and goes to the only dentist in town, a mouse named Dr. DeSoto. Dr. DeSoto has a policy of not treating cats and other dangerous animals, but Dr. DeSoto's wife is moved by pity for the fox, who is in tremendous pain, and they decide to treat the fox. When it becomes clear that the fox plans to eat the mice after they fix his tooth, Dr. DeSoto and his wife devise a plan to trick the fox so he will not be able to eat them. They paint his teeth with a "secret formula" and tell him it will prevent him from ever having toothaches again. But the secret formula is really glue, and they glue the fox's teeth together, making it impossible for him to eat them. Children generally think it is great that the mice out-fox the fox. After reading the story, Coreen Samuel asks kindergarten children, "Was it okay for Dr. DeSoto to trick the fox like that? Should the DeSotos have lied to the fox?" Most children say yes, that the mice did not want to be eaten. However, some children take the perspective of the fox. They worry that the fox will starve with his mouth glued shut. One child is concerned that the fox will still get toothaches because the glue is not really a secret formula. The children are able to look at this story from the fox's point of view and think about his rights as well as the mice's rights.

After reading the book in Peige's class of 4-year-olds at the Human Development Laboratory School, the second author (Zan) asks the same question. The responses are unanimous. All the children think it is okay, and they cheer at that part of the story. However, one child surprises us by her reasoning. While most children state that it is okay because the mice do not want to be eaten, this child states that it is okay because if the fox eats Dr. DeSoto, then there would be no one to fix teeth in the town. She takes the perspective of the larger community. Although probes did not go further to explore her thinking, this suggests Kohlberg's Stage 4, remarkably high-level reasoning for a 4-year-old.

When children all take one point of view, it becomes the teacher's responsibility to represent other perspectives. If no one mentions the fox's position, the teacher can ask a question such as "Do you think the fox might have a problem?" or "Is that fair to the fox?" This approach can help children decenter to consider more than one point of view.

4. Ask Open-Ended Questions

Open-ended questions are those with more than one possible answer. Examples are "What do you think ___ should do?" "Can you think of something else ___ might have done?" When constructivist teachers ask children whether something is fair or right or okay to do, they follow it up with questions such as "Why do you think that was a fair thing to do? What would happen if ____ does that? How will the other people in the story feel?" It is important to probe in order to understand children's reasons and encourage them to explain their reasoning. Sometimes children cannot, but when they do, it usually spurs further discussion. This kind of questioning is very different from asking comprehension questions.

The discussion about *Heckedy Peg*, begun above, continues as Peige probes children's reasoning about why they think it is okay or not okay for the mother to trick the witch.

E: Uh-uh, it's—she's lying.
T: Is it okay to lie in this case?
E: Huh-uh.
Children: No!
T: No? Why? Can you tell me why it's not okay?
E: Because it's bad.
J: It's bad, and she will look at her and say, "You have feet," and she'll say, "Yes I do." That's a lie, right?
T: That's a lie? Well, Carol, what do you think about it? Do you think it's okay for the mother to tell the witch she does not have feet?
C: [Unintelligible] she does.
L: She's tricking her.
T: The mother does have feet. But she told Heckedy Peg she cut them off. Is that okay for the mother to say?
L: Yeah.
T: Yeah? Why is it okay?
C: 'Cause it's not [unintelligible] anything.
T: Because it's not [unintelligible] anything? Why do you think it's okay that the mother told Heckedy Peg that she cut her feet off?
N: I think she was lying because—because she just told Heckedy Peg that she was hiding her feet behind her.
T: She was sly, huh?
H: She's just lying.
T: She was lying? Was it okay for her to lie, or was it not okay for her to lie?
H: Yes, it was okay.
T: Why?
H: If you're just, if you're not [unintelligible], then it's not okay, but if you're just tricking people so they wouldn't do something like that, then you can, it's okay.
T: I see.
E: Huh-uh! You're wrong! You know nothing! (Strong tone of voice).
T: Allen, I see that your hand is raised.
E: I know better! You can't come to my house!
A: I think that she's just trying to trick the witch. I think that she's just trying to get her children back.
T: She's just trying to get her children back? So it's okay to lie in that case?
A: Yeah.
H: That's what I meant.
Children: Yeah.
E: Huh-uh.
A: Only if it's very important.

T: (To Hal) That's what you meant?
H: Yes, that's what I meant. I meant what she said.
T: Okay, Earl has a disagreement. (To Earl) Tell us what you think. Do
    you think Allen and Helen are right, that it's okay to lie to save your
    children?
E: Huh-uh, it's not.
T: It's not?
E: It's bad.
T: Is it ever okay to lie?
E: No!
J: No.
T: Never?
Children: Yes.
T: Yes? Well, we have a difference of opinion.
C: You could call someone to help.
T: Yes, you could call someone to help. Let's see what the mother does
    (continues reading).

Peige's questions are worded so as to encourage children to develop an
opinion and elaborate the reasons why they believe as they do.

5. Help Children Clarify Their Reasoning

Sometimes children's words are disjointed, garbled, or otherwise
difficult to interpret. It is helpful (not just for moral discussions, but for
all discussions) to repeat back to children what they said, with a questioning inflection, especially if they are not well understood. This will often prompt them to elaborate what they have said, offering reasons or
corrections.

Repeating children's ideas in a clear way helps other children better
understand and inspires them to formulate their opinions. The teacher
should strive to foster open discussion *among children* of the issues being
presented, not simply discussion between a child and the teacher. Becoming aware of classmates' differing opinions can promote reassessment of
ideas and growth in perspective-taking.

6. Accept All Opinions and Positions

It is important, but enormously difficult, for the teacher not to place
value judgments on children's reasons. Doing so sends the message that
the teacher knows and seeks the right answers. In the discussion about
Heckedy Peg quoted above, Peige does not pass judgment on the children's

reasons why lying is or is not okay. She questions, probes, and repeats, but she refrains from approving or disapproving children's ideas, knowing children will not be convinced just because she says so.

It is important to resist the urge to try to get the class to come to a consensus about a hypothetical issue. The goal of a discussion is to foster children's awareness of different points of view, not to convince them of a particular moral view. Consensus is neither necessary nor particularly desirable. The teacher can, however, restate the opposing positions at the end of the discussion. This serves to wrap up the discussion, and to emphasize the point that people's opinions can differ. For example, at the end of the discussion about *Doctor DeSoto*, the teacher can state something to the effect of "So some people think that it was okay for Dr. DeSoto to trick the fox because he did not want to be eaten. But some people think it was not okay because the fox's teeth were glued together and he couldn't eat, and he might starve." Opposing positions should be stated in a neutral way. Constructivist teachers do not worry about leaving an issue unresolved.

REAL-LIFE MORAL DISCUSSIONS

An active social environment inevitably provides real-life dilemmas. These are situations in which the rights of one child conflict with the rights of another child or of the group. Conflicts involving access to toys, supplies, and space to play can become moral issues. We encourage teachers to take advantage of these situations as opportunities to focus children's attention on rights, fairness, and consideration of all persons concerned. We describe two examples of real-life moral discussion: misusing colored markers and sophisticated bullying.

Misusing Colored Markers

In the kindergarten class at the Human Development Laboratory School, the assistant teacher, Karen Amos, introduces consideration for the feelings of wrongdoers. Children had been leaving the caps off markers, causing them to dry up. Karen brought her own personal markers to school, with the understanding that if the children could demonstrate care for the markers, then they could ask the assistant director to buy them some new ones. However, one child suggests a new rule: If children leave the caps off the markers, they will not be allowed to use them. A moral discussion ensues. The discussion is moral in the sense that it pits justice against mercy. The child who suggests the rule that children who misuse markers cannot use them takes the side of justice, and Karen argues for mercy by presenting the perspective of those who occasionally forget the rules. At first, children suggest that those who misuse the markers should never get to use them again. Karen asks the children to specify a length of time, and they suggest 3 days. Karen believes that 3 days is too long to deprive children of markers, and she goes on to defend children who forget to replace caps by stating, "I know that sometimes I forget, too." Popular opinion is against her, however. They vote and decide that the rule will state that children who leave caps off the markers will not be allowed to use them for 3 days.

Often, what appears on the surface to be a moral dilemma is actually a conflict between children, although the distinction between the two may be fuzzy at times. (See Chapter 5 for a discussion of conflict resolution.) Usually in a conflict between children, one child's rights have been violated by another, and the victim protests. But in a moral dilemma, the conflict is not so much between children as between rights. For example, one year in the kindergarten class at the Human Development Laboratory School, children had 1 day each week assigned to them as their sharing day when they could bring items from home to show to the entire class. One child, showing his item to his classmates while walking around the circle, selectively allowed some children to touch it but not others. Children protested, "That's not fair!" The question was who has the right to decide whether children can touch someone's possession. Some children thought that it should be an all-or-nothing proposition. Either everyone can touch, or else no one can touch. Other children thought that the owner of the object had every right to decide who can touch. Issues such as this are difficult to solve, and there are no easy answers. We discuss in Chapter 6 why we decided to eliminate sharing time as a regular part of the daily routine. This example illustrates one kind of problem that can arise.

Sophisticated Bullying

Beth Van Meeteren reports on a problem with bullying in the Freeburg 1st- and 2nd-grade classroom. We quote from her written account.

Day 1: We've been having an increase in bullying behaviors in the classroom through subtle and not-so-subtle attacks. It has been ruining the learning atmosphere as many children were afraid to contribute during group discussions or express themselves freely, mostly out of fear of being laughed at. The laughing was done in a manipulative manner, not clear and obvious, but covered up with mock sincerity. There was also an escalation of arguing and aggression, with accusations of "He did it first." No amount of working at the Peace Bench was resulting in any progress. It seemed like the bullies were using it to their advantage, mocking sincerity while laughing behind the victims' backs. They began to laugh at adults, too. Christie, Shari, and I had been laughed at. When I confronted them, they mocked surprise and "reassured" me they were not laughing at me, but just having fun together.

Shari and I attempted a puppet play, with Shari's puppet being the victim. I handled two puppets laughing at Shari's. It was semi-successful, as the kids all thought it was funny, but it did allow Shari and me to demonstrate we knew the inner workings of the bully circle. Christie [Sales] suggested we use the word *power* to talk about how a bully wants power, and when we acquiesce or cower or fight back, it gives them the power they want. Christie came in at group time and shared that she was hurt when people in the classroom wanted her to do the Hokey-Pokey for the sole purpose of laughing at her, and it made her not want to come into our classroom any more. Shari and I then both shared our experiences of being laughed at.

One of the suggestions the kids had was to tell the teacher when being bullied. We did another short piece where we asked Waynette to be the teacher, and my bully puppets were kind when Waynette was looking, but mean when she wasn't. I had the puppets pretend to be nice to the "teacher" by giving her hugs and then turning around and being mean behind her back. What I was trying to do was let the bullies know that I knew I was being manipulated. I don't know if I was successful.

Day 2: Today we watched a short video about some birds bullying another bird. It is from a film called *Monsters, Inc.* by Pixar. In it, some small birds make fun of, laugh at, exclude, hit, and punch a big, goofy-looking bird who wants to be their friend (but is too stupid to understand he is being made fun of). At the end of the film, the small birds are humiliated when, after trying to hurt the big bird, they lose their feathers and are left embarrassed and naked. The goofy bird laughs at them after handing them leaves to hold in front of them. We watched all the way through and then went section by section, pausing to talk about how the birds are sometimes like them. In the course of the discussion, Javon laughed at Dante's suggestion. I stopped him and confronted him about this publicly. After admitting he hurt Dante, Javon said he was no longer going to laugh at people's suggestions. I was proud of how Javon admitted his fault and decided to make a change in his behavior and told him so in private.

As we state above, the teacher's task in moral discussions is to uphold fairness, equality, and reciprocity. One problem with moral discussions that arise in real life is that it is not always clear what is fair, and yet solutions are needed. As in the situation about touching sharing items, a decision is called for regarding how the class will handle the problem. Submitting moral issues to a vote is generally not appropriate. Often the best thing the teacher can do is to conduct a thorough discussion and then have the class vote to decide how to handle the situation. The important point is to discuss the issue thoroughly because it is in the discussion that children will challenge each other's reasoning and perhaps come to a new understanding of the moral issue.

HYPOTHETICAL DILEMMAS DRAWN FROM REAL-LIFE EXPERIENCES

When discussing the book *When a Friend Refuses to Share* (Goolsby & DeVries, 1994b) with kindergartners at the Human Development Laboratory School, Coreen Samuel found that children at first were sympathetic primarily with the child who wanted more blocks and suggested various ways of sharing or finding more blocks. When Coreen introduced the question of whether it would be fair to expect the three children to tear down their zoo, some children switched loyalties and defended the children building the zoo. In general, children took one side in the story and, except for one child, could not coordinate the competing claims. One child suggested a compromise, that the children make shorter houses and a shorter fence for the zoo, thus freeing up some blocks for the new child. The difficulty children have in seeing more than one perspective in this story makes clear why children have such problems in real-life conflicts.

Our goals in this dilemma were, first, that children would be led to think about the problem from both perspectives. We wanted the children to see that both parties had a valid argument, and that sometimes problems cannot be solved simply by finding out which side is right. Second, we wanted children to think about how the children in the story might feel about what was happening. Often, young children can think of only a small repertoire of feelings (we refer to this as "mad, sad, glad" because this seems to be the extent of their thinking about feelings). We want children to think in more differentiated ways about feelings. We have tried to introduce words such as *disappointed, frustrated,* and *afraid,* to describe children's feelings. Finally, we hoped that children would begin to explore different ways to solve the problem, whether taking turns, sharing, or some other solution, and how these proposed solutions would cause the children in the story to feel.

Another story, titled *When a Friend Steals* (Goolsby & DeVries, 1994c), tells about a young boy, Jack, who comes to school hungry every day because he does not get up in the morning early enough to eat breakfast. His solution is to take items of food from his classmates' lunches while they are outside playing. Eventually, the teacher discovers him stealing food, and they have a class discussion. Children tell Jack that they do not like having their food taken. The teacher in the story asks children if they can think of any solutions to Jack's problem.

In Coreen's Human Development Laboratory School kindergarten, children suggest numerous solutions to the problem of what Jack can do about being hungry in the morning. They suggest things that Jack can do, such as getting up earlier, getting an alarm clock or a rooster to wake him up, and packing a breakfast to eat in the car on the way to school. They also suggest things that the entire class can do, such as writing a note to his parents asking them to pack him a breakfast to eat at school and bringing extra food for Jack to eat in the morning. This leads to a moral question: "Should Jack be punished for taking the children's food, or should the children try to help Jack?" In the kindergarten class we find a difference of opinion. One child is very clear that Jack should be punished, because "he takes stuff out of people's lunches." The injunction not to steal is powerful, and, in his view, punishment is the expected consequence—no justification necessary. Another child, however, disagrees. He thinks that the children should help Jack. When asked why, he explains, "Because then he'll stop doing it. If they punish him, then he might take two things out of people's lunches." We were amazed that a 5-year-old could understand that punishment is ineffective and that cooperative methods are more successful. This reflects the kind of reasoning we hope to promote in children. Other children's books by Goolsby and DeVries include *When a Friend Eats More Than Her Share* (1994a) and *When a Friend Steals* (1994c).

In his research on children's moral judgment, Piaget (1932/1965) cited informal observations indicating that children can often reason at a higher level when focusing on their own experiences than they can in hypothetical story situations. In personal experiences, children are likely to feel and think that it is not right to be hurt, humiliated, embarrassed, shamed, or called names by others. Ideas of justice can also be born when children are unjustly punished for a sibling's crying when, in fact, they had not caused this, or when they are punished for something a sibling or classmate actually did. Research on the moral development of adults shows that it is when facing personal moral dilemmas that they, too, can make progress in terms of moral development (Power et al., 1989). It is the disequilibrium in personal experiences that can often lead to reflection, struggle, and eventual progress.

However, it should be noted that the findings of higher reasoning in real life considered situations when emotions were in fairly good control. When emotionally overwhelmed with strong feelings, a person may not be able to reason at a higher level but revert to a lower level. For example, during a tantrum or when a child is extremely angry, reasoning at all may be impossible. In such cases, it is later, when feelings are more under control, that a teacher or parent may be able to appeal to children's reflection. We have also observed that even in situations of high emotion, young children, to their credit, may be able to calm themselves enough to respond positively when an adult offers help.

We have also observed children who at times respond more reflectively to hypothetical situations. Some rather consistently aggressive children in Sherice Hetrick-Orton's kindergarten at the HDLS responded at higher levels when confronted with aggression on the part of puppets than in situations when they were aggressive.

10

Cooperative Alternatives
to Discipline

Discipline usually refers to methods of controlling and punishing children in order to socialize them. A dictionary definition of the verb *discipline* lists two usages, including (1) "to train by instruction and control; teach to obey or accept authority" and (2) "to punish or penalize" (Morris, 1973). As these usages imply that adults do something *to* children, we therefore say that we do not "discipline" children. Rather, we *work with* children cooperatively to help them gradually construct moral feelings and convictions about relations with others. The general theoretical rationale for our efforts to develop a cooperative alternative to discipline is presented in Chapter 3, where we emphasize our goal of development through self-regulation. Throughout this book, we stress that children's self-constructed social and moral convictions are rooted in the richness of their everyday interpersonal experiences. The challenge of socializing children is to figure out how to help them control impulses, take others' perspectives, and become able to reflect on the interpersonal results of their actions. In Chapter 5 we deal with misbehaviors that are often involved in children's conflicts.

The first edition of this book emphasized some logical consequences that seem more like "doing to" children than "working with" children. As we see it now, that emphasis was misplaced. We are grateful to Alfie Kohn (1996/2006) and Jane Nelsen (1981/2006; Nelsen, Duffy, & Erwin, 2007; Nelsen, Lott, & Glenn, 2000) for challenging us to be more specific about our stance toward logical consequences. The use of logical consequences for misbehaviors is often punitive, and we do not advocate punishing children. We revised our principles of teaching to emphasize how teachers can use reciprocity sanctions, rather than expiatory sanctions, to help children change behaviors. In our current view, the use of logical consequences should be limited to situations in which young children need to be challenged to help them take account of the ideas, feelings, and rights of others (see examples in Chapter 5). Such an approach not only helps children correct their misbehaviors but also helps them to develop affective, intellectual, and moral self-regulation—that is, to develop autonomy.

The issue of discipline is basically one of how to use the power of adult authority. Piaget's notion of heteronomous adult-child relationships (see Chapter 3) refers to an adult wielding power, with children having little possibility to make choices or decisions to regulate their own behavior. In contrast, where no constraints are imposed on children, teachers have abandoned their legitimate authority. Such classrooms have sometimes erroneously been called *constructivist* but are more correctly called *permissive*. Contrary to myth, children in constructivist classrooms are not allowed to "run wild" and do whatever they like. Certainly, all teachers must develop abilities in managing a classroom of children and dealing with inevitable breakdowns in cooperation. Adult exercise of authority is sometimes necessary in all classrooms. When children are unable, for whatever reason, to regulate their behavior, then the adult must step in and, when necessary, provide the external regulation that is temporarily needed. The issue is, How and when should constructivist teachers use external regulation?

Constructivist teachers are not passive in the face of misbehavior. On the contrary! Their actions, however, do not take unilateral forms (such as lecturing, punishing, and rewarding). Instead, cooperative forms (such as engaging children in conflict resolution and discussing with children how to solve classroom problems) offer children possibilities to exercise self-regulation and construct social and moral convictions.

Essentially, *cooperative alternatives to discipline* describes an approach in which the adult acts with the goal of children's self-regulation in mind. Certainly, we want children to hold values broadly shared in our society— for example, the Golden Rule. However, in our view (following Piaget), moral convictions cannot be achieved by authority but require cultivation through countless personal interactive experiences and reflection on these at school and at home.

When cooperation breaks down into misbehavior, it is easy to focus on trying to externally regulate/change undesired behavior. However, this focus is transformed when the teacher's deeper question becomes "How can I help this child become more self-regulating?" More specifically, the question becomes "How can I help this child change his or her thinking (as well as behavior) concerning respect toward others?"

In this chapter, we consider Piaget's distinction between two types of sanctions and address the issue of how to implement cooperative alternatives to discipline by suggesting principles of teaching. Finally, we discuss situations that often lead to children's misbehaviors and how to avoid these. We give examples from classrooms throughout.

TWO TYPES OF REACTION TO CHILDREN'S MISBEHAVIOR

Piaget's (1932/1965) interviews of children (mainly from low-income families) about how adults react to children's misbehaviors showed that children think in terms of two types of adult reaction: punitive (expiatory) and cooperative (reciprocity) sanctions. Piaget described *expiatory sanctions* as an adult's reaction to transgressions with coercion or painful punishment or both. Expiatory sanctions are intended to make the child suffer in some way. Punitive or expiatory sanctions include spanking, yelling, making a child stand in a corner, and making a child write "I will not __" 100 times. Humiliating children and chastising them in an emotionally overwhelming way are also expiatory. Any punishment designed to make the child suffer physically or emotionally falls in this category. Expiatory sanctions are arbitrary in the sense that "there is no relation between the content of the guilty act and the nature of its punishment. . . . All that matters is that a due proportion should be kept between the suffering inflicted and the gravity of the misdeed" (p. 205). These sanctions may express revenge or vindictiveness on the part of the adult. Although some people think that making the child suffer is a preventive measure, Piaget found that older children view such punishments as ineffective and as simply making "the offender insensitive and coldly calculating" (p. 225). The attitude is "Daddy will punish me, but he won't do anything afterwards!" (p. 225). Piaget further commented, "How often, indeed, one sees children stoically bearing their punishment because they have decided beforehand to endure it rather than give in" (p. 225). Constructivist teachers try to understand children's views of punishment and let this inform their work with children. For example, Beth Van Meeteren found that some 1st-graders new to the idea of the Peace Chair viewed it as punishment, and she had to explain, "This is the way we solve our problems."

Piaget (1932/1965) found that younger children believe that punishment is necessary and just, and the sterner the better. This results from moral realism—centering on the material result of a misdeed and not on intentions, for example (see Chapter 2). Younger children believe that the punishment invoked should be related quantitatively to the misdeed—the worse the misbehavior, the harsher the punishment should be. In his research, Piaget told children two stories of children breaking china. In one story, a child accidentally broke many china cups, and in the other story, the child broke one cup while attempting to steal something. Younger children tended to believe that the child who broke more cups should be punished more severely than the child who broke only one. Older children, in contrast, believed that intentions matter: The child who broke many cups accidentally was not at fault, but the child who broke only one cup while trying to steal something should be punished more severely.

One of us (Zan) has a friend who told her a personal story of having been forbidden by her parents to get her ears pierced when she was a teenager. One weekend when her parents were out of town, she had a friend pierce her ears. When her parents returned and saw her ears, they were furious. Her punishment was to do the family ironing for 6 months (and this before permanent press!). Many years later, she still insists that it was worth the punishment.

It is not unusual for an adult to feel that a child should be made to suffer for a misdeed. This view reflects the common idea that if the child suffers, he or she will remember the punishment and will not do the misdeed again. However, suffering may lead the child simply to resent the perpetrator of the punishment. Such punishment may also lead the child to feel inwardly that he or she is bad and can thereby have a negative effect on self-esteem. Or it may lead the child to be more calculating next time so the adult does not find out about a misdeed. From the point of view of the child's psychological development, punishments are risky and most likely counterproductive if the adult wants to promote the child's moral development.

In contrast to expiatory sanctions, *sanctions by reciprocity* emphasize the social bond broken by a child's misbehavior. Feelings of disappointment, anger, or loss of trust reflect such a break. For example, when someone lies, others may feel that they no longer can trust the one who told the lie. In other words, mutual good will in a relationship has been interrupted. To reestablish goodwill, the wrongdoer must act to compensate the bad feeling and repair the relationship. Willingness to make the repair arises from a child's valuing of a relationship with another. Thus, the close personal relationships of attachment between teachers and children provide a necessary foundation for the effective use of reciprocity sanctions. Similarly, children's relations with one another are crucial to the effectiveness of reciprocity sanctions among children. For example, children sometimes say to an offending child, "I don't trust you any more." If children do not care about others, reciprocity sanctions will be ineffective. When children do not care about the teacher or other children, the goal must become to establish caring relationships.

Sanctions by reciprocity have in common the communication of a break in a social bond They are related to a misdeed rather than being arbitrary and are not intended to be punishments. However, the reader should keep in mind that reciprocity sanctions can be implemented in punitive ways that short-circuit reciprocity and turn them into punishments. Moreover, despite a teacher's best efforts to present a sanction in a cooperative way, children may still interpret it as unfair or as a punishment.

PRINCIPLES OF TEACHING

A cooperative alternative to discipline goes a long way toward establishing a constructivist sociomoral atmosphere. Underlying all the principles of teaching is a teacher's attitude of helpfulness. "How can I help you?" is often heard in constructivist classrooms when teachers intervene in a situation of misbehavior. (This basic idea is discussed by Watson, 2003.)

We conceptualize the following seven cooperative teaching principles:

1. Provide a general and pervasive context of warmth, cooperation, and community.
2. Minimize coercion to the extent possible and practical.
3. Try to understand the child's point of view.
4. Avoid ambiguous or unenforceable rules and expectations.
5. Use reciprocity sanctions when misbehavior requires attention.
6. Promote children's reflection on rules and expectations.
7. When power struggles occur, disengage or find a way to give the child power.

We discuss these principles of teaching below.

1. Provide a General and Pervasive Context of Warmth, Cooperation, and Community

We place this principle first as a guideline for teachers who want to implement a cooperative approach to discipline as a reminder that dealing with misbehavior does not occur in a vacuum. This principle involves what we referred to earlier in the book as "a way of being with" children. We have argued that moral development is optimally supported when children feel that adults in their lives care for them and cooperate with them. It is in situations of misbehavior that teachers are most challenged to protect the cooperative sociomoral atmosphere, especially their relationships with children.

Although we draw inspiration for this principle from the work of Piaget, we recognize that many others recommend cooperation, beginning with pioneers in early education (Read, 1976; see Weber, 1969). Almost all recent books on discipline stress the importance of cooperation and community (review by Charles, 2002; Kohn, 1999, 2006; Marshall, 2001; Nelsen, 1981/2006; Nelsen, Duffy, & Erwin, 2007; Nelsen, Lott, & Glenn, 2000; Watson, 2003), and we leave to the reader the task of determining similarities and differences between our approach and that of others.

2. Minimize Coercion to the Extent Possible and Practical

This general constructivist principle is the one with which we, and the teachers with whom we have worked, struggle the most. It involves everything the teacher does. In Chapter 3, we discuss Piaget's view that an excess of external regulation has disadvantages for children's social and moral development. Yet Piaget (1932/1965) also pointed out that "however delicately one may put the matter, there have to be commands and therefore duties" (p. 180). Herein lies the problem—how to decide what is necessary control and what is unnecessary control. We say to reduce or minimize coercion, rather than saying to eliminate it because at times it is impossible to avoid controlling children (such as for reasons of health and safety and pressures on the adult). Examples include the following: "After you blow your nose, you must wash the germs off your hands because they can make people sick," "I can't let people hit each other because I have to keep everyone safe," "We have to do the handwriting exercises because in our school, all children in 1st grade have to learn how to make letters correctly so other people can read what they write." These are necessary coercions (external regulations) where children (and sometimes teachers) are given no choice in the matter. Permissive teachers who make the mistake of eliminating almost all adult authority may fail to react firmly even when unsafe behavior occurs.

The challenge for teachers is to judge when external regulation of children is legitimate and necessary. Clearly, in the following situations, a teacher cannot avoid being coercive:

- When a child hurts or threatens to hurt someone
- When a child violates another's rights
- When a child is in imminent danger

Constructivist teachers we know constantly ask themselves, "Is this coercion necessary?" Sometimes conscientious teachers overregulate children—that is, they control them unnecessarily. In addition to explicit rules about sitting with crossed legs at group time (discussed in Chapter 6), we have also observed overregulation when helpful teachers provide too much direction to children who set tables for snack or lunch, telling exactly how many napkins, plates, and cups they need (rather than allowing them to grapple with this mathematics problem). Overregulation such as this robs children of their autonomy and keeps them dependent on adults to tell them what to do and how to do it. It deprives children of the opportunity to figure out how to do something. Finally, it dilutes a teacher's legitimate authority because children may hear so many directives that they learn to tune them out.

When external regulation is necessary, it is important to use the least amount possible to secure compliance. Research on child rearing shows that when parents use the least amount sufficient to secure compliance (see review by Maccoby and Martin, 1983), this approach to child rearing results in significantly better outcomes for children, compared with child rearing characterized by more external regulation than necessary for gaining compliance. When the adult pressure is mild, children have the opportunity for at least some autonomy. That is, a child feels that he or she has a choice about whether to accede to mild pressure. Willing compliance is autonomous.

To give an example of using the "least amount necessary" in contrast to "more than necessary" external regulation, consider the situation in which a child is precariously standing on a chair to reach something on a high shelf. In the case of the "least amount" of external regulation necessary, an adult might come close, loosely wrap his or her arms around the child, and say, "I know you're good at climbing, but I'm worried that the chair might tip over and you will fall. Remember our rule to ask a grown-up to get things off those tall shelves? Let me help you. Tell me what you need." In the case of "too much" external regulation, an adult might rush over and pull the child off the chair without warning or yell, "Get off that chair right now! You're going to fall and hurt yourself."

Instead of using external regulation, it is usually possible to find a way to give a choice rather than a command. If a child is oblivious to a runny nose, teachers usually tell the child to get a tissue, give the child a tissue, or even wipe the child's nose. Instead, a teacher can help the child become more self-regulating by asking, "How can you take care of your nose?" or, if this question is too subtle for the child, "I see that your nose is running. Do you want to go get a tissue or take care of your nose in the bathroom?" This allows the child to decide what to do but also communicates that the child must do something to correct the situation.

When teachers must exercise control over children, it is important to do so with a sympathetic attitude that helps mitigate negative effects of the coercion. The child's experience of control is very different when the adult is hostile or punitive in contrast to when the adult is sympathetic with the child's feelings. Giving explanations for necessary control respects the child and helps minimize the harmful effects of coercion. Adults who say, "Do it because I say so!" may not realize that this tells children not to think and promotes their heteronomy rather than autonomy. Sympathetic control is communicated when the adult recognizes the child's feelings and explains, "I know you don't want to clean up, but we need to clear toys from table tops and the floor so we will have a place for lunch and cots (for nap time)." When a child cannot understand the adult's reason or resists complying, the cooperative adult can only appeal to the personal bond based on mutual affection. For example, a teacher might say, "We need to put the Legos™ away, and I can't do it by myself. Will you help me?" Autonomy is preserved when a child is able to respond willingly to this appeal. If a child continues to refuse and resist, the next step might be to raise the issue of problems with cleanup at a class meeting, without, of course, mentioning the child's name, and bring peer feelings to the child's attention.

External control (coercion) can be mild or strong. It can be communicated with a look or a tone of voice as well as words. Teachers trying to minimize coercion guard against expressing impatience or anger because such emotion on the part of the adult can intensify the child's fear or anxiety about the adult's power. Normally, most teachers are professional about holding their negative emotions in check in the classroom. Nevertheless, teachers sometimes become angry and frustrated with children. If these feelings are expressed in an uncontrolled way, they can have an intimidating and coercive effect, damage the teacher-child relationship, and make the child feel unsafe. This does not mean that the teacher should never let children know that he or she is angry. However, the anger must be expressed in a controlled way, as discussed in Chapter 5.

Sometimes adults find it difficult to make the distinction between being firm and being mean when trying to exercise necessary control. It may help to ask another adult to provide a "reality check" for the teacher, to let the teacher know if his or her tone of voice or body language was mean or simply firm. Another source of a "reality check" is video. When teachers reflect on their own teaching in private, they often become conscious of behaviors that they were unaware of, such as using a harsh tone of voice or glaring.

When a teacher has to control a child's behavior externally, it is important to find a way to return some control to the child as quickly as possible, to avoid the undesirable effects of heteronomy. This means opening the way for the child's voluntary action such as giving the child a choice or an opportunity to solve a problem. Proposing restitution for causing harm to another is also a way of returning autonomy to a child.

3. Try to Understand the Child's Point of View

Piaget's research and theory on sanctions informs our views of a cooperative alternative to discipline by giving us information on how children think about punishments and consequences of misbehavior. The constructivist teacher makes a special effort to understand how a child views what the teacher calls "misbehavior." Trying to understand children's points of view enriches teachers' efforts to minimize coercion.

An example of thinking about misbehavior from the children's points of view is given by Christina Sales when she was a teacher of 3-year-olds at Freeburg. She describes becoming frustrated and uncomfortable at the beginning of the year because she was spending her time largely in regulating children—telling them constantly what to do and what not to do. Realizing that she had fallen into a controlling pattern of interacting with children, she pondered these problems: "What can I do to get children to do what I expect them to do? Specifically, what can I do to get children to flush the toilet and to flush only toilet paper?" (They threw paper towels and plastic lids in the toilet, and a plumber had to be called.) "What can I do to get children to clean up after activity time?" (Children ran around the room instead of cleaning up.) "What can I do to get children to stop splattering water everywhere at the water fountain?" (Children were placing a flat palm underneath the spout so that water splattered out in all directions.) "What can I do to get children to eat family style as Head Start requires?" (Children were grabbing what they wanted rather than passing serving dishes.) Christina concluded that children were not deliberately misbehaving. Rather, her expectations were out of line with what her children knew about how to behave at school. For example, teachers encouraged children to explore water when they were at the water table during activity time. Why not at the water fountain or the toilet? When she viewed this from the children's points of view, she understood better how to intervene. She shifted her focus from children's behavior to their knowledge and decided that her expectations should become her goals. Then she systematically addressed these expectations. She taught children how to use the classroom bathroom (see her list of bathroom expectations in Chapter 7), how to use the water fountain, how to put materials away on shelves, and how to pass and serve foods family-style. Knowing what to do gives children the power and possibility to act autonomously by following the rules and to comply with teacher expectations without external regulation.

Trying to understand children's points of view leads to efforts to change children's thinking and feeling and, as a result, to change their behavior. This is very different from simply trying to change behavior. Beth Van Meeteren writes about an incident in her Freeburg 1st-grade class when she tried to change a child's thinking rather than punish him for misbehavior.

Tracy, a child who walked with crutches, leaned across Dequavious' paper to get some markers. Dequavious took her action personally and gave her a shove that knocked her to the floor. (Tracy sometimes stopped breathing, and her full-time nurse had to resuscitate her, so any fall was of concern.)

After helping Tracy back in her chair and making sure she was all right, I said to Dequavious, "I need to talk with you. We need to keep Tracy safe." Dequavious refused and resisted my efforts to talk with him by yelling at me. I got him to sit down and began to explain how dangerous it was for Tracy to fall and how she cannot feel her legs. He was very interested. Later, I noticed he was over at the Peace Bench with her. I kept my eye on them, not knowing what he would do. Apparently, he wanted to find out more about Tracy. She came and got me, saying, "Dequavious needs your help to talk." I asked how I could help, and he said he was afraid Tracy would yell at him if he asked her questions. I asked him what he wanted to know, and he asked her if it was true she couldn't feel her legs. Tracy was very frank and answered every question he had for her from not feeling the backs of her legs to stopping breathing and needing rescue breaths and how much that scares her and how being knocked down sometimes makes her stop breathing. I asked them both if the other 1st-graders should know this information, and they both agreed we should talk about it at group time.

If the teacher had punished Dequavious, he would not have had the possibility to develop a deeper understanding of another and to experience his resulting empathetic feelings.

We have often heard teachers in early education classrooms say to children who are misbehaving, "You are making a choice to hit [or use an outside voice, talk to a friend during group time, etc.]." The problem with this type of comment is that it cuts off discussion and does not address children's real needs and intentions that are reflected in the behavior. We recognize that some children intentionally do misbehave, defy the teacher, and so on. However, when this sort of intentional defiance occurs repeatedly, it may be an indication that the child needs additional support from mental health consultants, special educators, or other specialists. In general, we do not think most young children consciously make choices to misbehave in these ways; rather, they simply act out impulses they cannot yet control. When this is the case, a teacher's assumption that a child is making a conscious choice to misbehave gets in the way of understanding the behavior and making efforts to help the child. Constructivist teachers try to help children become more conscious of internal impulses and their external consequences. For example, one Freeburg kindergarten teacher, Sherice Hetrick-Orton, talked with a frequently impulsive child, Chris, about how he felt before he hit someone. When Chris said he felt mad, Sherice asked where he could feel that "mad." Chris responded that it was in his tummy, and Sherice began a conversation about what he might do next time his tummy felt mad, to help him refrain from hitting. This finely tuned approach enabled him to become conscious of his feelings and what they meant. Influenced by Jane Nelsen's *Positive Discipline* (1981/2006), the teacher suggested Chris might give her a signal instead of hitting and helped him to select what the signal would be (touching his earlobe, his chest, etc.). They discussed how she could signal back (thumbs up, forming a circle with thumb and forefinger, etc.), even from across the room when she saw him but was engaged with other children. Sherice thus supported Chris in becoming more conscious of his feelings and exerting self-control when he became angry.

4. Avoid Ambiguous or Unenforceable Rules and Expectations

Although constructivist teachers minimize the exercise of coercion whenever possible, when they *do* use necessary control, they want it to be effective. Legitimate authority is undermined when teachers give children instructions and then do not enforce them. When this happens, children learn that the teacher's instructions do not necessarily have to be followed. This dilutes and squanders the teacher's legitimate authority. As mentioned in Chapter 6, early childhood teachers sometimes make rules governing how children should sit at circle—on their bottoms with their hands in their laps and their legs crossed. Anyone who has conducted a group time with wriggly 4-year-olds knows this is unrealistic for many. If a teacher tried to be consistent in enforcing this rule, he or she would spend the entire group time correcting how children are sitting! An expectation the teacher has to ignore is probably not a reasonable expectation. Whenever rules and expectations are enforced only sometimes, children become confused about when they apply and when they do not apply. Teachers must be clear about exactly what are the bottom-line non-negotiables, striving to establish only those that are necessary and developmentally appropriate. Then they must be consistent in insisting that these expectations be followed. This is not a new idea but should not be overlooked.

A common type of unenforceable rule or expectation is the ambiguous direction. This leaves the child wondering exactly what is expected. For example, the teacher might say to a child wandering around the classroom, "Aaron, what do you need to be doing right now?" This question conveys to Aaron that he is doing something wrong, but it does not tell him what that is, or what he should be doing instead. When using this question, the teacher assumes the child knows what he should be doing, but if Aaron does not know, he is left to guess what it is the teacher wants. It is more respectful to the child to state explicitly what is expected (and why, if that can be done briefly). "Aaron, it is Writers' Workshop right now. You need to get your journal and sit at a table to write."

5. Use Reciprocity Sanctions When Misbehavior Requires Attention

Piaget's (1932/1965) moral judgment interviews of children revealed six types of reciprocity sanctions that the children considered just reactions to misbehaviors: (1) natural consequences, (2) doing to the child what he or she has done, (3) depriving the transgressor of a thing misused, (4) exclusion, (5) restitution, and (6) censure. To say that children view these as just does not mean that we advocate using them. Instead, we recommend using them only when they can be invoked nonpunitively. This is tricky because, as Piaget (1932/1965) noted, reciprocity sanctions do contain an element of suffering. However, the suffering is not inflicted for the purpose of suffering, but "is simply an inevitable result of the breach of the bond of solidarity" (p. 206). The purpose of the reciprocity sanction is to communicate that the wrongdoer has disrupted an interpersonal relationship. Nevertheless, the young child may interpret a reciprocity sanction as punitive, or a teacher may invoke a reciprocity sanction with the intent to punish. When this is the case, it becomes an expiatory sanction and does not convey reciprocity. With time, clear explanation, and emotional support, however, the child can gradually come to understand and accept the moral logic of reciprocity involved in this type of consequence.

Natural or Material Consequences

Natural consequences are immediate and material (or physical) consequences of a child's action. They are not invoked by an adult; they just happen as a result of something the child does. When a child is careless at snack time and knocks over a glass of milk, it spills. When children dump all the sand out of the sandbox onto the grass, they no longer have sand to play with. When children do not follow the pretzel recipe carefully, the class snack may be inedible. These consequences become reciprocity sanctions when the child realizes that others also suffer the consequences. If pages are torn from a book, no one can read it. If carelessness results in damaged or lost game pieces, the game is less enjoyable to use or cannot be used at all. If tops are left off the colored markers, they dry up and no one can use them. It is the teacher's responsibility to articulate how the consequence affects others (for example, "What a shame that somebody tore/lost our game pieces. Now we can't play the game.") and to propose possible restitution ("Is there something we can do to fix it?").

When an immediate and material consequence can in good conscience be allowed to occur, it can be a powerful teaching tool. Teachers sometimes rescue children from natural or material consequences and lose an opportunity for children to construct the mental relationship between action and result. For example, the teacher may constantly put the caps back on markers. We understand the concern for waste but believe that the lesson on natural consequences is well worth a wasted marker. Karen Capo let her 3-year-olds at the Human Development Laboratory School experience the consequence of not cleaning up their toys and materials. The room was a mess when they came in the next day! No one enjoyed this, and most children began to take cleanup more seriously, reminding each other and helping each other.

In Coreen Samuel's kindergarten classroom at the Human Development Laboratory School, two boys were careless during a cookie-making activity (which might not be allowed by today's nutrition regulations) and did not pay close attention to the recipe. They put in one cup of baking powder instead of one teaspoon. The teacher observed their error and could have prevented it. However, she felt that the only way the boys would become more serious and careful about cooking was to experience the result of their carelessness. At snack time when everyone tried the cookies, children were disappointed and said they tasted "yucky." The teacher was able to review the recipe with the boys and help them realize their error. The next time they made cookies, they were more careful.

Many natural or material consequences are too dangerous or too expensive to be allowed to occur. We could not put eyes at risk by allowing children to work at the woodworking bench without their wearing protective goggles. However, some natural or material consequences that adults tend to prevent are not actually dangerous to children. For example, a teacher might remind children about putting on their mittens before going outside. If a child refuses to wear them and gets cold hands, this may make him or her understand the next reminder. Going outside without ones' mittens when it is only moderately cold may not be dangerous for a short period of time.

Children do not always make the cause-effect connection when natural consequences occur. Then it is the teacher's job to make the connection for children. At the Human Development Laboratory School Peige (T) brought such a consequence to children's awareness when she showed them a broken classroom holiday decoration at group time.

T: Before we get started on the story, we have a little problem. Do you remember we had talked about how careful we needed to be if we had delicate decorations in our class (holds up broken decoration)?

Children: Yes.

T: And we decided we liked this one?

Children: Yes.

T: (In a matter-of-fact, nonjudgmental tone) Well, this delicate decoration has been ruined and will have to be thrown away because people didn't take care of it.

This kind of follow-up allows children the opportunity to make a mental relationship between carelessness and resulting damage to objects.

Doing to the Child What the Child Has Done

This sanction is used mainly among children. A child who hits another may be hit back. Yet children may not recognize the reciprocity in this vengeful "eye-for-an-eye" response. For example, at the Human Development Laboratory School, 4-year-old Zelda was remorseless when she hurt Carol, but complained to the teacher when Wayne hurt her. Peige Fuller pointed out to her that Wayne had done to her what she had done to Carol earlier. Such interventions give children the possibility to decenter and to think about the other's perspective. Zelda has the possibility to make a comparison (a mental relationship) between her feelings when Wayne hit her and Carol's feelings when Zelda hit Carol. This relationship is not so easy, especially when children feel upset.

This sanction is rarely appropriate for adults to use with children. However, we have seen a situation in which a teacher appropriately reminded children that they had earlier refused to help her, and that made her reluctant to help them. Reading the story *The Little Red Hen* (Miller, 2004) may engender passionate discussion about whether the Little Red Hen should share her bread when no one would help her plant, harvest, and grind the wheat or make the bread.

Depriving the Transgressor of a Thing Misused

When used sensitively and with care, depriving the child of objects and opportunities when these are misused can help children construct attitudes of responsibility. An example of depriving transgressors of a misused opportunity occurred in the Human Development Laboratory School Investigators class, when Kenny and George run around in a dangerous way on the carpet. Peige withdraws the opportunity to play on the carpet and explains why to the children: "Kenny and George, sit down, please. Running in the classroom makes people fall down. I need for you to be safe. It is my job as the teacher to help you be safe." She goes on to tell the children that they have 5 more minutes of activity time left and that although they cannot play on the rug, there are other activities available to them.

It is important to note that this sanction is not just a matter of taking away an object or opportunity. It must be accompanied by an effort to help children recognize the reciprocity of the relationship between the transgression and the consequence. Crashing a tricycle into another means giving up a turn and waiting for another turn. In the case of children fighting over an object, conflict resolution should always be the first approach. Depriving the children of the object in question should be used rarely and only in cases when the children cannot come to an agreement or when they repeatedly fight over an object. Even in such a case, the constructivist teacher who takes away an object or privilege temporarily does so with explanation and efforts to help children figure out a solution. Over time, children can learn that the advantage of cooperation is continuing to play with a desirable object. The teacher who encounters repeated conflict over a particular object may consider whether more of this material should be added to the classroom. If this is not possible, consultation with children about new rules governing use of the coveted object may be necessary. Some teachers of 5- or 6-year-olds are reluctant to solve the problem by providing more materials because they believe that working on a solution is more educational.

Exclusion

Exclusion from the group is a sanction that children frequently use when children violate the rights of others. For example, 3-year-old Zelda responds to Riana's pinching by telling her that she doesn't want to be her friend. If a child cheats in a game, the partner may refuse to play again. If a child behaves aggressively on the playground, the teacher may require him or her to play alone for a while, with efforts to help the child grasp the cause-and-effect relationship between his or her behavior and the reactions of the other children. Peige used the consequence of exclusion when Sean continued unwelcome touching of Clark at group time. Peige enabled Clark to move, and when Olivia sat next to Sean and was similarly bothered, she, too, moved. Peige emphasized the exclusion consequence to Sean when she said, "You keep touching all the children, and they don't like it, so they move away, and now you don't have anybody to sit by."

At group time, young children sometimes talk or play and disturb others. In earlier chapters, we discuss how to approach children in respectful ways in order to give them opportunities for regulating their behavior voluntarily. If a child causes serious disruptions, and efforts such as having the child sit beside the teacher or asking an assistant to sit beside the child are ineffective, the teacher may have to ask him or her to leave. How can this exclusion be implemented to reduce its potentially coercive effects? One strategy is to discuss with the group how children can take themselves out of circle when a teacher asks them to leave, sit quietly at a table, and return when they feel ready. It is necessary for the teacher to discuss with the group this idea so that children understand that they can decide when to return. The teacher thus cooperates with the child by offering a way in which to withdraw and return that protects autonomy. If an assistant is not available to help, the teacher may have to dismiss group time and have children engage in activity time while addressing the child who disturbed group time. This conversation should focus on helping rather than blaming the child. For example, the teacher might say, "I could see that you were upset when I asked you to leave circle. What did you think about that?" After the child responds, the teacher might use an "I" statement such as "When you were talking and laughing, I was worried that children could not hear the story. It's my job to make sure people can hear. What do you think we can do about this problem if it happens again?" By trying to learn and work with the child's perspective, the teacher may be able to lead the child to understand something of the perspectives of others in the group, including that of the teacher. This conversation should be relaxed and sympathetic but firm about the need for change. It is clear that this kind of effort to change how a child thinks and feels is very different from the arbitrary and punitive use of "time-out."

The exclusion sanction is difficult for adults to invoke without making it a punishment. Time-out is a widely used form of exclusion that is *not* a reciprocity sanction. Time-out involves no reciprocity because it is unilateral (invoked by the teacher), arbitrary (having no relation to a misdeed), and perceived by children as punishment. For these reasons, we do not advocate its use.

Exclusion by itself can be experienced by children as rejection and can damage relationships. To be effective in helping children recognize that their behavior has caused a rift in a relationship, sometimes teachers must be explicit in describing for children exactly what happened. This must be followed by letting the child know how to be reinstated with a wronged person or group. For example, Peige Fuller adjusts her Human Development Laboratory School lesson plans in order to help a 4-year-old reinstate himself after he is excluded from field trips. Ryan was a problem whenever the Investigators went on a field trip, running away from the group and violating other rules. As a class they discussed field trip rules and decided that any child who could not listen to the teacher's words and follow the rules on field trips would not be allowed to go on the next field trip. On a trip to visit the campus newspaper, Ryan refused to hold hands and ran away from the group. Peige knew she had to enforce the rule in order to impress upon Ryan the seriousness of the problem. However, a big field trip to the zoo was coming up, and she did not want Ryan to miss it. So she planned two small campus trips before the zoo trip. On the first, Ryan was not allowed to go on a walk across campus to play on some favorite trees. Peige emphasized that this was the consequence on which the group had agreed. Before the second campus trip, Peige talked with Ryan about his behavior, explaining that if he did not follow the rules, he would not be allowed to go on the zoo trip. She asked him if he could demonstrate to her that he could be trusted on field trips now. He said that he could. Peige gave him the opportunity to regain trust on the second small campus walk so that he would not experience the disappointment of missing the trip to the zoo. We should add that her strategy worked: Ryan followed the rules on the second walk and was allowed to go on the zoo trip.

Restitution

Restitution means paying for, repairing, or replacing an object in order to restore the situation to its condition prior to the misdeed. For example, Harry brought a new dinosaur to the Human Development Laboratory School kindergarten, to replace the one whose tail he had bitten off. Kathy, who tore Ellen's picture, repaired it and gave it to her. Restitutions also include actions taken to repair broken relationships. Apologies, when freely offered in a spirit of contrition, can be a form of restitution. Although constructivist teachers never require apologies (see Chapter 5), they rejoice when they witness sincere requests for forgiveness as a sign that children recognize how their own actions affect others' feelings toward them. (See Chapter 5 for other examples of restitution.)

When Dillon, a Freeburg 1st-grader, deliberately stepped on Grace's hands at the top of the slide, Beth Van Meeteren intervened, to take care of not only physical needs but moral needs as well. First, she comforted Grace and then tried to engage Dillon in conflict resolution. Because the perpetrator seemed belligerent, she took him aside and talked with him about how his actions caused physical pain and hurt feelings. When Dillon began to show remorse, Beth asked what he could do to make Grace feel better. Dillon suggested an "I'm sorry" card, and Beth encouraged him to carry out this project. Dillon presented the card to Grace, and she accepted his apology.

Censure

Piaget (1932/1965) found among older children the idea that sure (that is, the expression of disapproval) alone is a reciprocity sancti when it makes "the transgressor realize how he has broken the bond of solidarity" (p. 209). According to Piaget, for these children, "censure no longer needs to be emphasized by means of painful punishment: it acts with full force in so far as the measures taken by way of reciprocity make the transgressor realize the significance of his misdeeds" (p. 2006). The first author remembers vividly that day at about age 4 or 5 years when her mother responded to a wrongdoing by pulling her close and, with a note of sadness, telling her how disappointed she was in her. She cried with far greater remorse to this communication of a break in the relationship than she would have to a spanking. We must caution strongly that to be a sanction by reciprocity, censure cannot be presented as based on coercive authority. It must be based on disruption in a relationship that the child genuinely cares about. The disapproval of peers can be especially effective in making a child realize "the significance of his misdeeds."

Reciprocity sanctions are sometimes the same as what is often termed logical consequences in that they can be clearly and understandably linked to the child's behavior. However, Jane Nelsen writes in the 2006 revision of her book *Positive Discipline* that she has become aware that many parents and teachers following her advice to use logical consequences are actually punishing children. She now recommends that logical consequences be used only as a last resort. To avoid turning logical consequences into punishments, Nelsen (1981/2006) suggests using the following criteria. They must be related, respectful, reasonable, and revealed in advance (of a misbehavior) (p. 107). Finally, Nelsen concludes that she has seen consequences misused more often than she has seen them used effectively.

Because of the danger that children may experience these consequences (the six reciprocity sanctions discussed above as well as those generally referred to as logical consequences) as punishment, we agree with Nelsen that teachers should not leap to using consequences to solve every discipline problem. The challenge is to determine when these consequences are appropriate.

The first author interviewed Freeburg teachers about when they used logical consequences. Their responses can be grouped into two overlapping categories: (1) when misbehavior is very serious and (2) when the consequence can be closely related to the misbehavior. The first category included dangerous behaviors. The rule in one classroom was, If you hit, kick, bite, or do anything to make the room unsafe, you have to leave the room. This consequence is meant for the seriously out-of-control child and is intended to place the child in a setting where he or she can calm down. The child might leave the room and stay with an assistant or the school director. An out-of-control child may not be able to regain control in the classroom situation. Removal offers an opportunity for the child to regain control, prevents escalation, and protects the child's reputation from further erosion among peers. Another rule in this first category at Freeburg was, If you hurt other children, you have to play by yourself until you can play without hurting. This consequence is meant for children who repeatedly use aggression to get what they want. For example, a child may go from center to center, pushing others out of the way and grabbing things from other children. If the child continues to use physical means after the teacher intervenes to help the child learn other ways to get what he or she wants, the teacher may decide to use the consequence of exclusion. One teacher said to such a child, "I can't trust you to be with other children right now. When you play with other children, you hurt them. So you are going to have to play by yourself right now. When you are ready to play with other children without hurting them, come and get me, and we can talk about what you can do so that I can trust you to play safely."

In the second category, a consequence is closely related to the misdeed. Examples of rules or expectations in this category include the following:

- If you throw water at the water table, you have to leave the water table
- If you make a mess, you have to clean it up
- If you throw sand in the sandbox, you have to get out

During the 1st year at Freeburg, new tricycles arrived. Three-year-olds thought it was great fun to play something like bumper cars outdoors. The teachers, Christina Sales and Marilyn Luttenin, disagreed. They decided that the possibility of children getting hurt was great and that drastic measures were called for. Christina introduced the teacher rule: If you crash your trike into something, you have to get off and wait for another turn. (Children were using a sign-up list for turn taking.) Teachers reported that children learned very quickly how to maneuver the trikes to avoid crashes.

6. Promote Children's Reflections on Rules and Expectations

Part of intervening with children's self-regulation in mind includes promoting children's reflection on rules and teacher expectations. We want children to understand why a rule or expectation exists. Otherwise, they will not be motivated to follow it. When children do not understand the reasons for their compliance with teacher expectations, they are behaving heteronomously—being controlled by external power. When they understand reasons, they can begin to regulate their behavior autonomously. Following this principle leads teachers to provide children with explanations of why they are required to behave in certain ways that may seem arbitrary to them. It becomes almost second nature for constructivist teachers to explain the reasons when they present expectations or directives. For example, "I can't let you hurt children. I have to keep everyone safe. I don't want anybody else to hurt you, either. When you hurt children, you cannot be with them. That is why you are working/playing by yourself, away from the children right now."

7. When Power Struggles Occur, Disengage or Find a Way to Give the Child Power

Power struggles are situations in which two parties vie for control. A child who resists or defies a teacher is trying to be in control. The teacher who responds by putting more pressure on the child to comply is also trying to be in control. This cycle defines a power struggle. Many writers on discipline have discussed this problem that seems to arise in almost all classrooms (Dreikurs, Grunwald, & Pepper, 1976/1998; Gordon, 1989; Nelsen, 1981/2006; Nelsen, Duffy, & Erwin, 2007). The basic reason to avoid a power struggle is that no one wins. If the adult does use superior size and strength to overpower a child, the child has still won, having wielded power to make the adult lose his or her temper, feel frustrated, helpless, and so on. Overwhelming another person (whether adult or child) physically or emotionally is coercion.

Teachers (and parents) often find themselves in a power struggle before realizing it. That is because the child can begin a power struggle simply by resisting what the adult directs the class or the child to do. For example, the teacher might ring a bell or sing a song to begin cleanup, and a child might continue playing or working, refusing individual requests to help. The first step toward avoiding power struggles is to try to intervene before the behavior gets out of control. Once a situation is identified that triggers a child's resistance, the teacher can plan how to deal with it, to prevent or defuse a power struggle.

A child's struggle for power often arises from either too little or too much external control. Children who get into power struggles often do so out of feelings of powerlessness. Therefore, one way to avoid power struggles is to find ways to give children legitimate power. In constructivist classrooms, teachers constantly look for ways to empower children. In one preschool classroom, a particular child always got into a power struggle with the teacher at cleanup time when he refused to clean up. The teacher defused his defiance by putting him in charge of turning the sand clock over when it was time for the 5-minute warning, watching the clock until all the sand had run through, and then telling everyone that it was time to clean up. This power and responsibility transformed him and ended the power struggle around cleanup.

SITUATIONS THAT CAN LEAD TO MISBEHAVIOR

Some classroom situations that can make misbehavior more likely can be avoided. These include the following:

- Crowding in a part of the classroom
- Insufficient amount of engaging activities or materials
- Too much time spent waiting

We discuss why these can lead to misbehaviors.

Crowding in a Part of the Classroom

When insufficient space prevents children from engaging in an activity, elbows fly, bodies push, voices rise, and tempers flare. Sometimes the pretend area or the block area is not large enough and needs to be expanded so that children do not unintentionally interfere with others. Classrooms are sometimes small and present special challenges to finding enough space for activities. Every teacher has had the experience of many children flocking to a new activity. At that moment, a teacher can suggest a sign-up list or call everyone back to the group time area to discuss the problem and find a solution. When teachers understand and anticipate the problem that crowding can cause, they can plan for it. Some ways to plan for the possibility that many children will want to do a new activity include discussing the potential problem before activity time and asking children to decide what to do, organizing a sign-up list before activity time, planning several centers with the same activity so that all who want to can do the activity right away, and making sure that all centers are appealing to children so that the rush to one is less likely.

Insufficient Amount of Engaging Activities or Materials

Sometimes curriculum in early childhood classrooms is not engaging because it is either too far above or too far below children's levels of competencies. Frustration or boredom can result. Children often misbehave when they have nothing they want to do. Insufficient materials lead to the same problems. Unfortunately, we have seen many classrooms where rowdiness and misbehavior result from competition for a limited number of interesting or desirable materials/activities. Instead of dealing with this as a behavior problem, teachers should view it as a curriculum problem and (1) plan activities for the range of developmental levels in the class and (2) make materials available in sufficient quantities for the whole class.

Too Much Time Spent Waiting

In many schools, children often are required to wait. They must wait in line for recess, lunch, a drink, to go home, and so on. In addition to wasting precious time, waiting invites misbehavior. To minimize wait time, teachers must plan carefully and make decisions about how to organize situations that do not include waiting. When wait time is unavoidable, teachers can prevent the negative effects of waiting by giving children something interesting to pay attention to. For example, they may read a funny poem or engage children in singing to occupy the time. Some teachers have found appealing and educational ways to dismiss children from group time such as by using the first letter in children's names, a color that appears in their shirts, or the type of shoes they are wearing. If an assistant teacher can lead the first children dismissed on to their destination, little time is wasted in waiting.

11

Activity Time

Children in constructivist classrooms spend a significant portion of each morning and afternoon engaging in activities of their choice such as group games, physical-knowledge activities, pretend play, literacy and mathematics activities, block building, and art. How the teacher manages activity time is extremely important for the sociomoral atmosphere.

This period of the day is sometimes referred to in early education as *free play*. In the best classrooms, what is "free" about free play is children's freedom of choice among a variety of activities. In the worst classrooms, what is "free" is the teacher's freedom from teaching responsibility. A teacher new to the Human Development Laboratory School understood free play in this second way and commented that free play did not occur in our classrooms. She saw free play as a time when the teacher reads or gets caught up on records or housekeeping chores while the children play by themselves. In this sense, our activity time is not free play. Although activity time in a constructivist classroom may look a lot like free play to the untrained observer, a trained observer will note the constructivist teacher's very active role and the educational purposes of the varied activities provided.

Over the years, we have observed three particular mistakes in implementing activity time. One is to spend such a large proportion of time in classroom management that the teacher has little opportunity to observe children's reasoning. When the teacher's preoccupation remains solely with cleaning up, keeping the paint jars filled, and engaging in overall classroom supervision, he or she does not become intimately involved in the activities themselves. The complexity of activity time, with many activities and many active children, makes this mistake an easy one to make. Without closely observing or engaging with children, the teacher will not find out what children are learning and what difficulties they have. This knowledge is necessary for productive intervention and future planning.

A second mistake is to provide few activities that inspire children's reasoning. When children do not have intriguing possibilities, their reasoning remains at a low level, and management problems arise. Without activities that inspire interest and personal purpose, children will not benefit from activity time, and the sociomoral atmosphere will deteriorate.

A third mistake is to relate to children in an authoritarian way so that children are oriented to figuring out what the teacher wants them to say or do. As discussed in Chapter 3, authoritarian engagement with children cuts off or circumvents the flourishing of their spontaneous honest reasoning in a cooperative atmosphere.

Hoping this chapter helps teachers avoid these mistakes and enriches activity time, we discuss objectives, categories of knowledge reflected in activities, and principles of teaching.

OBJECTIVES

Specific objectives for different activities vary according to what is provided on a given day. Constructivist teachers plan activities in which children are likely to experience the disequilibrium that Piaget argued is necessary for learning (see Chapter 2). For example, a teacher might decide to promote disequilibrium by asking children in a ramps-and-pathways activity (DeVries & Sales, 2010) if they can make a marble go uphill without pushing it. Disequilibrium is also the objective when encouraging children to consider contradictory opinions and supporting the search for truth through experimenting and discussing results. The constructivist teacher has disequilibrium as an objective when asking children to figure out how to take turns with the activity when space is limited and helping them become conscious that many want this privilege at the same time. And, finally, the teacher guides children as they cope with disequilibrium and try to figure out a way to agree and establish a new interpersonal equilibrium.

One way to state our fundamental objective for children during activity time is to refer to Eleanor Duckworth's chapter "The Having of Wonderful Ideas" in her book by the same title (1987/2006). We want children to be so engaged in pursuing their interests and purposes that they will be inspired to have wonderful ideas. This is the essence of the constructive process.

KINDS OF KNOWLEDGE REFLECTED IN ACTIVITIES

Piaget's (1964, 1969/1970) distinction among kinds of knowledge is useful to teachers in thinking about activity time. We discuss physical knowledge, logico-mathematical knowledge, and conventional knowledge in relation to the construction of mental relationships.

Physical Knowledge

One type of psychological experience is physical experience that involves acting on objects and observing their reactions, leading to knowledge of the objects. Knowledge that has its source mainly in objects is called *physical knowledge.* This may be action simply to find out what will happen (without a preconceived idea) or to find out if the object will react as one expects. The source of physical knowledge is therefore the object. The child cannot construct physical knowledge without information about the object's reactions to actions. For example, physical knowledge about sinking/floating requires observing how various kinds of objects behave in water and making and revising mental relationships in the course of these observations.

Conventional Knowledge

Conventional knowledge is arbitrary truth agreed upon by society (such as that December 25 is Christmas Day in the United States and the rule that cars stop when a traffic light is red). The source of conventional knowledge is other people, through various means of communication.

Logico-Mathematical Knowledge Revisited

In the first edition of this book, we referred to a third kind of knowledge—*logico-mathematical knowledge*—a term we now prefer not to use. To explain, let us recall that Piaget distinguished between physical *experience* and logico-mathematical *experience.* Logico-mathematical experience, in contrast to physical experience, consists of mental actions on objects that introduce characteristics that objects do not have into the individual's understanding of those objects. For example, number is not a property of any group of objects but consists of mental actions or relationships created by an individual. That is, the "twoness" of two objects does not exist in either object, but consists of relationships made by the individual who confers on them this characteristic of quantity. As stated elsewhere, "Logico-mathematical knowledge consists of relationships which the subject creates and introduces into or among objects" (Kamii & DeVries, 1978/1993, p. 16).

This terminology has been a stumbling block for many teachers who think of knowledge in terms of content. However, in a certain sense, content is irrelevant to logico-mathematical knowledge. That is, one can mentally organize pebbles, blocks, friends, or whatever objects by ordering, classifying, or enumerating them. The same mental action can be used to organize any content. What is important about logico-mathematical knowledge in Piaget's theory is that this is the structure of knowledge—actually, the intelligence. More on this below.

Part of the reason for discomfort in using the term *knowledge* to refer to mental structure is that Piaget referred to *logico-mathematical knowledge* only a few times, much more frequently referring to *logico-mathematical relationships*. We want to state clearly that logico-mathematical *knowledge* and logico-mathematical *relationships* both refer to the organization or structure of the mind. Piaget also used the term *logico-mathematical* in other ways, but always to refer to structure. He thus spoke of logico-mathematical connections, framework, and so on.

Now back to the issue of knowledge as usually understood in education. Pointing out that one cannot have a structure without content, Piaget used the term *mental relationships* in talking about both this structure of knowledge and its content. Many examples from the research of Piaget and his collaborators might be cited where they describe developmental levels in children's construction of mental relationships. To illustrate how Piaget (1974/1976) thought about content, let us consider one study in which children were asked to figure out how to make a 50-centimeter sailboat (with a keel, rudder, square sail, and hair drier for wind power), floating in a large circular bowl, move from a starting buoy to two other target buoys. They could rotate the sail and also slide it across. Children were also asked to describe and explain their actions and results. Without recounting the levels here, we want to point out that these describe a gradual progression in grasping the practical significance of the various factors and coordinating the geometrical and causal relationships among these. Piaget talks about how at Stage 3, children are able to make and coordinate relationships among the positions of the rudder or the sail, the directions of the boat, the directions of the water or the wind, and their relative movements and, finally, are able to come to "a geometrical and dynamic (causal) interpretation of the system as a whole" (p. 149). It is clear in this example that knowledge content and logico-mathematical organization cannot be separated. Every mental relationship has both structural and content aspects.

Piaget (1936/1952) defined intelligence as "the construction of relationships" (p. 418). This statement refers to mental structure. He also commented that "making a new relationship involves invention of something novel in the child's organization of the world" (1969/1970, p. 77). This statement refers to both structure and content. When Piaget talked about his "general theory of intelligence *or* of knowledge" (Piaget & Garcia, 1983/1989, p. 184, emphasis added), he complicated our understanding of these interdependent terms. We therefore find it useful to talk about a hypothetical coin (representing the mind) with indissociable sides. One side represents knowledge, and one side represents intelligence. Mental relationships related to content are on the knowledge side, and mental relationships related to organization or structure are on the intelligence side of the coin. Piaget emphasized that intelligence and knowledge of the universe progress together and are transformed simultaneously.

Having made the distinctions between kinds of knowledge, Piaget quickly points out that it is difficult to conceive of pure physical or conventional knowledge. All knowledge content involves logico-mathematical organization. For example, the child who pushes a ball on an incline may notice that this object reacts differently from a cube or other object. The *difference* does not exist in either object. It is created mentally by the child. The child putting objects in water may notice that most wooden things float and most metal things sink; this categorization is logico-mathematical organization of observations. A child who knows that Houston is in Texas has constructed a logico-mathematical relationship of inclusion. The first author is reminded of a 5-year-old seated next to her on an airplane. He looked out the window as the plane flew over Houston and asked, "Is Houston by Texas?" This question showed that he was puzzling over the spatial relationship between Houston and Texas but did not understand the spatial inclusion of Houston *in* Texas. He also lacked the conventional knowledge of the political organization into city and state that requires a logico-mathematical relationship of inclusion.

Thus, we can talk about children's thinking in terms of its logico-mathematical organization or mental relationships of which the thinker is unaware. We can also talk about mental relationships in terms of the content of which the thinker is aware. In the examples above, content involves movement of a ball, whether objects stay on top of water or go to the bottom, color, and geographic areas. When we want to talk about children's conscious thinking, we focus on the knowledge content.

In trying to understand children's thinking in the classroom, we prefer to focus on mental relationships in the minds of children—content relationships they consciously make—while recognizing that organization or structure relationships lie behind and make possible the content relationships.

How are these distinctions useful to a teacher? First, they are useful because they help the teacher understand that young children construct intelligence as well as knowledge in the course of physical experience. Constructivist teachers recognize that the young child is still dependent on contexts involving physical action for construction of mental relationships that constitute both knowledge and developing intelligence. This leads the teacher to plan physical-knowledge activities in which children can act on objects and observe their reactions.

Second, the teacher can think about what kind of knowledge is involved in curriculum topics. For example, a study of dinosaurs involves knowledge that is conventional in nature, such as the names of dinosaurs and the class names *carnivore, herbivore*, and *omnivore*. Children can construct content knowledge of herbivores, carnivores, and omnivores only if the teacher explains the meaning of these words that describe what dinosaurs eat. Although the names are arbitrary conventions, the classification is a logico-mathematical organization of the content. That is, children have the possibility to construct the mutually exclusive nature of the subcategories *herbivore, carnivore*, and *omnivore* and their hierarchical relation to the superordinate category of *dinosaurs*. In contrast, in sinking/floating activities children are motivated to construct mental relationships about how objects act in water. Although the teacher would not hesitate to inform children of the definition of *herbivore*, he or she would not tell children the principle of specific gravity because children cannot observe this principle. They can only observe the reaction of each object to its placement in water. Piaget's distinctions between kinds of knowledge therefore help the teacher make decisions about how to engage with children in activities. We discuss this further in the section below on fostering reasoning.

PLANNING FOR ACTIVITY TIME

Managing a productive activity time requires careful planning. The teacher plans only one activity in which teacher assistance and intervention are required and all other activities that children can do on their own. For example, sinking and floating and parachute making would not be planned for the same day because each of these requires a great deal of teacher intervention to promote children's reasoning.

In order to help parents understand the educational objectives of activity time, rationales for general categories of activities were written by the first author and teachers at the University of Houston Human Development Laboratory School. These were posted in the hallway on a parent bulletin board so teachers did not need to repeat these in weekly lesson plans (see Appendix). Examples of rationales for specific activities are given below in the section on planning for children's reasoning.

Constructivist education is not a "cookbook curriculum." Therefore, we talk about a general approach and offer examples of planning, to aid teachers in creating their own curriculum that will be tailor-made for their children. For further guidance with regard to objectives, planning, and intervention, the reader can consult previous books on constructivist early education: group games (DeVries et al., 2002; Kamii & DeVries, 1980), physical-knowledge activities (DeVries & Sales, 2010; DeVries et al., 2002; Kamii & DeVries, 1978/1993) and activities involving number and arithmetic (Kamii, 1982, 1985, 1994, 1989/2004). The secret of a successful activity time is planning to appeal to children's interests, purposes, reasoning, and cooperation. We discuss these below.

Appeal to Children's Interests

We discuss in Chapter 4 the importance of interest as the affective fuel of activity that leads to intellectual and sociomoral progress. How does the constructivist teacher select activities that will interest children? It is not always possible to be sure ahead of time. Constructivist teachers take an experimental attitude.

Careful observation of children's spontaneous activities can be a source of new ideas for activities that appeal to children's interests. Children's direct suggestions are also excellent resources for activities. We describe in Chapter 4 how one constructivist teacher consulted children about what they wanted to know. Human Development Laboratory School teachers routinely did and found that it is an important way to communicate to children that they can find out what they want to know in school. Children bring a special energy to activities derived from their own expressed interests. However, children may be interested in materials and activities they cannot think of on their own. In addition to taking children's expressed interests seriously, the teacher's responsibility is to offer activities and then pay attention to whether children are, in fact, interested.

Appeal to Children's Purposes

Interest is the springboard for purpose. General interest in materials leads children to explore them and find purposes. Constructivist teachers help children find *their* purposes in activities. This principle, however, does not mean that the teacher should never suggest purposes. When children are interested in materials, the teacher then has the opportunity to suggest a specific purpose.

When we say that activities must appeal to children's purposes, we mean that children must find in the activities something that they are motivated to do out of their own interest, not because they are being asked to do them by the teacher. For example, when a teacher sets out a boat-making activity, the goal is for the activity to be so fascinating that children will want to figure out how to make a boat and test it to see if it will float.

In contrast, consider an activity once described to us in which the teacher's goal was for the children to learn their colors. One week, the theme was "blue." Everything the children did related to the color blue. They made blue play dough, made and drank blue Kool-Aid for snack, painted with blue paint, and so on. The problem with this type of approach is that "blue" in itself does not appeal to children's active purposes. Rather, the children's purposes were to experiment with the play dough, mix and enjoy the Kool-Aid, and create paintings. Recognizing and naming the color blue is not a difficult task for a young child and is best taught as a secondary objective in activities such as art in which children have something to figure out how to do. If the teacher's objective is limited to teaching when to use the conventional color name, more worthy objectives may be lost.

Appeal to Children's Reasoning

After appeals to children's interests and purposes, reasoning is close behind. The constructivist teacher plans in terms of possible purposes that will engage reasoning. For example, Marti Wilson, the Explorers' (18 to 30 months) teacher at the Human Development Laboratory School, wrote about her plan one week in the following way:

In Art, children will explore different media to figure out how they work. We will be experimenting with chalk, pastels, crayons, and markers. The children will be figuring out the best way to hold these to produce marks on their paper. If the tool is held in a different way, will they still be able to produce the marks? Does the amount of pressure used affect the marks produced? Through these experiences with the different media, the children may begin to construct some cause-effect relationships such as "When I move my hand a lot, I get many big marks, but when I move my hand a little bit, I get fewer small marks." I do not expect the children to verbalize these relationships, but I do believe they will be able to observe these differences. I will verbalize what I see children doing, to help them become conscious of their actions (for example, "I see that you are pushing harder").

Stephanie Clark, the Investigators' (3- to 4-year-olds) teacher, wrote the following:

Physical-knowledge activities will focus on sprinklers. Monday, I will put containers without holes in the water table. Tuesday, I will ask the children if they have any ideas about making sprinklers out of these containers. We will use a variety of tools to make these changes. Where do I need to make the holes? How many holes do we need? Can we use these sprinklers for something useful like watering plants? Thursday, I will put out a variety of tin cans perforated to facilitate the flow of water. Which do you think will pour the most water? I expect the children to guess the largest can (with only one small hole). Then I will show the children the perforations (some just around the edge of one can, some in a straight line across the middle of one, and many all over the bottom of a small can).

Peige Fuller, when she was the Investigators' teacher, wrote as follows:

We will play "Sardines" outside. This game is sort of like Hide-and-Seek in reverse. One person hides, and everyone else sets out to find him or her. When a child finds the hider, he or she joins him or her in the hiding place, until eventually everyone is jammed into the hiding place. Children experience disequilibrium when they see that they cannot choose the same kind of spots they do for regular Hide-and-Seek because the places are not big enough.

It is clear in these plans that teachers take into account children's levels of reasoning and think about what children might be challenged to think about.

One key to planning activities that promote children's active reasoning is to choose materials that are open ended and can be engaged at more than one developmental level. Children at a variety of levels can thus find something challenging to do. For example, in activities involving shadows, very young children will just begin to see the correspondence between the shapes of objects and their shadows. Somewhat older children will find it challenging to figure out how make a shadow bigger by backing away from a screen on which their shadow falls without losing their shadows (by staying in the path of the light). Children who can do this may still find it difficult to figure out how to make a shadow on the ceiling. Still others who have figured out the spatial relationships among light, object, and shadow will puzzle over changing densities in shadows, whether merged shadows are still there, and the nature of light. In any one class, teachers may have children at several developmental levels (see DeVries, 1986; DeVries & Kohlberg, 1987/1990), and the same activity can appeal to all of them.

In planning, it is important not to underestimate or overestimate what will challenge children's reasoning. The goal of teaching "blue," for example, is too easy for children. Although the blue activities offer challenges, the teacher did not plan for any learning beyond the color name. Had she thought of the educational advantages of blending color in paints and play dough, the color name objective would have shifted to a secondary emphasis. Without planning for children's reasoning, it is unlikely that the teacher will intervene in ways to promote it.

In contrast with activities that are too easy, many preschool programs set goals that are much too advanced for children. For example, for most children, it is not particularly useful to teach 4-year-olds to count to 100. Even mastering the rote memorization will have little effect on their ability to understand number as a system of relationships or solve a numerical problem. Instead, it is more useful to use activities such as those suggested by Kamii (1985, 1989/2004, 1994).

Appeal to Children's Cooperation

In Chapter 4, we discuss why it is important to appeal to children's cooperation. Planning for cooperation involves thinking about what kind of cooperation may be possible or necessary in activities. This can range from simple preparations such as deliberately setting out only one stapler for four children to share at the art table to devising physical-knowledge activities that require two children to work together, such as building and talking to each other over paper-cup-and-string telephones. Cooking is a particularly good activity for promoting cooperation if it is set up as a team effort in which children have to negotiate who gets to read out the ingredients needed, gather them from the pantry, read the recipe, measure ingredients, stir them, and so on.

We do not mean to imply that all activities should be cooperative or that children should not work or play alone. Children sometimes want and need to be alone, and their wishes should be respected. Constructivist teachers do, however, stay on the lookout for ways to facilitate cooperation between children during activity time.

PRINCIPLES OF TEACHING

The implementation of activity time is a different kind of challenge in comparison with group time where the teacher is clearly the leader. During activity time, the teacher's leadership is more subtle as children are encouraged to take the lead. Because children are so active during activity time, it is guaranteed that problems will arise. The challenge for the teacher is to take advantage of this opportunity to cultivate a sociomoral atmosphere of mutual respect and cooperation. We suggest five principles of teaching related to implementing activity time.

1. Pique children's interests.
2. Allow children to choose activities.
3. Encourage reasoning and intervene in terms of it.
4. Foster self-regulation and cooperation.
5. Be flexible.

We discuss each of these principles below.

1. Pique Children's Interests

Activity time begins, in a sense, at the end of group time when the teacher introduces the special activities that will be available that day. We can think of three general ways in which to pique children's interests.

Suggest Possible Purposes

We discuss above the importance of considering the possible purposes children may pursue in an activity. Sometimes, especially with materials unfamiliar to children, the teacher wants to open an activity to any and all purposes. For example, in the rollers activity at the University of Illinois at Chicago's Children's Center, Maureen Ellis introduced the materials by saying, "See whatever you can think of to do with these things."

When materials are familiar or when the teacher wants to promote a particular purpose, this can be suggested to children. For example, in shadows activities, we noticed that children were thinking about the shadow, the object, and the light, but not about what happens in the space between these. We therefore worked with Coreen Samuel at the Human Development Laboratory School to develop situations that would inspire children to think about what happens between the light and the object and between the object and the shadow. In one activity, Coreen hung a two-dimensional cutout of a house from the ceiling and cut out a door and windows, leaving shutter flaps so these openings could also be closed. She made a figure of "Uncle Wiggily" (inspired by the book *Uncle Wiggily's Happy Days*, by H. R. Garis, 1947/1976, which children knew well) and glued him behind the shutters of one window. Two scenes were prepared on movable dividers to represent the Forest and the River. These dividers were placed behind each other between the house and the wall. The wall had a permanent rainbow painted on it. Finally, a slide projector was positioned behind the house with a paper cone over the lens to focus the light in a circular spot on the back of the house. The purpose suggested to the children was "Can you figure out how to make Uncle Wiggily's shadow appear in the Forest, then in the River, and finally, in Rainbow Land?" Children were intrigued by these materials and eagerly took up the purpose as their own, figuring out how to open the shutters in the house to make Uncle Wiggily appear in the Forest, and moving the barriers one at a time to make him appear on the River and Rainbow.

Suggest Possible Techniques

When introducing activities, it is sometimes helpful to show children some examples of what they might want to try to do in an activity. For example, to introduce paper sculptures, Dora Chen showed 4-year-olds in the Human Development Laboratory School an example of strips of paper forming inverted U-shaped loops pasted at each end on a flat piece of construction paper. Some strips were fringed, some accordion pleated, some plain. She asked children how they thought these were made and suggested that they might try some of these ideas and think of others in order to make a sculpture.

Marti Wilson introduces activities carefully to her HDLS Explorers (18 to 30 months), in order to inspire them to reason. For example, she brings to group time a small container of paint, a sheet of paper on which she has made some potato prints, and a blank sheet of paper. She suggests the technique as follows:

In the art center, I made this picture this morning. Look. You know how I made these pictures? I took this potato and put it in the paint and I pushed it on my paper (demonstrates two prints and holds paper up to show the result to children). We have potatoes and paints in the art center. If you want to make a picture, what do we need to wear? (Children chorus "Smocks!")

In another center, Marti shows the children a container of animal cutouts, some laminated and some made of felt.

I have some animals in here (tilts container to show contents to children). Some of these animals will stay on the board when you put them up here (puts felt animal on flannel backed board). Some of them will not stay up (puts laminated picture of animal against felt; it falls). Some of them fall down when you put them up (tries another laminated animal). See if you can figure out which ones will stay on our board and which will fall off. There are lots of different animals here to try.

Conduct Discussion of Children's Ideas

In some cases, it is fruitful to conduct a short discussion of children's ideas about a physical phenomenon with which they will have the opportunity to explore and experiment. This serves a diagnostic purpose for the teacher to find out how children reason at the beginning of experimentation. It also serves to make children conscious of their own and others' ideas. At the beginning of what turned out to be a 10-week project on shadows, Coreen Samuel conducted a discussion with her 5-year-old HDLS Inventors. Announcing mysteriously, "Today, we're going to Shadowland," she invited children's ideas about shadows, asking, "What is a shadow?" Roddy said, "It's a thing who comes on your body when you're walking around." Brandon said a little wooden horse "might get to make a big shadow if it wants to," but the big horse makes a big shadow because "that's what it wants to do." Some children predicted that in the shadow of a large die, the dots would show, but others disagreed. Coreen then encouraged an experimental attitude: "You get to see what happens."

During an activity time in a public school in Waterloo, Iowa, just prior to a group time, 2nd-grade teacher Cory Levendusky had taken photographs with a digital camera of children's work with lengths of cove molding in a ramps-and-pathways activity (DeVries & Sales, 2010; Zan & Geiken, 2010). Cory used a projector to show these photographs on the classroom wall at the beginning of group time and asked children to think about them. He had noticed that many children were standing up long blocks as precarious supports for the cove-molding track and wanted children to reflect on better methods (T is the teacher; C is various children).

T: What were people doing to keep their cove molding up—their track?
C: Um, they were using blocks to keep, like two pieces standing up.
T: (Calls on another child who has hand raised)
C: Um, some of the colorful blocks. Sometimes they had to stand on top of each other to make it taller.
T: You had a lot of tall, high constructions. These colorful blocks: Were they solid, or were they cardboard, or—
C: Cardboard.
T: People who were using the colorful blocks, what would you say? Pamela?
C: We were using it to stack up so we could, like, make some crisscrosses so we could keep it up, so we could go two different ways.
T: Did anybody experience a problem—something that was not working for you?

C: We were kind of using one of those boxes until one of them were kind of tilty. We didn't have enough room to put them until one of them fell down because the other block was kind of tipping over until the block fell down, and the whole thing almost fell down.

T: Interesting that you said that some of the blocks were tipping, and it was hard for them to stand up. Anybody have any ideas about what we can do to make sure that wouldn't happen?

C: Put other blocks on the side of it.

C: Put it down by the sides of it so it makes it stay up more.

T: You think it would give it strength?

C: (Nods)

T: I saw a lot of people working as a group, sharing ideas. That's something that's worked, to think of how to solve a problem. You can get really good at building the same structure every time, but you can make different structures. You have to make the marble do different things.

C: You mean like crisscross?

T: All kinds of things—whatever you want it to do, you're going to have to come up with a way to make it do what you want it to do. And by listening to other people, you're going to have to come up with ways to do that. That's what we're doing right now. We're sharing what works well—some solutions and ideas—and we can apply that information to our structures. All right, who has something that worked that they were kind of surprised—"Boy, I didn't think that would work"?

C: Um, like, I put it on the suitcase that—we were even using the table with the overhead projector, and when we done that, we were surprised that it actually didn't roll off into the garbage can.

T: Who else found a surprising thing that worked well?

C: When we first tried, we used it straight (level), and the marble wouldn't move, but then we had a little slant to it, and it made it slide down more.

T: What I want you to think about now is what you liked the best about this. Think about it in your head. Then you can raise your hand.

C: I like it because we're all doing what we think that could have worked to make the marble go faster and faster as it rolled.

T: I'm glad to hear that. What's one thing you want to try next time?

C: We could kind of put two blocks together, and then so we could have enough of them to put the things so the marble couldn't fall, and the thing won't tip over.

T: We'll definitely have a chance to try that. I can't wait to see what you do next time. Thumbs up if you are excited for next time!

Everyone: (Shows thumbs up)

In this discussion, the teacher conversationally encourages children to think of what they tried to do, problems they encountered, surprises, and ways to make their structures more stable. He also asked them to think about what they valued in the activity and encouraged them to build different structures, ending by focusing them on what they want to try the next time.

2. Allow Children to Choose Activities

We cannot emphasize too strongly the importance of allowing children to move freely about the classroom, pursuing activities of their own choosing. This is important for children's developing autonomy in all domains. The child with solid experience in regulating the pursuit of interests is also more likely to become active in self-regulation through cooperation to settle disputes fairly.

We mention in Chapter 4 our disagreement with the practice of assigning children to activity centers and rotating groups after a certain period of time. We object to this practice because it does not respect children's interests or promote children's purposes. Even if a child is interested in an assigned activity, interest must stop at the moment determined by the teacher for moving to the next center. In response to this kind of management, some children simply do not invest themselves in the activities because they know they will be forced to leave them.

In Chapter 1, we noted that the Manager of the Factory classroom allowed children to choose activities only after they completed their worksheets or other work. We disagree with this practice because it also fails to respect children's interests. It reflects the teacher's interest in academics as the highest priority. While some value may be attached to center activities, they were used as rewards for academic work, and little effort was invested in making them appealing and challenging.

We do not mean to imply that constructivist teachers should never have periods of time set aside for required activities. For example, at Sunset-Pearl Elementary School, teachers were concerned that children were not reading enough on their own. Partly, this seemed due to the noise level during activity time. After much discussion with children, they decided to institute a schoolwide reading time called Solitary Quiet Uninterrupted Individual Reading Time (SQUIRT). SQUIRT happened every day (usually after lunch). The length of time for SQUIRT varied according to the age of the children, but during SQUIRT everyone, even the adults, engaged in quiet reading. Children could choose anything they wanted to read. They could read at tables, desks, or even sprawled on pillows on the floor. The only requirement was that they read alone. SQUIRT became a popular time of day for the entire school.

Although constructivist teachers want children to have control over what they choose to do during activity time, occasionally teachers may want to influence children's choices. For example, Peige Fuller noticed a group of three girls in her class of 3- and 4-year-olds who spent all their time in the pretend center with the baby dolls. She wanted to interest these girls in other activities without being coercive and decided to begin by expanding pretend activities. Removing everything from the pretend center, she engaged the class in discussing the types of pretend centers they would like to have. Over the course of about 3 months, they had a restaurant, a doctor's office, a florist shop, a museum, an office, a beauty shop, a library, and a grocery store. Pretend play was enriched, and the pretend center became linked to other centers. The museum (which was familiar to everyone because they visited the art museum on the university campus) led to creating art objects to display. When the teacher finally brought the baby dolls back into the classroom, the girls still played with the dolls, but their interests had been widened to the pursuit of many other activities as well. In Sherice-Hetrick Orton's kindergarten class at Freeburg, a beauty shop led to writing a list of services offered (including doing nails and hair and giving hand massages) and their costs, writing appointments, and calculating the cost (in play money) to each customer.

3. Encourage Reasoning and Intervene in Terms of It

Throughout this book, we try to point out that the sociomoral atmosphere that promotes moral development also promotes intellectual development—and vice versa. Essentially, this atmosphere is characterized by respect. That is, the teacher's acceptance of and openness to children's ideas encourage children to have ideas and to express them. To foster reasoning, we suggest four considerations. These are to respect preoperational reasoning, consider the kind of knowledge involved and the mental relationships children have the possibility to construct, assess developmental level in children's activities, and intervene in terms of children's reasoning. We discuss these briefly below. These provide useful examples of how constructivist teachers have encouraged reasoning as well as sociomoral development in these activities.

Respect Preoperational Reasoning

In Chapter 2 and throughout this book, we describe children's reasoning, which is qualitatively different from the reasoning of older children and adults. Adults often laugh when children say, for example, that the weather forecaster made it rain or that their shadow sleeps under their bed at night. These ideas, however, are the product of children's honest thinking. To dismiss children's preoperational reasoning as just cute is to devalue children's thinking and, therefore, to devalue children as thinkers. The sociomoral atmosphere is enhanced when the teacher respects children's ideas and reasoning.

Consider the Kinds of Knowledge

Constructivist teachers use the distinction among the kinds of knowledge to help them respond to children's wrong ideas. If a child's wrong idea is arbitrary conventional knowledge, the teacher does not hesitate to correct the child. For example, if a child incorrectly says he or she is painting with blue paint, the teacher may say teasingly, "I thought that was green paint." When a child's wrong idea involves physical knowledge, the teacher refrains from correcting, instead steering the child toward testing the idea with objects. For example, if children think that water can flow up a hill as well as down, then physical-knowledge activities involving the movement of water in tubes might offer children an opportunity to experience conflict between their expectations and what happens (see Kamii & DeVries, 1978/1993). When an error in thinking involves content that is logico-mathematical in nature, the teacher does not correct, but plans for more opportunities for children to go on reasoning about the issue. For example, if a child makes the logical error of addition in a board game (counting as 1 the space occupied at the end of the last turn instead of moving forward one space), the teacher makes a die with only 1s and 2s, so that the child will experience more frequently the contradiction of counting 1 and going nowhere. Correction of this wrong idea must be made by the child through thinking. Wrong ideas about physical knowledge and logico-mathematical content are not corrected because children may learn to mistrust their own thinking and look to adults as the sole source of knowledge. We want children to be confident in their ability to be thinkers and learners.

Assess Children's Developmental Level

We have emphasized that children construct many wrong ideas in the course of moving toward advanced reasoning about the world of objects and the world of people. While observing and engaging in activities with children, the constructivist teacher continually assesses how children reason.

We often state that constructivist education takes development as its aim (see, for example, DeVries, 1992). Essentially, this means that when possible, constructivist teachers think about children's progress through sequential and qualitatively different stages. However, Piaget's descriptions of developmental stages are often not helpful, because the tasks used for research interviews are usually not appropriate for classroom activities. We do not, for example, try to teach children to conserve substance (see Chapter 3) because this is an example of knowledge where, as Eleanor Duckworth (1987/2006) put it, "Either we're too early and they can't learn it, or we're too late and they know it already." We need more research that will help us recognize development in classroom activities, but some research exists. Examples are stages in children's practice of rules in marbles (Piaget, 1932/1965), stages in children's play of Tic-Tac-Toe (DeVries & Fernie, 1990) and Guess Which Hand the Penny Is In (DeVries, 1970), and stages in children's conceptions of shadow phenomena (DeVries, 1986). The reader may want to see a summary of these (DeVries, 1992). Here, we give a brief overview of Piaget's stages in the practice of rules because these apply to all group games.

In his research on children's play of Marbles, Piaget found four stages in the child's practice of rules. At the first stage of *motor and individual* play, the child's practice of rules is not even social. The child simply plays with the marbles, dropping them one by one onto a carpet, throwing them, or pretending with them.

The second stage of *egocentric* play is definitely social because the child tries to follow rules, feeling an obligation to play according to the authority that comes from others. However, the social character of play lies more in the child's intention than in practice. That is, children practice rules egocentrically—without realizing when their ideas about rules are different from those around them. In Marbles, for example, children may sometimes keep the marbles they knock out of a square and may sometimes replace them. Children imitate the observable features of others' play in a way that is correct in general but incorrect in detail. At this stage, children may play with others without trying to win. No competitive attitude exists, and "winning" means simply following some rules or having fun. Children playing together may even play by different rules without noticing it.

The third stage Piaget called *incipient cooperation*, characterized by the appearance of a competitive attitude. Children try to win and are concerned with cooperating by playing according to rules that are mutually agreed upon. Competition at this stage thus exists within a broader framework of cooperation to agree upon, accept, and abide by the rules. Competition is not the primary motivation for playing the game. Rather, the motive is to play together at a game in which everyone has an equal chance of winning. At this stage, children do not know all the rules, and their incomplete rule system results in a simplified game.

The fourth stage involves *codification of the rules*. Children are interested in cooperating to anticipate all possible instances of conflict of interest and in providing a set of rules to regulate play. When disagreements occur, players see the issue as one that can be settled through negotiation. Rules can be whatever players decide.

This research on children's play of games helps the teacher assess children's developmental level. A child's effort to play by rules is progress in feeling obligation to a social system of rules coming from outside the self. This attitude develops before children have a good understanding of rules and before they play competitively. Research shows that the emergence of a competitive attitude is developmental progress and should not be discouraged (though some children need special help in developing a cooperative perspective on competition). This is but one example of how it is useful for the teacher to think about developmental stages in assessing children's activities.

Intervene in Terms of Children's Reasoning

The way to deal with children's incorrect reasoning is to acce, . . . and then, when possible, set up a situation in which it is necessary for children to call into question their own ideas. The main thing to keep in mind is that children construct many wrong ideas in the course of moving toward advanced reasoning about the world of objects and the world of people.

We have noticed that the most successful constructivist teachers pay close attention to the details of children's activity. They try to figure out what children think in order to understand and decide how or whether to intervene. In a boat-making activity, for example, Rebecca Peña Hines provides 3-year-old Experimenters at the Human Development Laboratory School with a variety of materials on a table next to the water table. She asks, "What do you think would make a good boat?" Children select and try many materials, and Rebecca converses with children individually as they try cardboard, Styrofoam, and wood. When Andrea tries a strawberry basket several times (appearing surprised that it sinks), Rebecca asks, "Is there anything you could do to make that float?" Eventually, after error-informed experimentation, Andrea triumphantly sets the basket on a piece of Styrofoam.

Playing group games with children provides an excellent opportunity for assessing and promoting children's reasoning, both moral and intellectual. For example, when children all want to go first, it is an occasion to help children confront the fact that others have similar desires that conflict with their own. This can also be the occasion for helping children begin to realize the value of negotiating an agreement satisfactory to everyone. In playing a game of strategy such as Tic-Tac-Toe, the teacher can verbalize strategies that lead children to become more conscious of temporal and spatial relations. For example, "I'm going to put my X here because if I don't, you will finish your line on your next turn. I have to block you."

4. Foster Self-Regulation and Cooperation

Self-regulation and cooperation may be fostered by referring children to other children for help, supporting negotiation, promoting shared experiences, and responding to incidents of cheating by assessing intentionality. We discuss these recommendations below.

Refer Children to Other Children for Help

During activity time, the teacher will inevitably be barraged by requests for information, assistance, and intervention: "Hold this for me while I glue it," "Where is the tape?" "James won't let me play." Teachers cannot possibly respond to every overture and must decide which needs really require adult help. Children can learn to see each other as resources and not depend solely on the teacher: "I'm helping Sylvia right now. Maybe you can ask Lonnie to hold it?" "I think I saw Kadarion with the tape. Why don't you ask him where it is?" "Try saying to James, 'I want to play. When can I have a turn?'"

In Korea, constructivist education is managed by one teacher with 40 children. Young-Ae Choi, director of the Moon Kyung Kindergarten in Seoul some years ago, pointed out that one advantage of this teacher-child ratio is that children must depend on each other, and cooperation reaches a higher level than in classrooms with fewer children or more teachers where the teacher responds more frequently to children's appeals. Although we do not advocate putting 40 children in a room with one teacher, we respect our Korean colleagues' ability to successfully implement a constructivist program with this ratio.

Support Negotiation

Opportunities to foster children's negotiation abilities abound during activity time. Chapter 5 provides guidance on dealing with conflicts. Here we discuss a general approach to dealing with problems of sharing materials and turns with activities.

We would like to point out that we do not advocate forced sharing in constructivist classrooms. Especially if the item in contention belongs to one child (for example, a child-made boat) or has been chosen first by one child (for example, a puzzle), forced sharing is coercive and disrespectful to children. We believe that individual rights should be respected and that the teacher's interventions should focus on negotiation. "Did you ask Donell if he wants to use the boat with you or if he wants to use it by himself?" "You can ask Pauly if he wants help with the puzzle. He doesn't? Well, maybe you can do one by yourself, too, or find another friend to help you." If an item in contention belongs to the entire class, teachers can still facilitate sharing without being coercive. The way to do this is to give children the responsibility for regulating fair use of materials. For example, at the art table, a single stapler can lead to conflicts. The teacher can support children's rights and foster cooperation through negotiation. "I see that Kadeisha is using the stapler now. You could ask her to give it to you when she finishes." (See Chapter 5 for more guidance on conflict resolution.)

The problem of how to share limited resources can often be handled informally with children who want turns. For example, Mary Wells once brought a real parachute in a backpack to her kindergarten class in a Houston public school, and the children had the chance during activity time to try it on. In this incident, Mary (T) helps Nolan negotiate with Alan in order to get a turn with the parachute.

N: He won't give me it.
T: You haven't had a turn, Nolan? (To Alan, who has the parachute) Have you had a turn yet, Alan?
A: No.
T: Well, then you need to tell Nolan that he can have it when you are finished.
N: He won't.
T: Alan, what did you say to Nolan?
A: I said after I get through.
T: Okay. (To Nolan) Come listen to his words. He says when he gets through. (To Alan) When will you be through, Alan? Let's look at the clock and see when you're going to be through. Nolan, let's look at the clock, and let's see when Alan's going to be done, so you'll know. Okay, it's on the 2 right now.
A: I'll give it up on 4.
T: On 4, okay. (To Nolan) When the big hand is on the 4, he'll give it to you. Okay?
N: Okay.
T: So watch for it to go to the 4.

Mary shows respect for Alan's right to use the parachute while acknowledging Nolan's desire for a turn with it as well. She treats Alan as a reasonable person who will give the parachute to Nolan as soon as he is through using it. She also treats Nolan's desire to try on the parachute as reasonable and asks Alan to respond to Nolan. With Mary's help, Alan and Nolan negotiate a resolution satisfactory to both.

Other ways of dealing with the issue of sharing include using sign-up lists and choosing rhymes such as Eeney, Meeney, Miney, Moe (discussed in Chapter 5). When an activity is particularly popular, a sign-up-list procedure is one fair way to regulate turns. Children sign a list if they want a turn at the activity, and children and the teacher consult it to see who is next after someone finishes. The list removes some of the arbitrariness from deciding who gets a turn next and allows children to predict when they will get a turn, avoiding pleas such as "When do I get a turn?" "Can I be next?" "But I asked first." The teacher simply answers, "We're going down the list. Look to see where your name is."

Promote Shared Experience

Children's interactions during activity time include shared experiences as well as negotiations. As discussed in Chapter 2, friendly or shared experiences occur when there is no disequilibrium or tension to be resolved in an interaction. Children engaging together in absorbing activities have many opportunities for companionable sharing. It is the pleasure of shared experiences that provides a prime motivation for the kinds of interactions that lead to progress in sociomoral development. When children experience special friendships and the satisfaction of playing with others, they are motivated to prevent and work out conflicts. For example, in Chapter 5 we describe an intense argument between two 5-year-old friends over whether a jump in checkers was legitimate. It was a misunderstanding in which both boys were absolutely certain they were right. The strength of the friendship may be credited for the fact that they did not come to blows. However, the conflict became so intense that they screamed, cried, swept the checkers onto the floor, put their hands over their ears, and could not listen to or talk with one another. When her efforts to mediate proved unsuccessful, the teacher asked them to separate until they could listen and talk. Within a few minutes, Kerrick was trying to catch Jordan's eye, and when he did, he blew on his arm to make rude "raspberry" noises. This amused Jordan, and the two boys approached each other. The teacher asked if they wanted to talk first or clean up the checkers. Grinning with relief, they began to pick the checkers up off the floor. Kerrick continued to blow "raspberries" while Jordan shook with laughter. This illustrates the role shared experience can play in conflict resolution.

For young children, this kind of Level 0 shared experience serves a bonding purpose and should not be dismissed as mere silliness or discouraged. We have to remember that preoperational thought is also expressed in child humor that is very different from that of adults.

As they play, children engage in all levels of shared experience, from burping and other funny noises, to reciting together a naughty bathroom rhyme, to sharing a secret, to reflecting on how best friends fight "but then we get over it, don't we?"

Respond to Cheating by Assessing Intentionality

The problem of cheating is most often encountered in group games (see Kamii & DeVries, 1980). The issue of cheating is a delicate matter because it is easy to misjudge a child's behavior as cheating. Cheating is an intentional violation of rules in order to benefit the self. Young children often violate rules, however, without intending to cheat. Unintentional rule violations are often due to inadequate understanding of rules which reflects what Piaget (1932/1965) terms the child's egocentric practice of rules, discussed above. We give some clues for assessing intentionality and provide some guidelines for dealing with rule violation.

Clues to assessing intentionality. To determine whether a child is cheating, the teacher must consider various clues to the child's intention. Sneaky violation is definitely a sign of intentional cheating! For example, a child may surreptitiously turn the die to a 6 and pretend it was a fair roll. Blatant rule violation, however, is often not cheating. It is probably not cheating if the child makes no attempt to conceal a violation. For example, unselfconscious turning of the die may simply reflect an intelligent approach to succeeding in the game. Figuring out that getting a 6 is an advantage is cognitive progress!

The teacher should also be aware of a form of cheating that is midway between innocent and sneaky cheating. We have in mind those occasions when a child knows that turning a die to 6, for example, is against the rules, but does it openly without seeming to realize or care that others may notice. Similarly, in card games children may go through the "draw" pile until they find the card they want. Such violations can reflect the child's failure to appreciate the idea that respect for rules is necessary to fair and satisfying play. Intellectual and moral aspects are not coordinated into a system. At times, a conscious decision to violate a rule wins out as an intelligent way to succeed.

Children often violate rules because they have not yet constructed an understanding of them. Breaking a rule you do not understand is not cheating. Therefore, it is important for the teacher to figure out how children understand rules. In the board game Candyland, players can take a shortcut if they land on the shortcut's beginning space. Children sometimes, however, misunderstand the rule to mean that you take the shortcut every time you touch it, no matter on what space you land.

Mistakes are not cheating. In games involving counting, children often make mistakes that simply reflect lack of construction of numerical notions. For example, in counting, a child may recite the sequence of numbers incorrectly. Correspondence may be imperfect between the spoken numbers and pointing to dots on a die or spaces on a board. A child may make the "logical error of addition," as described above. A child may skip the space occupied by another player, failing to count it because of lack of the logic that all spaces must be counted on the path to the final winning space. One clue suggesting these behaviors are not cheating is that they sometimes operate to the player's disadvantage. The teacher can determine whether counting errors are cheating only by observing the child's counting throughout a game. If the child always counts correctly except when the mistake benefits him or her, then the child is probably cheating.

It is important to assess whether a child has a competitive attitude. As indicated above, sneaky efforts to cheat indicate progress in this aspect of game playing. Although adults often see a different kind of competition for resources, such as calling, "Me first!" young children are not naturally competitive in games. They often think, for example, that the goal of a path game is to get to the end. When everyone reaches the end, everyone wins. For these noncompetitive children, no race occurs.

It is curious that children having a competitive attitude often play in what seems to be a noncompetitive manner. A competitive attitude often coexists with noncompetitive strategies. For example, in card games they may openly show their cards or look at another's cards. Before concluding that this is cheating, the teacher can observe whether or not knowing an opponent's hand helps the child play. Strategies may not be developed to the point that a child can understand how to use this information. In the absence of being able to use the information to advantage, there is no reason either to hide one's own hand or not to look at the opponent's hand. Children may want to win without knowing what strategies will produce a win. The competitive attitude is often the inspiration for a child to figure out strategies to win.

Guidelines for dealing with rule violations in group games. So what should the teacher do when a child violates rules? We suggest four guidelines.

- *Make sure the child knows what the rule is.* This can be done by referring to the rules. "Oh, I thought the rule said to roll the die like this (demonstrating). Let's check. Yes, it says to roll the die." If the child continues to violate the rule, he or she is either cheating or lacks the ability to understand the rule. Keep in mind that children often lose track of where they are on the board, and that going in turn can involve complex spatial and temporal reasoning. With three or more players, we often observe that children have difficulty in following the order of turns. For example, one 4-year-old saw her position as "next" in relation to both of the other players. She therefore explained, "It's Sue, me, Tracy, me, Sue, me, Tracy, me." When the children do not feel there is a problem with inconsistent ordering of turns, it is best to allow them to regulate turns, even when they make errors.
- *Find out if other players object to the violation.* "Is that right? Is that what we are supposed to do?" If all children are happy playing by a particular rule, or if children do not even notice that they are all playing by different rules, then the teacher probably should not insist on the conventional rules. However, the teacher can emphasize the rules in his or her own play and try to make children conscious of the rules.
- *If there is a dispute among children about the rules, uphold the value of mutual agreement.* "Doneisha thinks we should play it this way, and Nolan thinks we should play it that way. What shall we do? We have to agree on what the rule is."
- *As a player in the game, protest rule violations.* This is especially called for when children protest as well but can be done when the teacher thinks a child should be confronted with a different point of view. "If you can set the die down on 6, then can I do that, too?" If the child answers, "No," then the teacher can go on to question the fairness of this. "It doesn't seem fair that you get any number you want, but I have to roll the die. If you get to do it, then I should be able to, too." If the child says, "Yes," then the teacher should play by the child's rule and eventually point out the disadvantage of all players moving 6 on every turn. The teacher can also model correct game playing by stating, "I like to roll the die around in my hand and let it land on any number. I think it's more fun when I don't know what number I'm going to get. I like to be surprised."

When a child tries to be deceptive in cheating, the teacher should protest, but keep it light. "Are you trying to look at my cards? Oh, no, you don't!

I'm going to hold them real close so you can't see them." If a child cheats consistently, the teacher may want to point out to that child privately that the consequence of cheating may be that other children will not want to play games with him or her.

In summary, cheating reflects cognitive developmental advance in young children. It requires an understanding of how to play and how to win. What is missing, of course, is recognition that cheating violates the rights of others and that winning by cheating is not really winning. In the course of play, children gradually construct these fine points. When children are cheating and no one seems to mind, the teacher should not make an issue of it. But when children cheat and others object, the teacher should uphold fairness and reciprocity. "Nora doesn't like it when you skip her turn. You wouldn't like to have your turn skipped, either."

5.   Be Flexible

One key to a successful activity time is to be flexible. Children often do not do what you expect, and you have to shift your focus. For example, kindergarten children in Mary Wells's class were testing the boats they had made to see if they floated in water. Most children experimented in the expected ways. Then some children put pecans on their boats to represent people, and Mary asked how many they could put on and still keep their boats afloat. This led one child to try to make her boat sink! Seeing that it popped back up when the child held it on the bottom, Mary shifted to the child's goal. "How could you make it stay down? What would you have to put on it to make it stay down?" A child suggested a brick, and the search was on for ways to make boats sink.

It is also important to be flexible when children do not want to engage in a planned activity. Sometimes an activity falls entirely flat. When this happens, the constructivist teacher tries to figure out why the activity did not appeal to children. Sometimes modifications are possible to salvage the activity, but sometimes the teacher just scraps the idea. Sometimes an activity that appeals to one group of children does not appeal to another. The constructivist teacher takes an experimental attitude and tries to learn from these experiences.

The Sociomoral Atmosphere
of the School

It is impossible to realize fully the constructivist sociomoral atmosphere in the classroom if the sociomoral atmosphere of the school is not consistent. Unless the sociomoral atmosphere of the entire building is compatible with the constructivist approach, children will have contradictory experiences. The classroom does not exist in a social vacuum, and contacts with others outside the classroom form part of the sociomoral atmosphere children experience in school. In this chapter we discuss the work of Kohlberg and his colleagues on assessing the moral culture of institutions, especially high schools. In addition to studying how moral atmosphere relates to individual sociomoral development, they have conceptualized levels of moral atmosphere in institutions. Then we comment on children's and teachers' experiences of the larger sociomoral atmosphere in preschools and elementary schools and suggest principles for principals who wish to cultivate a constructivist sociomoral atmosphere in their schools.

KOHLBERG AND COLLEAGUES'
WORK ON ASSESSING MORAL CULTURE

In their book *Lawrence Kohlberg's Approach to Moral Education*, Power and colleagues (1989) describe the "Just Community." Implemented in high schools and prisons, the Just Community invites participation in democratic decision making concerning the life of the group together. In this approach, teachers can be advocates of a particular point of view, but they avoid indoctrinating students. Instead, they present positions that can be criticized, encourage students to formulate their own views on issues, and accept as binding the democratic judgment of the majority. Study of the Cluster School, a Just Community school within a larger high school, showed dramatic results. In addition to significant increases in the moral reasoning of individuals, racial relations improved and interracial conflict became almost nonexistent. Stealing ceased. Drug use virtually ceased. Cheating was curbed as students adopted an honor code. Educational aspirations were enhanced. In contrast, Power and colleagues commented:

> Our data indicated that the culture of the large public high school actually undermines effective moral education by subjecting students to negative peer group influences and by alienating them from adults. In such a context adult authority tends to reside more in adults' status and coercive power than in their moral persuasiveness. (1989, p. 300)

Kohlberg and his colleagues conclude their book by saying that the experience in a Just Community leads to a responsibility orientation characterized by awareness of and concern for relationships, the welfare of others, and the public interest. This research provides further evidence, in addition to our own study of sociomoral atmosphere and sociomoral development at the kindergarten level (see Chapter 1), that cooperative adult-child relations promote, and coercive relations impede, the development of moral understanding.

Kohlberg and his colleagues developed several ways of assessing moral atmosphere in an institution. For example, they describe five levels of teenagers' institutional valuing of the school reflecting increasing perspective-taking:

Level 0: Individuals do not value the school
Level 1: Instrumental value (school helps individuals meet their needs)
Level 2: Enthusiastic identification (school valued at special moments such as when a team wins a sporting event)
Level 3: Spontaneous community (school valued for closeness or friendliness of members where members feel inner motivation to help others)
Level 4: Normative community (school valued for its own sake where membership involves a social contract to respect the norms and ideals of the group) (Power et al., 1989)

In their research on the Cluster School, Power and colleagues (1989) found change from Level 1 (before the Just Community was established) to Level 4 (by the 2nd year of implementation).

Power and colleagues also discuss how norms (generally accepted rules) differ according to the sociomoral atmosphere of a school. Norms of order are the collective rules that simply safeguard the survival and orderly functioning of the organization (for example, rules prohibiting stealing library books or disrupting the classroom). Norms of fairness involve respect for the equal rights and liberties of individuals and the processes through which rules are made. Norms of community involve caring (sharing concerns and affection), trust, integration (sharing of communication among subgroups), participation (sharing time, energy, and interest), open communication (sharing knowledge about matters that affect the group), and collective responsibility (sharing obligations, praise, and blame). Research on the Cluster School showed a shift by its 2nd year from norms of order and fairness to norms of community.

Research on prison inmates also provides data that inform our understanding of the effect of the moral atmosphere of the larger institution on individual development. Scharf (1973) showed that many prisoners reasoned at the lower level in their view of the prison's moral atmosphere even when they were capable of higher level reasoning. Kohlberg and his colleagues realized that the moral education of inmates would be ineffective unless it also involved working with the prison authorities to change the moral atmosphere of the prison experience.

Power and colleagues (1989) state:

> The aim of developmental moral education has to be a change in the life of the school as well as in the development of individual students. For the teaching of justice, as the teaching of reading or arithmetic, is set in a *context* of a classroom and a school, and how the students experience the life of the classroom and school will have a shaping effect on what they learn from what the teacher teaches. (p. 20)

These findings suggest that in preschools and elementary schools we must also be concerned with the sociomoral atmosphere of the larger school institution if we want to be maximally effective in influencing children's sociomoral development.

CHILDREN'S EXPERIENCE OF THE SCHOOL ATMOSPHERE

The larger school atmosphere may foster or impede the development of the classroom's sociomoral atmosphere. The Boot Camp and Factory classrooms of our program comparison study (see Chapter 1) reflected larger school atmospheres consistent with classroom practices. The Community classroom, however, was an island within a larger school atmosphere that implemented behavioristic practices and contradicted the children's classroom experience in many ways. For example, children from the Community classroom described in Chapter 1 were admonished to walk in the halls in a straight line and without talking. In the cafeteria children were managed by a "token economy" in which they were given play money for good behavior. Children could exchange their "bucks" for trinkets in the school store. Bucks were given to children mainly for quiet behavior. According to the assistant teacher who supervised the class in the cafeteria, Community children got few bucks because of their talking. The person in charge of the token economy even yelled at the assistant teacher for not insisting that the children refrain from talking. Community children had specialty teachers for art, physical education, and music. The music teacher maintained a positive dynamic in the classroom, but this cannot be said for art and physical education teachers. The P.E. teacher was heteronomous and promoted a negative sort of competition among children. The art teacher was extremely negative and critical toward children. She insisted that children "create" exact, perfect duplicates of her models. When children did not demonstrate skills such as use of scissors, she shamed them. Children often ended their art period in tears.

Even in this situation in which the constructivist program received ambivalent support and in which children also had nonconstructivist experiences, they still made more sociomoral progress than the children in Boot Camp and Factory classrooms. We therefore suggest that a constructivist classroom atmosphere can to some extent compensate for a contradictory atmosphere in the larger school.

THE TEACHER'S EXPERIENCE OF THE SCHOOL ATMOSPHERE

The sociomoral atmosphere for the teacher includes not only relations with the children in his or her class, but also relations with the administration and other teachers. The school atmosphere can reflect the attitudes of the larger administration (school district, child care center, community organization, Head Start agency, etc.), but such larger organizations frequently do not have a coherent philosophy. More important to school atmosphere is the philosophy implemented by the educational leader (principal or director), discussed in the following section.

Relations among teachers can provide a network of support or its opposite, a feeling of negation and isolation. In our program comparison study the constructivist teacher of the Community classroom enjoyed a friendly atmosphere in relation to other kindergarten teachers, but 1st-grade teachers were critical. They felt that the Community teacher was too lenient and that she should not give children choices. The principal, while willing to give us a chance to try a constructivist classroom, had some doubts that constructivist education could work in a public school. Nevertheless, she supported the Community teacher after an unfavorable evaluation by the district evaluator stated that the room was not quiet.

The larger administrative structure also constitutes an important sociomoral environment for the teacher by offering supportive or antagonistic attitudes, help or hindrance, praise or criticism. The system within which the school operates determines salaries, working conditions, and evaluation procedures that carry a message of respect or lack of respect for teachers.

PRINCIPLES FOR ADMINISTRATORS

The sociomoral atmosphere of the classroom is embedded in that of the larger organization, be that school, school district, and state education department; center, Head Start agency, and federal government; or other organizational structure. Yet just as teachers have latitude in how they operate a classroom, administrators have latitude in how they operate their programs. Some readers who are already administrators may be considering how to change a heteronomous sociomoral atmosphere into a more cooperative milieu. This is more difficult than beginning a new school with teachers already committed to the constructivist point of view. Sarason (1982), in discussing the problem of change in schools, refers to the principal as having "a key role in the educational change process" (p. 184). In agreement with this view, we therefore focus here on how administrators can foster a constructivist sociomoral atmosphere in their schools. In this section, we rely particularly on our experiences with Deborah Murphy (former principal of Maplewood Elementary School in North Kansas City, Missouri, and Edison Elementary School in St. Joseph, Missouri) who consciously tried to be a constructivist principal and influence teachers in a constructivist direction. We present four general principles for administrators wishing to work toward a constructivist sociomoral atmosphere in their buildings.

Respect Teachers

Murphy (personal communication) expressed the following rationale for her attitude as a principal toward the teachers in her school:

If I wanted teachers to respect kids, I had to respect teachers. If I wanted students to be free to challenge rules and ideas, I had to permit teachers that same freedom. If I wanted teachers to reflect on their educational beliefs and practices, I had to be open to the possibility that I could be wrong as well.

Although not taking a specifically constructivist perspective, Sarason (1982) provides a cogent description of how teachers treat children as they are treated. He conducted research on constitutional issues (the written or unwritten rules) in classrooms by having observers in six classrooms (grades 3, 4, and 5) record every statement by a teacher or child that related to rules. The results were as follows:

1.   Rules were invariably determined by the teacher. No teacher ever discussed why a rule was necessary.
2.   The teacher never solicited the opinions and feelings of any pupil about rules.
3.   In three of the classrooms the rules were verbalized by the end of the 1st week of school. In two others the rules were clear by the end of the month. In one it was never clear what the rules were.
4.   Except for the one chaotic classroom, neither children nor teachers evidenced any discomfort with the content of rules—it was as if everyone agreed that this is the way things are and should be.
5.   In all instances rules involved what children could or could not, should or should not, do. The issue of what a teacher could or could not, should or should not, do, never arose. (p. 216)

Sarason comments:

What I became aware of during the discussion was that these teachers thought about children in precisely the same way that teachers say that school administrators think about teachers; that is, administrators do not discuss matters with teachers, they do not act as if the opinions of teachers were important, they treat teachers like a bunch of children, and so on. (p. 217)

Sarason's argument is consistent with our constructivist view. He argues that failures in introducing and sustaining educational change "have foundered largely because they have not come to grips with the power aspects of existing relationships" (p. 218).

As a former administrator of schools, the first author can testify to the many positive outcomes of respecting teachers. Teachers become autonomous and take more responsibility for the education they offer children. This leads to increased creativity in curriculum planning, increased competence and confidence as professionals, more collaboration with other teachers, and higher morale.

Recognize the Necessity for a Paradigm Shift

In earlier chapters we have discussed how a teacher's world view or theoretical paradigm influences teaching. The predominant behaviorist paradigm has influenced all of us. This is why Piaget's theory is such an eye-opener for most people. Piaget's theory leads us to think in a new way about learning and development, and the implications of his theory lead us to think in a new way about teaching. We can speak about these fundamental changes in our worldview as a paradigm shift from behaviorism to constructivism.

To recognize the necessity for a paradigm shift is one way to respect teachers. That is, administrators must recognize that just as children construct their knowledge and sociomoral convictions, so do teachers. This construction takes time because for some teachers it involves a basic restructuring of fundamental beliefs and ways of being. However, many teachers already possess constructivist intuitions and tendencies. These teachers are relieved to find a scientific rationale for what they have believed all along. Still, old habits change slowly. Working with teachers who have been teaching in nonconstructivist ways challenges a constructivist administrator who would like to realize the constructivist vision right away. However, short-circuiting the constructive process can lead teachers to view constructivist education as a set of tricks or methods rather than a way of thinking. Our goal is a shared vision among all staff in a school. When this occurs, the result is a unified community of professionals who work together and work with children in ways that go beyond the vision of the administrator.

Engage Teachers in the Long View

Murphy (personal communication) described this principle as "head lifting," the result of moving one's focus from the specificities of day-to-day work with children to considering "where we are going and why, versus all the other possibilities." Murphy emphasized that "to shoot for long-term outcomes without articulated theories, beliefs, and principles that form the bedrock is shaky ground indeed. So a majority of our time together has been spent in this arena." In pursuing the long view, Murphy and her teachers have tackled the following questions:

- What do we really want our children to know, do, and value as a result of their time with us?
- What principles will guide us as we become a collaborative team?
- What do we know about child development that can inform our decisions?
- What do we believe truly and deeply about teaching/learning?

Strategies followed by Murphy and her teachers in order to "flesh out outcomes and belief statements" have included conducting anonymous surveys, engaging in group process (such as brainstorming and consensus building), forming study groups, reading journals, undertaking action research, consulting in classrooms, participating in workshops and other forms of in-service, developing a professional library and media center, and encouraging individual reflection on readings.

Model and Explain Constructivist Attitudes and Practices

Modeling constructivist attitudes and practices can be summarized as treating teachers with the same respect as constructivist teachers treat children and by showing how to treat children respectfully. We discuss these below in terms of governance, discipline, and shared experience.

Governance

In contrast to traditional decision making by administrators, Murphy's Maplewood School exemplified shared decision making. Murphy (personal communication) described the issue of governance in terms of who owns the school and recounts her first faculty meeting, in which she asked teachers to make rules she should live by. The rules teachers suggested were the following: Tell the truth; keep us informed; give us specific, helpful feedback on our teaching. From recommendations by teachers through committee structures, Maplewood evolved to decisions made by the staff as a whole, students, and interested parents. For example, they considered how basal and workbook money could be used for more appropriate instructional materials and equipment.

The student council at Maplewood was unusual in its power to consider real school problems and make real decisions about issues of concern to children. For example, in a round robin when members say how they think the school is doing, what needs to change, and concerns to think about, the issue of wearing hats in school was mentioned. Murphy followed her typical procedure of getting people to engage in dialogue before they made a decision they would have to defend. After a straw poll, students were asked to take a position opposite the one they took in the straw poll and to give reasons for the opposite view. Murphy reports that this method was more successful with children than with teachers, who tended to be polarized and to find it difficult to consider another viewpoint. Murphy asked whether other information might be obtained in addition to their initial opinions. Students suggested contacting other elementary schools and the high school they would later attend, to find out what the policy on hats was and why that policy was instituted. Eventually, students decided that hats would not be worn in common areas (hallways, gym, cafeteria) but that hats could be worn in classrooms if the class decided on this alternative.

Murphy put mailboxes in strategic places in the school so that students could anonymously submit an idea, complaint, or issue for student council consideration. Students therefore did not have to be on the student council to raise an issue. Teachers, too, could communicate a question, idea, or concern anonymously. Murphy notes that fewer letters were submitted to the student council at the end of the year than at the beginning, and that teachers used the anonymous communication less frequently. She believes this showed that the teachers were getting better at resolving issues at the classroom level and that people in the school were developing a sense of community in which they openly discussed concerns.

Discipline and Conflict Resolution

Murphy commented that the greatest challenge for a constructivist principal involves discipline. Teachers generally expect principals to resolve all situations referred to them. The principal who does not quickly fix a problem is not a good principal in teachers' eyes. In one instance, a teacher felt that a child was manipulating Murphy. Murphy invited the teacher to observe her problem-solving approach in which she listened and showed respect for the child's viewpoint. Afterward, Murphy and the teacher critiqued the process and developed a shared understanding of the problem. Murphy emphasized in her problem-solving approach that there is "no one rule or consequence that fits all situations." She explained to teachers that her concern was with long-term sociomoral growth and not just a "quick fix." According to Murphy (personal communication), "The point is to grow and not that someone wins. The long view leads to different strategies than just maintaining law and order for the day."

In our view, "discipline" is not appropriate in a constructivist school. As argued in Chapter 10, cooperative alternatives to discipline focus on nonarbitrary solutions. The establishment of a sociomoral atmosphere actually reduces the need for discipline because children do not have to struggle against adult authority in order to maintain their self-respect.

Shared Experience

We would like to point out the importance of shared experience in the sociomoral atmosphere of the school. We do not refer to school spirit as shared pride and identification when the school team wins a football game (Level 2 of institutional valuing, as previously described; Power et al., 1989). We refer, instead, to students' valuing the school because it is the kind of place in which people want to help each other and serve the community as a whole (Level 3) and to students' valuing the school as a community in which members feel an obligation to group norms and responsibilities (Level 4).

Student Council discussion of concerns led to the idea of a buddy system at Maplewood School whereby children would help other children with academic problems, emotional problems, and conflicts with adults in their lives. According to Murphy, students really took charge and decided what steps to take to bring this system about. Student Council members decided that three children should be elected from each class to be buddies. They emphasized to their classmates that a good buddy would have three critical attributes: be a good listener; be trusted not to tell; and have good ideas. Student Council members emphasized that a good buddy might not be the smartest, the most popular, or the best leader. After selection of the buddies, the next step was that the buddies decided they wanted high school students to train them. The wellness coordinator at the high school developed a group to come once a week and facilitate the buddy system. They did role playing and discussed issues such as how to identify themselves and whether to stay after school to pursue buddy activities.

THE SOCIOMORAL ATMOSPHERE
OF THE STATE DEPARTMENT OF EDUCATION

We have mentioned that the larger administrative organization can support or obstruct the implementation of a constructivist sociomoral atmosphere in a classroom or school. Obviously, the more philosophical agreement exists within the entire culture of the school, the easier it is to establish and maintain any type of sociomoral atmosphere. The state department of education sets mandates for schools that have a great impact on the sociomoral atmosphere within a public school or classroom. We pointed to the state of Missouri as a model in this regard for a time. There constructivist education (called Project Construct) was officially adopted by the State Department of Elementary and Secondary Education for pre-K through grade 1. Project Construct could be voluntarily adopted by school districts or by individual schools. Consultants (including the present authors) provided training to a core group of educators, who then offered Saturday workshops, summer institutes, and special sessions at the annual Conference on the Young Years. The state department published a curriculum guide (Murphy & Goffin, 1992), a framework for curriculum and assessment (Missouri Department of Elementary and Secondary Education, 1992), and a newsletter.

Missouri teachers wishing to implement Project Construct participated in training to which they took an administrator, a requirement that worked to ensure administrative support. Project Construct was for years implemented in more than 100 Missouri schools. The Project Construct National Center, located at the University of Missouri–Columbia, oversaw continuing development, including creation of assessment and evaluation methods that were consistent with constructivist objectives. In addition, early education teacher certification requirements and teacher evaluation procedures were developed to reflect Project Construct principles.

APPENDIX

Rationales for General Categories of Constructivist Activities During Activity Time

The following rationales were written by the first author and lead teachers in the Human Development Laboratory School at the University of Houston. We posted these on a parent board in the entry hallway to inform parents and visitors. In addition, teachers wrote rationales for selected activities in their weekly lesson plans.

Pretense

Pretense is the ability to think about a nonpresent object, person, or event and is a major step forward in cognitive development. Pretense involves decentering to consider the points of view of others. Through pretense, children experiment with situations, relationships, and emotions that are not well understood. In play, children are in control and can structure their experiences so as to work through personal concerns and interests. Pretense is a kind of "language" that is especially important in the years when children's verbal language is not fully developed.

Language and Literacy

The basis for language and literacy lies in general symbolic and representational development that begins in the 2nd year of life with spoken language and pretense. Throughout early childhood language develops through social interaction in a language-rich environment that includes children's stories, poetry, rhymes, and songs. Children are encouraged to use their words to express thoughts and feelings. Teachers model effective communication and refrain from speaking for children. Through entertaining stories children construct knowledge of book characteristics (author, illustrator, page progression), conventions of written language

257

(separation of print and picture, top-to-bottom and left-to-right sequencing, and correspondences between spoken and written language), and elements of story (setting of scene, introduction of characters, problem, and resolution).

Through all these experiences, children are constructing semantic and syntactical rules. The constructive process includes errors such as overgeneralization ("foots," "goed") that children correct with increased language experience.

Children begin to learn to read and write in ways analogous to learning spoken language—through stumbling first approximations. Teachers support these efforts in a variety of ways by encouraging and accepting children's: (1) writing from scribbling to pseudoletters to conventional letters, invented spelling, and conventional spelling; and (2) pretend reading, recognition of important words such as names of self, family, and friends, signs and labels in the environment, beginning hypotheses about relations between spoken and written language, and eventual construction of the alphabetic or phonetic hypothesis.

Blocks and Other Construction Toys

Construction toys—such as Waffle Blocks™, Legos™, Construx™, Tinker Toys™, Bristle Blocks™, Ramagons™, pop beads, wooden unit blocks, and cardboard blocks—offer many opportunities for development, including the following:

- *Physical knowledge.* Acting on objects in a variety of ways to observe the variety of reactions and to create certain effects. *Examples:* Creating windows and walls within a structure, balancing, bridging, stacking, and using inclines.
- *Representation and pretense.* Emergence and elaboration of representational or symbolic thought at different levels. The ability to let an object represent something else is important progress in the development of thought. With construction toys and props such as dolls and cars, children may also be inspired to engage in pretense. *Example:* The toddler may let a block be a house; a kindergartner may make an elaborate downtown scene.
- *Spatial reasoning.* Making things fit together, interlock, define open and enclosed spaces.
- *Logico-mathematical reasoning.* Noticing similarities and differences and classifying by creating equivalences that are possible in unit blocks and in Construx™.

Group Games

Playing games with rules contributes to children's cognitive and sociomoral development. To play a game with rules, children must cooperate by agreeing on the rules and accepting their consequences. When a rule is broken or a disagreement occurs, children have the opportunity to negotiate and figure out how to continue the game. Games are an excellent context for considering issues of fairness, the beginning of ideas of justice.

We select games for their potential in promoting children's reasoning.

- *Number.* Dice and card games offer opportunities for developing an understanding of 1-to-1 correspondence; more, less, and equal; and adding and subtracting. Some are games of chance, and some involve strategy. *Examples:* board games such as Hi-Ho Cherry O™ and Sorry™, and card games such as Uno™.
- *Physical-knowledge.* Many games also offer advantages found in physical-knowledge activities. *Examples:* Bowling, Topple™, Blockhead™, target games. Number, reading, and writing are involved in keeping score.
- *Social logic.* Some games challenge children to decenter or figure out what someone else may be thinking. *Examples:* guessing games such as I Spy, Guess Which Hand the Penny Is In; chasing games such as Hide and Seek, Simon Says.
- *Nonsocial logic.* As children get older, they are encouraged to figure out strategies in games not involving chance. These often involve spatial reasoning. *Examples:* Checkers, Tic-Tac-Toe, Connect Four™, Isolation™, Blokado™.

Art

Art activities such as painting, cutting, gluing, and creating with a large variety of media also offer various developmental possibilities.

- *Physical knowledge.* Acting on assorted materials to observe the variety of effects and reactions; figuring out how different materials combine.
- *Representation.* Emergence and elaboration of representational or symbolic thought at different levels. First representations do not usually resemble the thing represented. It is the representation in the child's mind that counts! As they grow older, children feel a need to achieve a resemblance.
- *Logico-mathematical relations.* Noticing similarities and differences among textures, colors, "tools," "canvases," and media.

References

Ainsworth, M., Blehar, M. C., Waters, E., & Wall, S. (1978). *Patterns of attachment: A psychological study of the strange situation*. Hillsdale, NJ: Erlbaum.

Bowlby, J. (1973). *Attachment and loss, Vol. 2: Separation*. New York: Basic Books.

Bowlby, J. (1980). *Attachment and loss, Vol. 3: Loss, sadness, and depression*. New York: Basic Books.

Bowlby, J. (1982). *Attachment and loss, Vol. 1: Attachment*. New York: Basic Books. (Original work published in 1969.)

Bowlby, J. (**1982**). Attachment and loss: Retrospect and prospect. *American Journal of Orthopsychiatry, 52*(4), 664–678.

Bretherton, I. (2005). In pursuit of the internal working model construct and its relevance to attachment relationships. In K. E. Grossmann, K. Grossmann, & E. Waters (Eds.), *Attachment from infancy to adulthood: The major longitudinal studies* (pp. 13–47). New York: Guilford Press.

Bretherton, I., & Munholland, K. (1999). Internal working models in attachment relationships: A construct revisited. In J. Cassidy & P. Shaver (Eds.), *Handbook of attachment: Theory, research, and clinical applications* (pp. 89–111). New York: Guilford Press.

Charles, C. (2002). *Building classroom discipline* (9th ed.). Englewood Cliffs, NJ: Prentice-Hall.

Colby, A., & Kohlberg, L. (1987). *The measurement of moral judgment*. Cambridge, UK: Cambridge University Press.

Developmental Studies Center. (1996). *Ways we want our class to be: Class meetings that build commitment to kindness and learning*. Oakland, CA: Author.

DeVries, R. (1970). The development of role-taking in young bright, average, and retarded children as reflected in social guessing game behavior. *Child Development, 41*, 759–770.

DeVries, R. (1986). Children's conceptions of shadow phenomena. *Genetic, Social, and General Psychology Monographs, 112*, 479–530.

DeVries, R. (1992). Development as the aim of constructivist education: How do we recognize development? In D. Murphy & S. Goffin (Eds.), *Understanding the possibilities: A curriculum guide for Project Construct* (pp. 15–34). Columbia: University of Missouri and the Missouri Department of Elementary and Secondary Education.

DeVries, R., & Fernie, D. (1990). Stages in children's play of Tic-Tac-Toe. *Journal of Research in Childhood Education, 4,* 98–111.

DeVries, R., Haney, J., & Zan, B. (1991). Sociomoral atmosphere in direct-instruction, eclectic, and constructivist kindergartens: A study of teachers' enacted interpersonal understanding. *Early Childhood Research Quarterly, 6,* 449–471.

DeVries, R., & Kohlberg, L. (1990). *Constructivist early education: Overview and comparison with other programs.* Washington, DC: National Association for the Education of Young Children. (Originally published in 1987 as *Programs of early education: The constructivist view,* New York: Longman.)

DeVries, R., Reese-Learned, H., & Morgan, P. (1991). Sociomoral development in direct-instruction, eclectic, and constructivist kindergartens: A study of children's enacted interpersonal understanding. *Early Childhood Research Quarterly, 6,* 473–517.

DeVries, R., & Sales, C. (2010). *Ramps and pathways: A constructivist approach to physics with young children.* Washington, DC: National Association for the Education of Young Children.

DeVries, R., Zan, B., Hildebrandt, C., Edmiaston, R., & Sales, C. (2002). *Developing constructivist early education curriculum: Practical principles and activities.* New York: Teachers College Press.

Dewey, J. (1975). *Interest and effort in education.* Edwardsville: Southern Illinois Press. (Original work published 1913)

Dreikurs, R., Grunwald, B., & Pepper, F. (1998). *Maintaining sanity in the classroom* (2nd ed.). New York: HarperCollins. (Original work published 1976)

Duckworth, E. (2006). *"The having of wonderful ideas" and other essays on teaching and learning.* New York: Teachers College Press. (Original work published 1987)

Garis, H. R. (1976). *Uncle Wiggily's happy days.* New York: Platt and Munk. (Original work published 1947)

Goolsby, L., & DeVries, R. (1994a). *When a friend eats more than her share.* Cedar Falls, IA: Regents' Center for Early Developmental Education.

Goolsby, L., & DeVries, R. (1994b). *When a friend refuses to share.* Cedar Falls, IA: Regents' Center for Early Developmental Education.

Goolsby, L., & DeVries, R. (1994c). *When a friend steals.* Cedar Falls, IA: Regents' Center for Early Developmental Education.

Gordon, T. (1989). *Teaching children self-discipline—at home and at school.* New York: Times Books.

Grossmann, K. E., Grossmann, K., & Waters, E. (Eds.). (2005). *Attachment from infancy to adulthood: The major longitudinal studies.* New York: Guilford Press.

Hamre, B., & Pianta, R. (2005). Can instructional and emotional support in the first-grade classroom make a difference for children at risk of school failure? *Child Development, 76,* 949–967.

Helm, J., & Beneke, S. (Eds.). (2003). *The power of projects: Meeting contemporary challenges in early childhood classrooms—strategies & solutions*. New York: Teachers College Press.

Helm, J., & Katz, L. (2001). *Young investigators: The project approach in the early years.* New York: Teachers College Press.

Howes, C. (1999). Attachment relationships in the context of multiple caregivers. In J. Cassidy & P. R. Shaver (Eds.), *Handbook of attachment: Theory, research, and clinical applications* (pp. 671–687). New York: Guilford.

Howes, C., & Ritchie, S. (2002). *A matter of trust: Connecting teachers and learners in the early childhood curriculum.* New York: Teachers College Press.

Jackson, P. (1990). *Life in classrooms.* New York: Holt, Rinehart, and Winston. (Original work published 1968)

Kamii, C. (1982). *Number in preschool and kindergarten.* Washington, DC: National Association for the Education of Young Children.

Kamii, C. (1985). *Young children reinvent arithmetic: Implications of Piaget's theory.* New York: Teachers College Press.

Kamii, C. (1994). *Young children continue to reinvent arithmetic: Third grade* (2nd ed.). New York: Teachers College Press.

Kamii, C. (2004). *Young children continue to reinvent arithmetic: Second grade.* New York: Teachers College Press. (Original work published 1989)

Kamii, C., & DeVries, R. (1977). Piaget for early education. In M. Day & R. Parker (Eds.), *The preschool in action* (pp. 363–420). Boston: Allyn and Bacon. (Original work published 1975)

Kamii, C., & DeVries, R. (1980). *Group games in early education: Implications of Piaget's theory.* Washington, DC: National Association for the Education of Young Children.

Kamii, C., & DeVries, R. (1993). *Physical knowledge in preschool education: Implications of Piaget's theory.* New York: Teachers College Press. (Original work published 1978)

Kohlberg, L. (1984). *Essays on moral development, Volume 2: The psychology of moral development.* San Francisco: Harper and Row.

Kohlberg, L., DeVries, R., Fein, G., Hart, D., Mayer, R., Noam, G., Snarey, J., & Wertsch, J. (1987). *Child psychology and childhood education: A cognitive-developmental view.* New York: Longman.

Kohlberg, L., & Mayer, R. (1972). Development as the aim of education. *Harvard Educational Review, 42,* 449–496.

Kohn, A. (1999). *Punished by rewards: The trouble with gold starts, incentive plans, A's, praise, and other bribes.* Boston: Houghton-Mifflin.

Kohn, A. (2006). *Beyond discipline: From compliance to community.* Alexandria, VA: Association for Supervision and Curriculum Development. (Original work published 1996)

Maccoby, E., & Martin, J. (1983). Socialization in the context of the family: Parent-child interaction. In P. Mussen (Ed.), *Handbook of child psychology: Socialization, personality, and social development* (4th ed.). New York: John Wiley & Sons.

Marshall, M. (2001). *Discipline without stress, punishments, or rewards.* Los Alamitos, CA: Piper Press.

Mead, G. (1934). *Mind, self, and society.* Chicago: University of Chicago Press.

Miller, J. (2004). *The little red hen.* New York: Random House Golden Books.

Missouri Department of Elementary and Secondary Education. (1992). *Project construct: A framework for curriculum and assessment.* Columbia, MO: Author.

Morris, W. (Ed.). (1973). Discipline. In *The American Heritage dictionary of the English language.* Boston: American Heritage & Houghton Mifflin.

Murphy, D., & Goffin, S. (1992). *Understanding the possibilities: A curriculum guide for Project Construct.* Columbia: University of Missouri and the Missouri Department of Elementary and Secondary Education.

Nelsen, J. (2006). *Positive discipline.* New York: Random House. (Original work published 1981)

Nelsen, J., Duffy, R., & Erwin, C. (2007). *Positive discipline for preschoolers.* New York: Crown.

Nelsen, J., Lott, L., & Glenn, S. (2000). *Positive discipline in the classroom.* New York: Random House.

Peek, M., & Giblin, J. (1985). *Mary wore a red dress.* New York: Clarion Books.

Piaget, J. (1964). Development and learning. In R. Ripple and V. Rockcastle (Eds.), *Piaget rediscovered: A report of the conference on cognitive studies and curriculum development* (pp. 7–20). Ithaca, NY: Cornell University Press.

Piaget, J. (1952). *The origins of intelligence in children.* New York: W.W. Norton & Company. (Original work published 1936)

Piaget, J. (1965). *The moral judgment of the child.* London: Free Press. (Original work published 1932)

Piaget, J. (1968). *Six psychological studies.* New York: Random House.

Piaget, J. (1970). *Science of education and the psychology of the child.* New York: Viking Compass. (Original work published 1969)

Piaget, J. (1973). *To understand is to invent.* New York: Grossman. (First published in 1948 in *Prospects,* UNESCO quarterly review of education.)

Piaget, J. (1976). *The grasp of consciousness.* Cambridge, MA: Harvard University Press. (Original work published 1974)

Piaget, J. (1977). Preface to the Second Edition. Ecrites sociologiques: I, Logique génétique et sociologie. In G. Busino (Ed.), *Les sciences sociales avec et après Jean Piaget* (pp. 44–80). Geneva: Librairie Droz. (Original work published 1965, published in English as *Sociological studies,* pp. 23–29, London: Routledge, 1995).

Piaget, J. (1981). *Les relations entre l'affectivite et l'intelligence dans le developpement mental de l'enfant.* Paris: Centre de Documentation Universitaire. (Published in 1954 in part in J. Piaget, *Intelligence and affectivity: Their relation during child development,* Palo Alto, CA: Annual Reviews.)

Piaget, J. (1985). *The equilibration of cognitive structures: The central problem of intellectual development*. Chicago: University of Chicago Press. (Original work published 1975)

Piaget, J., & Garcia, R. (1989). *Psychogenesis and the history of science*. New York: Columbia University Press. (Original work published 1983)

Pianta, R., La Paro, C., Payne, C., Cox, M., & Bradley, R. (2002). The relation of kindergarten classroom environment to teacher, family, and school characteristics and child outcomes. *The Elementary School Journal, 102*, 225–238.

Pianta, R., & Stuhlman, M. (2004). Teacher-child relationships and children's success in the first years of school. *School Psychology Review, 33*, 444–458.

Power, C., Higgins, A., & Kohlberg, L. (1989). *Lawrence Kohlberg's approach to moral education*. New York: Columbia University Press.

Raver, C. (2002). Emotions matter: Making the case for the role of young children's emotional development for early school readiness. *Social Policy Report, XVI*(3), 3–18.

Read, K. (1976). *Nursery school* (6th ed.). San Francisco: Jossey-Bass.

Sapon-Shevin, M. (1998). *Because we can change the world: A practical guide to building cooperative, inclusive classroom communities*. Boston: Allyn & Bacon.

Sarason, S. (1982). *The culture of the school and the problem of change* (2nd ed.). Boston: Allyn and Bacon.

Scharf, P. (1973). *Moral atmosphere and intervention in the prison*. Unpublished doctoral dissertation, Harvard University, Cambridge, MA.

Scieszka, J. (1989). *The true story of the three little pigs*. New York: Scholastic.

Selman, R. (1980). *The growth of interpersonal understanding*. New York: Academic Press.

Selman, R., & Schultz, L. (1990). *Making a friend in youth: Developmental theory and pair therapy*. Chicago: University of Chicago Press.

Steig, W. (1982). *Doctor DeSoto*. New York: Farrar, Straus, and Giroux.

Thompson, R. (1999). Early attachment and later development. In J. Cassidy & P. R. Shaver (Eds.), *Handbook of attachment: Theory, research, and clinical applications* (pp. 265–286). New York: Guilford.

Tuthill, D., & Ashton, P. (1983). Improving educational research through the development of educational paradigms. *Educational Researcher, 12*(10), 6–14.

Van IJzendoorn, M., Sagi, A., & Lambermon, M. (1992). The multiple caretaker paradox: Data from Holland and Israel. *New Directions for Child Development, 57*, 5–24.

Watson, M. (2003). *Learning to trust: Transforming difficult elementary classrooms through developmental discipline*. San Francisco: Jossey-Bass.

Weber, E. (1969). *The kindergarten: Its encounters with educational thought in America*. New York: Teachers College Press

Wood, A. (1987). *Heckedy Peg*. San Diego: Harcourt Brace Jovanovich.

Zan, B. (1996). Interpersonal understanding among friends: A case study of two young boys playing checkers. *Journal of Research in Childhood Education, 10,* 114–122.

Zan, B. (2002). Variations on a checkers theme. In R. DeVries, B. Zan, C. Hildebrandt, R. Edmiaston, & C. Sales (Eds.), *Developing constructivist early childhood curriculum: Practical principles and activities* (pp. 211–224). New York: Teachers College Press.

Zan, B., & Geiken, R. (2010). Ramps and pathways: Developmentally appropriate, intellectually rigorous, and fun physical science. *Young Children, 65*(1), 12–17.

Index

About the Authors

Rheta DeVries is professor emerita of curriculum and instruction at the University of Northern Iowa. For 16 years she taught there, conducted research, and for 13 years was director of the Regents' Center for Early Developmental Education, overseeing the building of the Freeburg School and implementation of its constructivist program. Previously, she taught and established constructivist programs at the University of Illinois at Chicago, the Merrill-Palmer Institute, and the University of Houston. A former public school teacher, she received her Ph.D. degree in psychology from the University of Chicago and did postdoctoral work at the University of Geneva, Switzerland. Previous publications include *Ramps and Pathways: A Constructivist Approach to Physics with Young Children* (coauthored with Christina Sales), *Developing Constructivist Curriculum in Early Education: Practical Principles and Activities* (coauthored with Betty Zan, Carolyn Hildebrandt, Rebecca Edmiaston, and Christina Sales), *Constructivist Early Education: Overview and Comparison with Other Programs* (coauthored with Lawrence Kohlberg), and *Physical Knowledge in Preschool Education* and *Group Games in Early Education* (both coauthored with Constance Kamii).

Betty Zan is director of the Regent's Center for Early Developmental Education at the University of Northern Iowa, where she is also associate professor of curriculum and instruction and director of the Center for Early Education in Science, Technology, Engineering, and Mathematics. She received her Ph.D. in developmental psychology from the University of Houston. She is the principle investigator on two federally funded research projects: Ramps and Pathways (National Science Foundation) and Coaching and Mentoring for Preschool Quality (Administration for Children and Families, Department of Health and Human Services), and is coauthor of *Developing Constructivist Curriculum in Early Education: Practical Principles and Activities*.